Changing Relationships

Routledge Advances in Sociology

For a full list of titles in this series, please visit www.routledge.com

Changing Relationships

**Edited by Malcolm Brynin
and John Ermisch**

Routledge
Taylor & Francis Group
New York   London

First published 2009
by Routledge
711 Third Avenue, New York, NY 10017

Simultaneously published in the UK
by Routledge
2 Park Square, Milton Park, Abingdon, Oxon OX14 4RN

Routledge is an imprint of the Taylor & Francis Group, an informa business

First issued in paperback 2012

Typeset in Sabon by IBT Global.

Library of Congress Cataloging in Publication Data

Changing relationships / edited by Malcolm Brynin & John Ermisch.
    p. cm.—(Routledge advances in sociology ; 45)
"Simultaneously published in the UK by Routledge."
Includes bibliographical references and index.
1. Interpersonal relations. 2. Man-woman relationships. 3. Family. I. Brynin, Malcolm. II. Ermisch, John.
    HM1106.C484 2009
    306.87—dc22
    2008028337

ISBN13: 978–0-415–96523–1 (hbk)
ISBN13: 978-0-415-54104-6 (pbk)
ISBN13: 978–0-203–88459–1 (ebk)

Contents

Figures

Tables

Acknowledgements

The support of the Economic and Social Research Council, which has made this research possible, is gratefully acknowledged.

To the memory of Alasdair Crockett, whose research at ISER would have made an important contribution to this book.

Part I
Forming and Maintaining Relationships

1 Introduction
The Social Significance
of Relationships

Malcolm Brynin and John Ermisch

Romeo and Juliet hide their marriage because it would dishonour their families. The family has to appear united, of one mind; each member is subordinate to it but also represents it. But in addition, and despite this power of the family itself, the two families are internally highly differentiated—by gender and across the generations—with power residing unequivocally with the fathers. The story resonates with us still because now, as in Shakespeare's time, the family can be seen as distinct from the relationships which comprise it. In the case of the families of Romeo and Juliet we observe several key relationship: between parents and children, wife and husband, boyfriend and girlfriend, cousins, nurse and child. We can therefore interpret the conflict of the play not as the outcome of two dysfunctional families but as one between different (and conflicting) forms of relationship.

Only twenty years ago, the British prime minister, Margaret Thatcher, said that 'The basic ties of the family at the heart of our society are the very nursery of civic virtue. It is on the family that we in government build our own policies for welfare, education and care' (quoted in Finch 1989: 3). But examine any relatively recent book in the social sciences on 'the family' to see that it is rarely about the family as a whole. We have moved from a concern with the family as a unit to a much more complex phenomenon, a network of relationships:[1] between members of a couple, between parents and children, less often between the children themselves or perhaps wider family members. For instance, as confirmed in many countries, cohabitation is more likely to arise where parents are divorced (Kiernan 2000: 55). This represents not a family effect but the effect of one relationship on another. There might even be doubt as to what counts as family, so that the boundaries of the network of relationships we call the 'family' are fuzzy. Take as an obvious example a young man and woman who might be described as boyfriend-girlfriend, but they sometimes live together, so some people would call them a couple—and therefore a family. The distinction between friendship and family relationship is nebulous (Spencer and Pahl 2006).

What do we mean by a 'relationship'? Robert Hinde's suggested route to an integrated science of relationships provides one such answer:

At the behaviour level, a relationship implies first a series of interactions between two people, involving interchanges over an extended period of time. . . . The interchanges have some degree of mutuality, in the sense that the behaviour of each takes some account of the behaviour of the other. However this mutuality does not necessarily imply 'cooperation' in its everyday sense: relationships exist between enemies as well as between friends, between those who are forced into each other's company as well as between those who seek it. (Hinde 1997, p. 37)

That is, a relationship is created by participants out of a series of 'interactions', by which we mean such incidents as one individual showing some behaviour X to another individual, who responds with behaviour Y. An essential character of a relationship is that 'each interaction is influenced by other interactions in that relationship. . . . A relationship exists only when the probable course of future interactions between the participants differs from that between strangers' (Hinde 1997, p. 38). We can perhaps add to this the idea that a relationship 'typically involves individuals who view themselves as a unit with a long-term commitment to continue their relationship' (Milardo and Duck 2000: xi)

This perspective provides an empirical basis for the analysis of relationships derived not from biological, legal, or normative definitions but in terms of observed interactions. We can therefore in principle abstract relationships out of observations we make of individuals interacting in the world that we experience directly. As Dunbar (2004, p. 66) explains:

> . . . we have to be able to move backwards and forwards between the physical world of interactions (real events) and the virtual world in which these events are constituted into relationships in order to be able to understand what the significance of specific actions is or might be, or how two relationships impinge on each other.

In this sense, relationships vary enormously in their significance and intensity. One way of looking at this is in terms of a nested hierarchical structure, with larger numbers of progressively less intense relationships maintained at higher levels (Dunbar 2004, p. 67). What might be called *human group size* has been claimed to number about 150 (Dunbar 1997, 2004)—the number with whom you have some kind of meaningful social relationship—not just by sight or a business relationship. The next level is sometimes called a *sympathy group*, numbering about 10–15 individuals. Finally, a subset of the sympathy group is what Dunbar and Spoors (1998) call the *support clique*, 'the inner clique of intimates that individuals would normally approach for advice and assistance when in difficulty' (p.275). Typical numbers in the support clique appear to be about 3–5 (Hill and Dunbar 2003, p. 67). Hill and Dunbar contend that there are cognitive constraints on the number of individuals that can be maintained at a given intensity of relationship, but from our point of view the important point is that people with whom we are linked through birth or marriage in what we call family may appear in any of these groupings. For instance, a spouse would undoubtedly be in most people's support clique as would the parents of dependent children, while adult children might appear only at the sympathy group level.

A related but different approach is described by Spencer and Pahl (2006), who call groups of relationships 'personal communities', which might be drawn from any of the preceding three groups. Each community contains individuals of different degrees of closeness and interreliance. Each therefore cuts across several levels of friendship (Spencer and Pahl 2006: 60), while friendship itself is defined in terms of intensity, ranging from simple ('associates', 'useful contacts'), through friends from whom either favours or fun might be sought, to complex friendships ('helpmate', 'comforter or confidant', 'soul mate'), many of whose members would be family.[2]

We can therefore see relationships in two ways: first, as biologically and/ or legally given connections between people, such as parent-child relationships or marriages; second, as connections formed by observable interactions, which can therefore additionally include other relationships such as cohabitation or friendship. But it is the interactions which make the relationship meaningful even if they do not define it. My sister is related to me, but if we do not interact it is difficult to see that our relationship is any different from a relationship between two strangers. Spouses almost certainly have a relationship, almost by definition while currently residing together, but here too the relationship might resolve to virtually nothing after a separation. Parents and children vary enormously in the extent to which they maintain an observable relationship once children have left home. In this book we look at some relationships—couples who have a romantic relationship but do not live together, and friendships—where we rely for information about these on observed or stated interactions. In respects of the family,[3] the relationships have some biological and/or legal force but interest is nevertheless always in the nature of the interactions associated with these. It is what people do in their relationships that counts.

Research on the family habitually starts with the concept of decline, attested primarily through change at the couple level, with the rise in divorce and cohabitation, but also in the view of some in the decline in the role of the family as a model and framework for young people (Popenoe 1988). Part and parcel of this perceived decline is the growth of the relationship, which, as Giddens observes in respect of the sexual relationship, is a term of relatively recent usage (1992: 58). Analytically, the one concept replaces the other. It is only through the analysis of these relationship dyads that we can observe power differentials, flows of influence, and the balance of individual welfare. It is the last of these in particular that forms the basis for this book. The questions of interest are now not what is the social function of the family, how stable it is, or even what can it provide for its members but how are relationships formed and dissolved, how long do they last, what are their effects on their members? Of course, there is much overlap between an approach based on the family and an approach based on relationships, because the former clearly comprises a number of the latter, but as a result of this focus it is clearer that what is at issue is not the decline of the family so much as the rise of the relationship.

At the heart of the approach based on this concept within economics is a concern for the analysis of individual welfare, and indeed the apparent decline of the family fits in naturally with the underlying theory of individualism.[4] As examples: for women in couples or for young people in relation to their parents, while inequalities in resources are still important, they are less so than in the past, enabling greater independence of action and bargaining power. Such changes have of course been a major source of analysis within sociology too, if nevertheless with entirely different theoretical and formal starting points. For instance, sociologists have been more concerned with family forms, within which the balance of power becomes more complex and contested. In this case the decline of the family is in part a story of the decline of the conventional family, defined by two married parents and their natural children.

There are, of course, other ways of looking at relationships. For instance, an approach based on psychology will in general relate to the emotions in couple relations and the nature of parenting. In the case of the latter there is a strong emphasis on measures of parenting rather than on social background as in sociology or the distribution of welfare as in economics. Yet the difference between these and psychology is often thin, and even more so when the field of study is called 'family studies'.[5] In order to demonstrate the areas of common ground but also the differences, we outline below some of the main building blocks of the two approaches, based in economics and sociology, used in this book.

AN ECONOMICS OF RELATIONSHIPS[6]

It is not obvious that economists, traditionally concerned with trade, prices, productivity, and so on, should be interested in the family at all. The family is an emotive thing. It is hedged in by laws, customs, morality. But economists have begun to argue that the family is subject to the laws of individual rationality like most other institutions, and they have applied the analytical methods of microeconomics to family behaviour. Even customs and moral duty may be the outcome of cultural evolution toward an equilibrium sustained by selfish people (Binmore 2005).

The aim of economics is to analyse the impacts of public policies, social change and technological developments on the welfare of individuals, the only unit for whom the word *welfare* is meaningful. Individualism is in fact the foundation of family economics. This means that the concerns of economists of the family are typically: how people become couples—involving the analysis of 'marriage markets'; the distribution of welfare within couples, especially of material resources; fertility—the decision if and when to have children; the devotion of material and other resources to children; and the factors that lead to marital breakdown. Uniting all these is the concern for individual utility or welfare. For instance, decisions about marriage and divorce must make comparisons between individual welfare within and outside a couple.

It is assumed that people seek to be at least as well off after a decision such as marriage as before. Such outcomes are not guaranteed but provide a baseline for analysis. In this context, the family is best viewed as a 'governance structure' for organising activities rather than a firm in which family members work, as has sometimes been suggested, or a set of long-term contracts (Pollak 1985). This approach is suitable for analysing any relationships within the family—e.g. between spouses, between parents and adult children—but also relationships more generally when they involve resource allocation and the distribution of the 'surplus' from interaction.

Regarding relationship dynamics, some family relationships, such as parent-child, are initially formed by the decision of one side of the relationship. Others are formed through purposive behaviour by both sides. Inevitably the couple is the starting point for analysis. The most obvious and most studied relationship within economics, therefore, is marriage. In addition to love and companionship, marriage offers two people the opportunity to share resources, to benefit from the division of labour, and to facilitate risk-sharing. How are marriage decisions made, and with what effect? What sorts of people do people choose to marry? Of course, the process of finding a spouse is often one in which information is scarce, and it takes time to gather it. Such market 'frictions' affect who marries whom, the gains from each marriage, and the distribution of gains between spouses, as well as fertility decisions. Nevertheless, we can predict certain outcomes on the basis of the assumption of rational behaviour (which holds *on average* even if many individual decisions might seem irrational to outsiders or even to the actors themselves).

Let us start with a simple example. Do people marry others like themselves? Suppose that people's utility from a marriage depends on the characteristics of their partner (which can be defined by various attributes, such as education) associated with their 'attractiveness' as a husband or wife, but also that there is no way to transfer utility between spouses. This assumption means that an individual who would obtain large gains from a match with a particular partner (because the former has less of one or more desirable attributes than the other, such as education) cannot compensate that potential partner to ensure the match is made. Then if marriage market frictions are not too large, positive assortative mating by attractive attributes emerges: that is, people on average do best in terms of their own welfare by marrying people like themselves.

Alternatively, and perhaps more realistically, if we allow 'transferable utility' and assume away any frictions, jointly efficient matches are made, so each match can be characterized by the 'total utility' it generates. They are efficient in the sense that neither party could do better marrying some-one else or staying single. What does this mean? Suppose that each person is endowed with a single attribute (again, such as education), which has a positive effect on total utility from the marriage—that is, both gain from each other's education. Positive assortative mating with respect to the attri-bute still occurs, but only in some cases—when attributes are complements (in the sense that the effect of one person's attribute is increased by the attribute of the spouse), in the production of total utility in the marriage. Anyone with more of this attribute would do better marrying someone with the same level because he or she can benefit from that attribute. However, negative assortative mating occurs when attributes are substitutes, such as the man's and woman's time.

What other factors can reduce the probability that like marries like? Mar-riage markets rarely operate without friction. With frictions in searching for a partner, it is no longer the case that complementary inputs necessar-ily generate positive assortative mating.[7] The positive correlation between desirable attributes like education is expected to be weaker when frictions are larger. Also, a higher divorce rate makes people less choosy when select-ing a spouse, because it reduces the perceived benefits from waiting for a better match by making it more likely that a person will return to the single state. Poorer matches ensue, there is likely to be less assortative mating, and marriages are more likely to dissolve.

In fact, the search for mutually beneficial relationships also characterises the formation of other relationships, such as friendship. For example, Belot and Ermisch (2008) study the creation and destruction of friendship ties in relation to geographic mobility. Of course what are considered as attractive attributes for friendship may be quite different from those that are desir-able for marriage, and as the costs of 'divorce' are lower, people will tend to be less choosy than when searching for a spouse.

The previous discussion places individual marriage decisions within a framework of gains and losses from marriage where these decisions ensure that *on average* people gain from the decision. But we have said nothing yet about the marriage or partnership itself. How do people get on once partnered? The idea of the family as a governance structure sug-gests a relationship based on bargaining. Indeed, a bargaining approach, along with attention to likely flows of information and the possibilities of monitoring behaviour, has made it relatively easy to think of family economics as an analysis of relationships. Models of bargaining between individuals, in which alternatives and 'threat points' affect intrafamily allocation of resources and the distribution of the gains from interaction, provide a fruitful framework for analysing relationships between family members. A bargaining approach naturally focuses on the structure of family membership and its internal organisation (e.g. comparing an intact nuclear family with divorced parents). It also allows the incorporation of ideas of power inequalities into the analysis.

Bargaining may or may not involve cooperation. In many circumstances (e.g. the coresident family) cooperative behaviour is likely to be a good representation of how couples get on because of repeated interaction between people, which facilitates information flows and monitoring. Cooperation achieves an efficient allocation of resources in the relationship, in the sense given earlier that one person cannot be made better off without making the other worse off. But cooperation does not entail lack of conflict: who gets what proportion of the gains from cooperation is still up for negotiation, and power in bargaining is likely to depend on the outcomes from noncooperative alternatives. In the case of marriage, this might be divorce in some circumstances, but not necessarily; a noncooperative relationship could produce higher individual welfare than divorce, and so divorce might not be a credible 'threat'.

Note that in these examples caring for the other party's welfare (e.g. of spouse, parent, or child) does not preclude the need for bargaining to determine outcomes, at least where the resources of the two parties are relatively similar. If, however, their resources differ sufficiently, caring produces transfers from the richer to the poorer party, and so the richer party effectively determines the distribution of resources and welfare.[8] In general, though, caring for others (as opposed to selfishness) is a special case of the cooperative model, not an alternative.

The analysis of intrahousehold allocation is a good example of the application of these ideas and illustrates the role of bargaining power in determining the outcomes. This area of household behaviour has often been seen as a black box and therefore preferences have usually been treated as the same for husband and wife, but this violates the foundation of individualism. Assuming cooperation and bargaining opens this black box. Bargaining power is often assumed to be related to the spouses' relative incomes, and empirical studies show that certain aspects of household consumption rise as women's share of household income rises (household food, children and women's clothing) while others fall (spending on men's clothing, on 'vices' and on support to children from the men's previous unions) (Lundberg, Pollak and Wales 1997; Ermisch and Pronzato 2008). Thus, individual consumption—clearly related to individual welfare—depends on relative power.

What about children? Most people wish to pass on their genes, but they are also concerned about the lifetime welfare of the children that they produce—the 'quality' of their children. Increasing the welfare of their children entails investment of parents' time and goods, and assuming that they wish to treat all of their children relatively equally, the more they have the more costly it is to raise the welfare of each. At the same time, if parents wish to raise 'higher quality' children, then the overall cost is higher. Indeed, as people's income rise, their desire for higher quality children increases, thereby raising this cost. This has contributed to a decline in fertility in most countries, and also to the tendency for higher income parents to have fewer children. The increase in women's attachment to the labour force and earning power has also raised the cost of children, because of the time intensity of investment in children, particularly when they are young. These changes in the desired number of children are also likely to affect the timing of childbearing in women's lives.

Of course, after children grow up they become independent agents themselves, but parents are still likely to care for their welfare, and they also are likely to value interactions with their children. The relationship between parents and their adult children, in terms of financial support for children and children's companionship with parents (or conforming their behaviour to their parents' wishes), may also be viewed as producing an efficient outcome through bargaining. A child considering leaving home will weigh up the relative costs and benefits, which depend on his or her human capital, preferences, costs, and the nature of the relationships with parents, which includes the benefits of affection. Parents have some sense of the level to which they will go financially to support their children both out of affection and to retain affection, based on relative resources. Only a proportion of this is given when the child still lives at home because it is cheaper to provide free or low-cost accommodation than money (Ermisch 2003: 222–5).

Cooperation and efficiency are not always appropriate characterisations of resource allocation in relationships, even if they provide the baseline for analysis. Information and monitoring constraints may play a role in parent–adult child relationships. While parents may wish to help their children financially when they need it, they also want them to behave responsibly in the sense of expending sufficient effort to support themselves. The parents' aim of providing an incentive for effort must balance altruistic and bargaining considerations in setting transfers to children. In this case, the inability to monitor the child's effort produces inefficient outcomes. Resource allocation to children after a couple's divorce is also likely to be inefficient. The mother usually obtains custody of the children and she decides the level of expenditure on them. Her former husband can only influence this by making transfers to his former wife. He cannot usually monitor the division of his transfer between expenditure on children and the mother's consumption, particularly expenditure on young children. The allocation of resources is not efficient, because the mother does not take into account the effect of her choices on the welfare of the father. The inefficiency can be interpreted as an *agency* problem—the father can only affect child expenditure indirectly, through his ex-wife's choices. The probability that a couple divorce is inversely related to the efficiency loss associated with divorce.

People come together (in the case of couples) and stay together (in the case of couples and also adult children) when this is to their individual advantage. There is a strong tendency towards equalisation within the relationship, firstly, in the choice of marriage partner, and secondly within marriage and in filial relationships. Bargaining and also caring models produce this outcome. However, any imbalance at one point in time, for instance in resources, means that bargaining is one-sided, indicating unequal power, which affects individual welfare.

A SOCIOLOGY OF RELATIONSHIPS

From a sociological perspective, economics is too concerned with formal models. It is unclear that people act as rationally as claimed. This does not mean that the fact that people fall in love or that children have emotional relationships with parents nullify the arguments, as things like altruism, poor or asymmetric information, and so on, can be built into the analysis. But to a sociologist it is questionable whether the rational basis for the maximisation of individual welfare produces sufficient regularity of outcomes to be especially useful. So many are the caveats (the result of the effects of laws, norms, ideologies, and emotions) that the empirical patterns predicted by the analysis might explain only a small part of social behaviour. For instance, countries differ enormously in marriage patterns, fertility, leaving home, support of children, and so on, and these differences are often of fundamental interest. That individual rationality plays a role is not an issue, but institutional and cultural factors probably explain more actual behaviour.

Nevertheless, the economic analysis of the family based on the individual has increasing resonance in sociology. As already indicated, the economics of the family, because of its focus on the individual, is already close to being an economics of relationships. Sociology too has been moving in this direction, whereas an earlier sociology of the family was primarily concerned with the structural role of the family in society. This could be seen in Marxist terms, where family forms support exploitative modes of production (e.g. Close and Collins 1985), a Parsonian sociology of the family which argues that the nuclear family is required by modern forms of production in a purely functionalist (and nonexploitative) sense, because it is more efficient than the extended family,[9] and many feminist accounts where, whether related to modes of production or not, the family is a means for the gendering of exploitation.

The sociology of the family has in the main moved away from deterministic approaches to the subject. What we observe is often too complex for such accounts. The family is multiple and combinative (Beck and Beck-Gernsheim 2002), the result of divorce, remarriage, and the coresidence of stepparent/stepchildren and half-siblings, and this provides more options for the individual (Giddens 1991). Various phrases have been used by sociologists to describe this process: 'post-familial family', 'post-modern family', 'patchwork families'. Further, if the decline of marriage encourages living alone, the family may reduce to the individual. As in economics, in fact, the individual becomes the baseline for understanding. Giddens emphasises this aspect of what he calls the 'pure relationship', which 'refers to a situation where a social relation is entered into for its own sake . . . and is continued only in so far as it is thought by both parties to deliver enough satisfactions for each individual to stay within it' (1992: 58).

If we reconsider the past, when extended relations were more common, or servants lived in-house and were often treated as extended family (Spencer and Pahl 2006), we can see that the really stripped-down family—the nuclear family—had a short history (Davidoff, Doolittle and Fink 1999). But this is not just a matter of the distribution of family types. Sociologists infer from the change to complex family forms a more flexible approach to family life whereby individuals can in a sense 'shop around' for the type of family that appeals to them.

> Whereas, in pre-industrial society, the family was mainly a community of need held together by an obligation of solidarity, the logic of individually designed lives has come increasingly to the fore in the contemporary world. The family is becoming more of an elective relationship, an association of individual persons, who each bring to it their own interests, experiences and plans and who are each subjected to different controls, risks and constraints. (Beck and Beck-Gernsheim 2002: 97)

But this also leads to unpredictability (Allen and Walker 2000; Beck and Beck-Gernsheim 2002). This becomes clearer if we take a longitudinal perspective. A woman might have a series of boyfriends, one or more of which might be serious relationships with many of the characteristics of cohabitation or marriage but with less commitment, more freedom. Perhaps two spells of cohabitation follow, then marriage, followed in turn perhaps by divorce and further cohabitations and even back to weaker relationships, and so on. Children might arise at different stages of these core liaisons, producing step-relationships in addition to the standard parent-child relationships. Similarly, a child might have a fully dependent relationship in a family, then earn money but remain at home and eventually bring in a live-in partner (or in different types of setup marry but still remain in the parental home), or move out intermittently (for study, for work), returning to the parental home every now and then, perhaps also after relationship breakdown. The individual is the sum of many moments and is effectively re-created over time. The family is a set of relationships defined by the intersection of individual biographies. Each association is one moment in two complex trajectories.

Individualization is a compulsion . . . to create, to stage manage, not only one's biography but the bonds and networks surrounding it and to do this amid changing preferences and at successive stages of life, while constantly adapting to the conditions of the labour market, the education system, the welfare state and so on. (Beck and Beck-Gernsheim 2002: 4)

The costs and benefits of a relationship are more fluid than in the past. Analytically, therefore, the view is similar to much that we find in economics. Sociologists can, for instance, argue that 'while family life is important, the family has evolved into a voluntary association. . . . If rewards are considered low, the relationships may not continue' (Brubaker and Kimberly 1993: 9). But the emphasis is very different, on variety rather than uniformity (and formal models seek out uniformity). Spencer and Pahl (2006: 108–27) describe the nature of partnerships, which begin as friendship, then might fluctuate uncertainly between friendship and a feeling that now not only a relationship exists but that a couple are *related*. This might result in marriage, but in turn this feeling of being related might fade, and presumably with it the feeling of friendship. There is little individual certainty. Cohabitation, for instance, is a clear manifestation of a more individual approach to partnership, where either commitment is reduced or the commitment of the other is tested. This can of course produce uniform patterns. Despite considerable differences in rates of cohabitation, there is a surprising similarity across many European countries in the time it takes for a cohabiting union to convert into marriage (Kiernan 2000: 52). However, such patterns mask a great deal of individual flux. The delay gives individuals more time to assess the effects of marriage on their own well-being, but the nature of this well-being varies considerably within every society.

This sort of uncertainty affects every stage of the life cycle, beginning with young children affected by divorce or separation. Adolescence is seen as marked by increasing uncertainty. It has often been pointed out that adolescence is being extended into what some have called a period of 'post-adolescence', through longer education, insecure job opportunities, growing individual choice in when and how to form a partnership, and delayed departure from as well as a higher probability of return to the parental home. There is a wider diversity of paths, but also greater risks of failure (Mortimer and Larson 2002). Because the traditional structures are declining, decisions are perhaps more likely to be made and unmade.

The family has traditionally been seen as providing a role within a social structure, but the dissolution of the family into a set of relationships appears to replace structure with process (Scanzoni et al. 1989). This has two quite contradictory implications. One is that the decline of the family is accompanied by a decline in regulation, in reliance on duties, in social pressures, and in a precise distribution of labour, in favour of more companionate relationships (e.g. Burgess, Locke and Thomes 1971). This change also effectively removes some aspects of behaviour from the gaze of the analyst. It is extremely difficult to measure or test affection. Paradoxically, therefore, the family is more of a black box than in the past, when it was assumed that the family was an indivisible unit. Second, this closer companionship implies weaker bonds. It suggests equality, the breaching of which potentially leads to relationship breakdown, whether within couples, between parents and children, or between siblings. In respect of couples, the pitting of one individual interest against another means that 'an inherent feature of the sexually based primary/close relationship must necessarily be conflict and struggle' (Scanzoni et al. 1989: 58).

Has the move towards seeing relationships in terms of process rather than of structure gone too far? Jones and Wallace, considering the 'deconstruction' of youth that appears in the sociological theory of individualization, argue that analytical reconstruction is needed, but also that 'to combine process with structure is a complex process' (1992: 17). 'Complex' does not mean impossible, but perhaps the change has gone too far, and this can be stated for two main reasons. First, social norms in respect of the family are changing, yet the structure of relationships is still highly normative. Even if people are increasingly inclined to see cohabitation as acceptable, they do not necessarily downgrade the value of marriage (Axinn and Thornton 2000). Stone (1990) traces the growth of 'affective individualism' as the basis for marriage back to the seventeenth century in Britain, where it probably had its earliest manifestation. This represents not the development of love itself but the normative role of love. Finch (1989) discusses a number of the sorts of norms which exist in relationships, such as degrees of shared understanding or even how need is defined. Even when people engage in extramarital relationships this is not a process of forming a 'pure' relationship; in Giddens's terms, not only are various benefits and costs weighed against each other (see also Duncombe et al. 2004) but so are different normative beliefs. As such affairs form and collapse, the actors switch between a 'myth' of romantic love and a myth of individualised self-justification, both providing a convenient normative framework in which to embed their actual behaviour (Lawson 1988). Giddens's pure relationship can never be pure because all relationships relate to a structure of norms (Morgan 2004).

We can see the effect of such norms in a very different way amongst the factors that determine marriages, such as the tendency towards homogamy (assortative mating in economists' parlance). While economists argue that in general people marry others like themselves because this is best for their individual welfare, for most (but not all) sociologists there is in addition to this idea of exchange a strong normative structure underlying homogamy. There is certainly a parallel to the economists' idea in sociology. For instance, well before Becker's work (1981), Goode argued that 'all mate-selection systems press toward *homogamous* marriages as a result of the bargaining process' (1964: 33). Otherwise, individuals lose out; but so do the social groups of which these individuals are members, who therefore prescribe rules of endogamy, and constrain the operation of love to ensure it operates within the group. At the same time, we can see in this line of thinking that marriage markets have always been highly social constructions. The restrictions might be weaker than in the past, but they exist.

Related to this is the critically important concern with the transmission of social values, for instance, to do with gender stereotyping, where change is slow. Gendered stereotypes are learned very early in childhood and are resistant to pressures, whether at home or school.[10] An important longitudinal analysis of family life in the US has argued that 'family transmission processes operate today much as they did in the past' (Bengtson, Biblarz, and Roberts 2002: 153) despite cultural shifts, the growth in divorce, and the evolution of new family forms. Divorce weakens the role of fathers, but overall, young people tend to hold the same social values as their parents. There is little real decline in cross-generational solidarity.

Second, the fundamental idea that individual relationships are less predictable than in the past because of the proliferation of family forms, is exaggerated. We can demonstrate this through contrasting a breakdown of individuals *within households* by family type in a large-scale survey (the British Household Panel Study) with a breakdown by relationship type. In the former, the family is the unit of analysis; in the latter, not the individual but a pair of individuals—many of whom therefore appear more than once. As an example, in a family with a mother, father and two natural children, we have four people but six relationships: the couple, two maternal and two paternal relationships, and one sibling pair. With another sibling this would become ten relationships. The results for the whole survey in 1991 (wave 1) and 2005 (wave 15), by family type, are given in Table 1.1. This gives a picture, often utilised in writing about the 'new' family, of the minority status of the conventional family. If we take this as couples with children, these form only one-third (to be precise, 33.1 per cent) of all household

Table 1.1 Household Structure in Waves 1 and 15 of the BHPS (%)

	Wave 1	Wave 15
Single, nonelderly	10.9	13.6
Single elderly	15.3	17.7
Couple: no children	28.3	28.4
Couple: dependent children	25.1	20.6
Couple: nondependent children	8.0	7.9
Lone parent: dependent children	5.7	6.2
Lone parent: nondependent children	3.6	3.7
2+ unrelated adults	1.8	0.9
Other	1.3	1.0
N	5,510	4,603

Table 1.2   Relationship Structure in Waves 1 and 15 of the BHPS (%)

	Wave 1	*Wave 15*
Spouses	21.5	20.1
Partners	2.2	3.9
Child-parent	51.6	49.7
Natural siblings	17.2	17.4
Other siblings	1.2	1.7
Grandparent-child	1.0	1.5
Stepparent-child	1.7	2.6
In-laws	0.8	1.6
Unrelated sharer	2.1	1.0
Other	0.7	0.4
N	*15,248*	*12,350*

types in 1991 and this falls to 28.5 per cent in 2005. 28% can be added for couples with no children

If we look at this from a relational point of view, though, as in Table 1.2, we get a different picture. The proportion of spouses in the sample falls slightly over time, compensated by the rise in other partnerships. The child-parent relationship declines slightly. But 'conventional' relationships, in fact, representing the nuclear family (the first, third and fourth rows) still form 90.3 per cent of all relationships in wave one (which goes down to 87.2 per cent 14 years later). Clearly, this is partly the result of the presence of two or more children. But while it is the case that over the life cycle people are more likely than in the past to experience a wider range of relationship types, from the point of view of the personal experience of people living in families *at any point in time*, the age-old forms of relationship outweigh the experience of additional or substitute forms. It is not the new family that is important so much as the increasing emphasis on relationships, whatever their type, in understanding people's familial and social networks, and their effects.

THE IRREDUCIBLE STRUCTURE OF RELATIONSHIPS

Can we say that society is *structured* around relationships in the way it has perhaps been reasonable to say that it might have been structured around families? There clearly is structure in the social phenomena which underlies relationships, and this comprises the most obvious building blocks of relationships—gender and generation.

One of the dominant forces behind the change in the conception of the family as a unit to the view of it as a network of relationships is the growth of feminism and the actual but also analytical emergence of women from the family. Goldscheider and Waite argue that women lose out through marriage in respect of loss of control over their lives, including the reduced chances of an independent income, and so 'the major barrier to getting married is marriage itself' (Goldscheider and Waite 1991: 62). Even if complete independence of resources is in practice not common, with women's increasing employment, the balance is changing (e.g. Chapman 2004: 107–15). This does not mean that conflict is more likely, as has been predicted by some, but rather that the balance of power has to be more carefully negotiated. In the past, women gained from access to men's higher resources. Now the man gains too and might even calculate his benefits from marriage on this basis (Brynin and Francesconi 2004). If some of the man's power has been lost, he gains materially from this loss through greater cooperation.

Becker argues that women work in the home while men undertake paid work because this is efficient for the household; generally women are more productive in the home than are men, and men are more productive outside the home. The specialisation is not so widespread today because, other than for mothers of young children, the marginal value of home production is nearly always lower than the returns to work. The only situation where it is economic to work in the home is where the man's income is especially high, or where women's education is so low that there is little practical difference in the benefits derived from care of the home and work. But in the latter case the husband is also likely to have low education and therefore both might be out of work. We know empirically that most women prefer to work for money than in the home for at least a part of their daily time, while women today have higher employment aspirations than did their mothers (e.g. Bengston, Biblarz and Roberts 2002: 149).

In fact, Becker predicted that as women's education and earning power begins to equal that of men, the division of labour he describes would begin to break down (and also divorce would increase). As discussed earlier, economic theory since then has developed models of bargaining and of cooperation which see the balance of outcomes less in terms of specialisation in a unitary family than of rules on how resources (time, money, goods) will be shared (Bourguignon, Browning and Chiappori 1993; Ermisch 2003). Broadly speaking, therefore, much emphasis has moved towards explaining and describing the allocation of resources and distribution of welfare within the couple. No longer is the outcome (any outcome of interest) the result of individuals acting rationally and producing a joint outcome almost invisibly, but rather of people explicitly and deliberately producing that outcome—bargaining, sharing, giving, sometimes exploiting.[11]

Across generations, key issues include parenting, resources, and family breakdown. While much researched, the effects on children of divorce are highly disputed. One assessment argues that it is not clear that there is on average anything other than a short-term effect of parental divorce on children in terms of psychological well-being—and even, it is argued, of resources (Fine and Demo 2000). The point here is that young people are adaptable, their resilience made easier by changing social norms in respect of the family towards greater liberalism. The 'combinative' family is not unequivocally second-best. Nevertheless, the effects of divorce have an impact on the parent-child relationship, not only on parents and children as individuals. For instance, Amato and Booth find that divorce lowers the feelings of affection of children towards their parents and that low marital quality does this too. If the parents get on badly, in later life their children will have weaker affection for them (1997: 45–83).

Transfers of resources are another important aspect of the parent-child relationship. Many factors intervene here, but the nature and timing of the balance are critical, determining not only welfare but ultimately decisions on whether or not to stay in the parental home. For instance, the more young people earn while still at home, the less their dependence on parents, but also the greater the dependence of parents on them, as they may then contribute to the cost of their board. It is clear that this is also an issue of power. Parents give to children, or defer giving, no doubt out of affection, but in addition the nature of the gift expresses power, helping to keep children at home or in line. Interestingly, this can apply even when the flow of resources is partially reversed, in the case of young people paying for their keep. While this also gives them some power, where they share substantially in the provision of household resources, the responsibility of such payments can be the basis for learning more general responsibilities. Thus, the transition to economic adulthood does not depend on leaving home (Jones and Wallace 1992).

More generally, the transition towards independence is becoming far more widely separated from other transitions, for instance, into education or work, than in the past, while the transition to independence, as already indicated, is also seen as becoming more unpredictable. Young people might stay at home longer to avoid early marriage in societies where independent living is frowned upon. Those who expect to leave education early might stay at home longer. In contrast, entry into higher education is often associated with early home-leaving and frequent returns (Iacovou 2004; Mortimer and Larson 2002: 36–8). Young people might have a variety of living arrangements available to them: the parental home, a temporary and intermediate household (sharing with others), independent living, or a partnership home (Jones and Wallace 1992: 96). There is little agreement, therefore, including in the psychology literature, whether leaving home should be viewed as a process of individuation (young people learning independence from parents) or of continued solidarity (family relationships simply change). It is possible that such relationships have a strong life-cycle element built into them, typified by a period of independence followed by solidarity, which does not simply follow an exchange model (Cooney 2000). Such patterns probably also outlast the complications of parental divorce.

THE STRUCTURE OF THE BOOK

We have emphasised previously the importance of viewing connections between people, where some sort of personal ongoing commitment is made, in terms of evolving relationships. What we observe is the effects of bargaining over time, of different degrees of cooperation, and of cohesion. Critical to the process to which these changes give rise is the balance of welfare, whether material or emotional, across gender and across the generations. In the following chapters the contributors to this volume look at these issues through examination of comparatively weak relationships such as friendship and 'living apart together', the gender balance in marriage and partnership in terms of employment, the domestic division of labour, how close couple members are to each other, or in terms of stress or shocks such as unemployment, poverty, and less traumatically, the need to move house. The balance of welfare works differently across the generations. The research in this area presented in this book covers the effects of parenting at very young ages of the children, the effects on young people leaving home, and material relations between parents and children when they leave home.

In the next section, we summarise in more detail the contribution made by each chapter to the sorts of arguments and issues we have outlined earlier. In Part I of the book we include chapters which discuss various aspects of social change in respect of relationships, or other factors which help set the scene, while in Part II we examine the welfare effects of these changes (although there clearly is some overlap between these two).

All these chapters are concerned with time, whether in terms of social trends, of change over time in individual relationships, or, more directly, the distribution of time within the household. In addition to the clear focus on relationships, this is the main contribution of this volume to what is, at least in terms of the family, already a considerable literature. The focus is not only on relationships but on relationship dynamics. A number of data sets have been used for this purpose, including the British census, the National Child Development Study, the Millennium Cohort Study, the European Community Household Panel, the German Socio-Economic Panel, a panel including a time-use diary (Home-OnLine), but most of all, the British Household Panel Study (BHPS). This is a nationally representative sample of some 5,500 private households recruited in 1991, containing approximately 10,000 adults. These same adults are interviewed each successive year. If anyone splits from their original household to form a new household, then all adult members of the new household are also interviewed. Children in original households are interviewed when they reach the age of 16. Movers are followed. As a result of this design, the sample as it evolves over time mimics changes in the population. The core questionnaire elicits information on income and earnings, labour market status, housing tenure and conditions, household composition, education, social and political views, and physical and mental health at each annual interview.

PART I: FORMING AND MAINTAINING RELATIONSHIPS

John Ermisch and Thomas Siedler investigate a phenomenon that has had considerable popular attention: 'living apart together', or LAT for short. These are couples who have a steady romantic relationship but do not live at the same address. While living at different addresses, they regard themselves as a couple and are recognised as such by others. Their analysis uses two sources of panel data: the BHPS, which carried questions about LAT in 1998 and 2003, and the German Socio-Economic Panel (SOEP), which asked questions related to LAT annually over the period 1991–2005. In addition to permitting similar analyses to the British data (with of course many more observations), these data allow analysis of the dynamics of LAT (e.g. how long do such relationships last, how do they end?) in more detail. They find that the LAT phenomenon is very similar in Britain and in Germany. It mainly involves young, never married people aged under 25, with the incidence being particularly high among students. But LAT also occurs after separation/divorce, with one-fifth of LATs coming from this group. LAT is a more common lifestyle for the better educated. The German evidence suggests that the average LAT lasts about four years with nearly one-half dissolving within 10 years. It also indicates that there was no trend since 1991. Thus, it appears that we mainly recognise it more; it has not become more popular. The British evidence suggests, however, that LAT may be shorter in duration in Britain, and that the LAT partner usually lives nearby.

Michèle Belot undertakes a not very common form of analysis, looking quantitatively at friendship networks. As already indicated, there are many ways of doing this. Here Belot makes use of the BHPS to see not only whom people choose (that is, in response to a survey question) as their three closest friends, but how these networks change over the life course and with change in life events. One of the central issues here is the gendering of social networks. Men, it has been argued, mix primarily with men, women with women. This does in fact turn out to be a gendered process, with women far more likely to have only women amongst their three closest friends than men are to nominate men. The idea mooted by Spencer and Pahl that relatives are not always distinguishable from friends receives some support, with 25 per cent of women reporting at least one relative as a close friend, but less than 18 per cent of men. This gendering is accentuated through life-course events, with childbirth tipping women away from friendships with people in full-time work. Thus, it is suggested, this sort of friendship segregation potentially reinforces women's labour-force exclusion, in the sense implied by Granovetter's work on 'weak ties' and much subsequent work. This overlaps with the effect, studied in this volume by Kan and Gershuny, of women's increasing emphasis on domestic work as a result of childbirth leading to continuing reduction in their earnings potential, but Jenkins' finding that women suffer financially from divorce or separation less than in the past, even if they still do suffer, shows that continuity of work is reducing the gender gap in other ways.

Maria Iacovou, with a contribution from Lavinia Parisi, looks at the timing and income effects of leaving home in a comparative context, using the European Household Panel Survey. Iacovou confirms that the timing varies greatly across Europe. This is in part to do with what young people leave home *for* (marriage/partnership, education, work, or simply to be independent), but the main aim of the chapter is to compare the relative effects of parental and child income on leaving home. In all countries, leaving home is more likely the higher the child's income, and in most countries the parents' income too. This suggests that both children and parents value the child's independence. Southern European countries and Ireland, where parental income does not appear to have this role, are, however, exceptions. Further, in the other countries where higher parental income encourages home-leaving, this separation entails a substantial risk of poverty for young people. This, to return to one of the arguments made earlier in the introduction, implies an 'independence' rather than a 'solidarity' model of the relationship between parents and adult children. However, this appears not to be the case from the final analysis of returns home by young people, which are at least as high in northern as in southern countries, and especially high in the UK. Independent relationships are an elastic concept.

In two chapters, Malcolm Brynin, Álvaro Martínez Pérez and Simonetta Longhi address the issue of how close couples are, first, in a chapter on homogamy, and, second, in a chapter on within-couple influences after partnership formation. They argue that homogamy is increasing over time, despite the growth of cohabitation and of remarriage, both of which trends might be expected to create less evenly matched relationships, and, further, that this increases over relationship time, that is, as the partnership develops. People are attracted to each other partly on the basis of similarity of attributes, and this similarity intensifies as the relationship progresses. In this sense, while the outcome might be interpreted as one of social closure (people are not willing to redistribute attributes through partnering people unlike themselves), this also suggests a continuing basis for affectionate relationships based on equality rather than on the potential power differential implied by unequal attributes. Some confirmation of this is apparent in the result, albeit not very powerful, that those who partner people unlike themselves suffer higher mental stress.

PART II: RELATIONSHIPS AND SOCIAL WELFARE

John Ermisch investigates how parents interact with their children and the consequences for their children's long-term welfare. The chapter demonstrates considerable variation across families in how parents interact with their children. Some of this variation is systematic. In particular, better educated mothers tend to 'score higher' on educational activities and better child-mother interactions with their young children. Such behaviour is likely to enhance the well-being of children during childhood. It also is associated with better cognitive development during the preschool years. Given the existing evidence that these early differences cast a long shadow over subsequent achievements, in the sense of a strong association between cognitive assessments at preschool ages and ultimate educational achievements, better parenting appears to have long-run welfare benefits for children. Supportive behaviour toward older children is also more evident among better educated mothers, and this behaviour is also associated with better educational attainments for the children.

In the following chapter, John Ermisch moves forward in the life course and investigates interactions between parents and their adult children, focussing on parents above retirement age. It analyses how help and contact between generations varies with the socioeconomic and demographic characteristics of the two generations, and it uses this analysis to shed light on the validity of theories of intergenerational family relations. It finds that more affluent parents are more likely to provide regular or frequent financial help to their adult children and more affluent children are less likely to receive it. Also, more affluent children see their mother or father less frequently and are less likely to provide them with regular or frequent in-kind help, and more affluent parents see their adult sons and daughters less frequently and are less likely to receive regular or frequent in-kind help. Among the theories studied, the only one consistent with the data suggests that adult children provide more frequent contact with and in-kind help for less affluent parents in order to reduce the inequity in well-being between parents and children. But these associations concerning contact and in-kind help primarily reflect a tendency for more affluent children and parents to live farther apart, with greater distance reducing contact and in-kind help. Thus, an important part of the story about intergenerational relations concerns parents' and children's location decisions relative to each other. The chapter also investigates how parental income is associated with the distance that children move when they leave their parental home. It finds that young people who leave higher income parental homes move farther away.

Man Yee Kan and Jonathan Gershuny utilise time-use data to analyse the relative roles of paid work and domestic unpaid work for both women and men. Their interest is in examining whether the birth of a child increases equality of work in general and the division of domestic labour in particular. This is a fairly well-researched issue, but effective measures of time use, especially over a period of time, are uncommon. To obtain theirs, Kan and Gershuny combine time-budget data with data from a large-scale household panel (the BHPS) to create a series of estimates of time use over the life cycle for men and women in couples. They confirm other findings, for instance, that while men increase their total workload after the birth of a child, women do so by more, but add to this finding that the outcome is cumulative in the succeeding years, with the gap between men and women rising. They further argue, in line with economists like Becker, that the gradual increase of unpaid work as a proportion of women's total work reduces their earnings capacity.

Priscila Ferreira and Mark Taylor look at the couple in terms of their geographical mobility. This is of interest because we would like to know whether moves are determined by the man or by the woman, or equally by both. This tells us something about the couple relationship, and specifically about their relative power. The authors use the BHPS to examine intended moves, actual moves, and their psychological consequences. They find that the presence (or otherwise) of dependent children is a major factor in influencing residential moves, with very young children inhibiting such moves. Over and above this, the mobility preferences of each partner have an important effect. Of most interest is that the relationship between intended and actual moves has an important effect on psychological well-being. Where people move because they want to while their partner does not (who are therefore 'tied movers'), they benefit psychologically. More remarkably, the partner does not suffer an increase in stress. When the man is a 'tied stayer', he enjoys an improvement in his psychological well-being, perhaps as a result of meeting his partner's preferences. A man whose wife is a tied stayer suffers more stress, implying a move towards equalisation of preferences. However, being a tied stayer is bad for women. Given that more women than men are likely to be tied stayers, this suggests some continuing inequality in preferences and outcomes.

Emilia Del Bono's main concern is to understand the influence of early labour market experience on the process of family formation. In particular, she is interested in understanding how the experience of unemployment might affect transitions towards marriage or the probability of having a first child. In general, one would expect employment to reduce fertility, as employed women place a high value on their time and limit the amount of resources they allocate to their family. Conversely, a woman experiencing an unemployment spell should be more likely to face a lower opportunity cost of her time and might be more likely to get married or enter motherhood. Using longitudinal data from the National Child Development Study, Del Bono exploits the exact timing of women's early labour market experience, distinguishing among full- and part-time employment as well as unemployment, to obtain a clear picture of how the process of human capital accumulation affects the probability of a first marriage or of a first birth. She finds that while employment always encourages transitions to marriage, it is only *recent* employment which reduces fertility. Moreover, she finds that recent unemployment spells do not increase, and might actually decrease, the probability of having a first child. As well as looking at the direct effect of labour market experience on marriage and fertility, Del Bono considers whether this operates indirectly by influencing future wages and employment opportunities. She finds that higher expected future employment is positively related to both fertility and marriage. This implies less of a trade-off between work and the process of family formation than might be expected.

All marriages and partnerships are subject to external, including economic, pressures. Morten Blekesaune reconsiders the problem whether unemployment leads to partnership dissolution, as indicated by previous research, looking, for instance, at whether length of partnership makes a difference. It is also possible, alternatively, either that causality is the other way round—marital breakdown causes unemployment—or that people prone to unemployment are liable to form unsuccessful marriages in the first place. Blekesaune investigates these associations using the panel properties of the BHPS. Interestingly, female unemployment does not have smaller effect than male unemployment on the probability of marital breakdown. However, the length of the partnership makes little difference, nor does controlling for unobserved heterogeneity. Finally, mental distress in either partner and financial dissatisfaction on the part of the woman increases the probability of partnership dissolution. Overall, the results imply not only that unemployment leads to marital breakdown but that the woman's experiences and concerns play a paramount role.

Stephen Jenkins's chapter provides evidence on what happens to people's incomes when their or their parents' marital union dissolves, using 14 waves of the BHPS. This long sequence of panel data is used in two ways. First, it is used to calculate the changes in income between the year before and the year after the marital split, and to examine trends over time in the distribution of these changes, updating earlier analysis by Jarvis and Jenkins (1999) based on only the first four waves of the BHPS. Second, it is used to examine six-year income trajectories, analysing how incomes evolve from the year before the marital split over the five years following the marital split. The research shows that marital splits continue to be associated with short-term declines in income for separating wives and children relative to separating husbands, but the size of the decline has declined over time markedly for women with children and this most probably reflects the effects of secularly rising employment rates and, related to this, the introduction of Working Families Tax Credit in 1998. The analysis of six-year income trajectories suggests that in the five years following a marital split, incomes for separating wives recover but not to their previous levels, on average. Women in paid work or who have a new partner fare best.

NOTES

1. See, for example, *Families as Relationships* by Milardo and Duck (2000), which, though, is extremely restrictive in what it appears to count as a relationship.
2. These methods imply an empirical basis for determining relationships—through observation of activity or of lists of relationships provided by respondents. This approach need not be qualitative. Techniques and software exist for the quantitative analysis of networks, where issues such as distance, clustering, and hierarchy become important (Carrington et al. 2005).
3. All families can, of course, be broken down into relationships, with the exception of the single-person 'family'. Yet people living by themselves must have lost family members over time. Alternatively, people either fail to form a (romantic) relationship or choose to live alone, if perhaps for a short time. Relationships are implied where they do not exist.
4. It is of note that some commentators blame the rise of individualism for the decline of the family. Economists cannot, of course, be blamed for this rise.
5. It is in the case of partnership analysis that the biggest divergence arises, with psychology often at least indirectly concerned with analysis of the effectiveness of guidance and therapy. It has been argued that the emotional content of these relationships can also be treated quantitatively. For instance, Gottman et al. (2005) seek to demonstrate the points at which observed negative interactions between partners are likely to escalate beyond a point where breakdown of the relationship is almost inescapable.
6. This section draws on Ermisch's (2008) entry in the *Palgrave Dictionary of Economics* for 'family economics'.
7. In the absence of search frictions, the equilibrium outcome is socially efficient. But search frictions produce 'sorting externalities', which lead to an inefficient equilibrium. When a man and woman meet, they only match if it is jointly efficient to do so, but by leaving the marriage market they change the composition of types in the market, which affects the expected returns to search for single persons in the market. Their failure to take into account the impact of their match on the welfare of singles in the market produces the inefficiency.
8. The outcome would be quite different if the richer party were selfish. The richer person would use bargaining power to allocate resources in his or her favour.
9. Becker's economic analysis comes to the same conclusion.
10. Though it has been argued that egalitarian parental models are likely to influence adult responses through persistent, invisible persuasion (Sedney, 1990).
11. And of course, loving, though this is not easy to separate analytically from questions of power (see, for example, Duncombe and Marsden 2004; Fischer and Sollie 1993; Sprecher 1990).

REFERENCES

Allen, K. and Walker, A. (2000) Constructing gender in families, in Milardo, M. and Duck, S. (eds) *Families as relationships*, Chichester, UK: John Wiley and Sons, 1–17.

Amato, P.R. and Booth, A. (1997) *A generation at risk: growing up in an era of family upheaval.* Cambridge, MA and London: Harvard University Press.

Axinn, W. and Thornton, A. (2000) The transformation in the meaning of marriage, in L. Waite (ed) *The ties that bind,* New York: Aldine de Gruyter, 147–65.

Beck, U. and Beck-Gernsheim, E. (2002) *Individualization: institutionalized individualism and its social and political consequences.* London: Sage.

Becker, G.S. (1981) *A treatise on the family.* Cambridge, MA: Harvard University Press.

Belot, M. and Ermisch, J. (2008). Friendship ties and geographic mobility: evidence from Great Britain, *Journal of the Royal Statistical Society,* Series A, Forthcoming.

Bengtson, V.L., Biblarz, T.J. and Roberts, R.E.L. (2002) *How families still matter: a longitudinal study of youth in two generations,* New York: Cambridge University Press.

Binmore, K. (2005) *Natural Justice,* Oxford: Oxford University Press.

Bourguignon, F., Browning, M. and Chiappori, P.-A. (1993) Collective models of household behavior. *European Economic Review,* 36: 355–64.

Brubaker, T. and Kimberly, J. (1993) Challenges to the American family, in T. Brubaker (ed) *Family relations: challenges for the future,* Newbury Park, CA: Sage, 3–16.

Brynin, M. and Francesconi, M. (2004) 'The material returns to partnership: the effects of educational matching on labour market outcomes and gender equality', *European Sociological Review,* 20: 363–77.

Burgess, E.W., Locke, H.J. and Thomes, M.M. (1971) *The family: from traditional to companionship.* 4th edn, New York: Van Nostrand Reinhold Co.

Carrington, P.J., Scott, J. and Wasserman, S. (2005) *Models and methods in social network analysis.* New York and Cambridge: Cambridge University Press.

Chapman, T. (2004) *Gender and domestic life: changing practices in families and households,* Basingstoke, UK: Palgrave Macmillan.

Close, P. and Collins, R. (1985) *Family and economy in modern society,* London: Macmillan.

Cooney, T. (2000) Parent-child relations across adulthood, in M. Milardo and S. Duck (eds) *Families as relationships,* Chichester, UK: John Wiley and Sons, 39–58.

Davidoff, L., Doolittle, M., and Fink, J. (1999) *The family story: blood, contract and intimacy, 1830–1960,* London: Longman.

Dunbar, R.I.M. (1997) *Grooming, gossip and the evolution of language,* Cambridge, MA: Harvard University Press.

———. (2004) *The human story,* London: Faber & Faber.

Dunbar, R.I.M. and Spoors, M. (1998) Social networks, support cliques, and kinship, *Human Nature,* 6: 273–90.

Duncombe, J., Harrison, K., Allan, G. and Marsden, D. (2004) *The state of affairs,* Mahwah, NJ: Lawrence Erlbaum Associates.

Duncombe, J. and Marsden, D. (2004) ' "From here to epiphany . . .": power and identity in the narrative of an affair', in Duncombe et al. (eds) *The state of affairs,* Mahwah, NJ: Lawrence Erlbaum Associates, 141–65.

Ermisch, J. (2003) *An economic analysis of the family,* Princeton, NJ and Oxford: Princeton University Press.

Ermisch, J. (2008) Family economics, *The New Palgrave Dictionary of Economics,* Steven N. Durlauf and Lawrence E. Blume (eds), Palgrave Macmillan, 2008, *The New Palgrave Dictionary of Economics Online,* Palgrave Macmillan. 20 March 2008.

Ermisch, J. and C. Pronzato (2008) Intra-household allocation of resources: inferences from non-resident fathers' child support payments, *The Economic Journal*, 118: 347–62.

Finch, J. (1989) *Family obligations and social change*, Cambridge: Polity.

Fine, M. and Demo, D. (2000) Divorce: societal ill or normative transition?, in R. Milardo and S. Duck (eds) *Family Issues as Relationships*, New York: Wiley, 135–56.

Fischer, J. and Sollie, D. (1993) The transition to marriage: network support and coping, in T. Brubaker (ed) *Family relations: challenges for the future*, Newbury Park, California: Sage.

Giddens, A. (1991) *Modernity and self-identity: self and society in the late modern age*, Cambridge: Polity.

———. (1992) *The transformation of intimacy*, Cambridge: Polity.

Goldscheider, F.K. and Waite, L.J. (1991) *New families, no families?: the transformation of the American home*, Berkeley, CA and Oxford: University of California Press.

Goode, W. (1964) *The family*, Englewood Cliffs, NJ, Prentice-Hall.

Gottman, J., Murray, J., Swanson, C., Tyson, R. and Swanson K. (2005) *The mathematics of marriage*, Cambridge, MA: MIT Press.

Hill, R.A. and R.I.M. Dunbar (2003) Social network size in humans, *Human Nature*, 14: 53–72.

Hinde, R.A. (1997) *Relationships: a dialectical perspective*. Hove, UK: Psychology Press.

Iacovou, M. (2004) 'Patterns of family living', in R. Berthoud and M. Iacovou (eds) *Social Europe: living standards and welfare states*, Cheltenham, UK: Edward Elgar, 21–45.

Jones, G. and Wallace, C. (1992) *Youth, family and citizenship*, Buckingham, UK: Open University Press.

Kalmijn, M. (1998) Intermarriage and homogamy: causes, patterns, trends, *Annual Review of Sociology*, 24: 395–421.

Kiernan, K. (2000) European perspectives on union formation, in L. Waite (ed) *The ties that bind*, New York: Aldine de Gruyter, 40–58.

Lawson, A. (1988) *Adultery*, New York: Basic Books.

Lundberg, S., Pollak, R. and Wales, T. (1997) Do husbands and wives pool their resources? *Journal of Human Resources*, 32: 461–80.

Milardo, R.M. and Duck, S. (2000) *Families as relationships*, Chichester, UK: Wiley.

Morgan, D. (2004) The sociological significance of affairs, in Duncombe et al. (eds) *The state of affairs*, Mahwah, NJ: Lawrence Erlbaum Associates, 15–34.

Mortimer, J.T. and Larson, R. (2002) *The changing adolescent experience: societal trends and the transition to adulthood*, Cambridge: Cambridge University Press.

Pollack, R. (1985) A transactions approach to families and households, *Journal of Economic Literature* 23: 581–608.

Popenoe, D. (1988) *Disturbing the nest: family change and decline in modern societies*, New York: Aldine de Gruyter.

Scanzoni, J. H., Polonko, K., Teachman, J., Thomspon, L. (eds) (1989) *The sexual bond: rethinking families and close relationships*, Newbury Park, CA: Sage.

Sedney, M. (1990) Development of androgyny: parental influences, in S. Carlson (ed) *Perspectives on the family*, Belmont, CA: Wadsworth: 406–20.

Spencer, L. and Pahl, R.E. (2006) *Rethinking friendship: hidden solidarities today*, Princeton, NJ and Oxford: Princeton University Press.

Sprecher, S. (1990) Sex differences in bases of power in dating relationships, in S. Carlson (ed) *Perspectives on the family*, Belmont, CA: Wadsworth, 102–13.

Stone, L. (1990) *The family, sex and marriage in England 1500–1800*. Abridged edition, Harmondsworth, UK: Penguin.

2 Living Apart Together

John Ermisch and Thomas Siedler

Personal relationships are increasingly marked by greater informality. In the case of couple relationships this is apparent in reduced reliance on the formality of marriage, reflected not only in the rise of cohabitation but in what can be viewed as an even more tenuous form of relationship, 'living apart together' (LAT). The latter might be the result of other possible social changes such as increased gender independence, so that, for instance, women might be less willing than in the past to follow their partner when the man moves for job reasons (see the chapter on this issue by Ferreira and Taylor in this volume). Work (or educational) demands might serve to keep couples apart in an age of increasing independence. But unwillingness to commit to a firm relationship might be a contributory or additional factor. The rise of LAT can then be viewed as a social change in the nature of what it means to be a couple.

In Britain, live-in partnerships, be they within marriage or not, have been forming later in people's lives. For instance, comparing women born in the 1950s with those born in the 1970s, the age by which one-half had their first live-in partnership (i.e. the median age) increased from 22 to 25.[1] Another big change over the last quarter of the twentieth century is that in the new millennium the vast majority of partnerships now begin as informal, cohabiting unions. These unions rose as a proportion of first partnerships from about one-quarter for women born in the 1950s to over four-fifths for women born in the 1970s. These two changes lie behind the large postponement of marriage and motherhood in women's lives. Cohabiting unions have a high dissolution rate, and it has increased over time: one-half of the cohabiting unions eventually dissolve, with the other half turning into marriage. In addition to union postponement and dissolution, the rate of re-partnering after dissolution affects the proportion of people who do not live with a partner. After a cohabiting union dissolves, one-half re-partner within about 2 years, but it takes over 7 years for one-half to have re-partnered after a marriage dissolves.

These developments mean that more people are spending time without a live-in partner. But to what extent are they without a romantic partner altogether? Most of us are aware of couples who have a steady relationship but do not live at the same address. While living at different addresses, they regard themselves as a couple and are recognised as such by others. This phenomenon has come to be called 'living apart together,' or LAT for short. The chapter addresses a number of questions. How important is the LAT phenomenon? For whom and where in the life cycle? Is it changing over time? What are the expectations of LAT couples regarding the future of their relationship? How does LAT relate to coresidential relationships? For instance, what role does it play in the formation of cohabiting unions and marriages? How long do LAT relationships last? What conditions and events (e.g. job and housing market changes) facilitate the conversion of LAT into a coresidential relationship?

We seek to answer these questions in a comparison of LAT in Britain and Germany. International comparisons of the phenomenon are extremely rare. There have been a number of studies of LAT in countries other than Britain and Germany (Levin 2004; de Jong Gierveld 2004; Milan and Peters 2003), but only two small British studies (Ermisch 2000; Haskey 2005) and three German studies (Schneider 1996; Traub 2005; Asendorpf 2008) have dealt with the issue. These studies do not provide an in-depth analysis of LAT. This chapter bases such an analysis on two sources of data. One is the British Household Panel Study (BHPS) that carried questions about LAT in 1998 and 2003. Using these responses and the other waves of BHPS data (1991–2005) we undertake analyses of LAT in relation to personal characteristics of partners and to past and subsequent patterns of coresidential relationships. The second source of data is the German Socio-Economic Panel (SOEP), which asked questions related to LAT annually over the period 1991–2005. In addition to permitting similar analyses to those based on British data (with of course many more observations), these data allow us to analyse the dynamics of LAT (e.g. how long do such relationships last, how do they end?) in more detail.

We find that the LAT phenomenon is very similar in Britain and in Germany. It mainly involves young, never married people aged under 25, with the incidence being particularly high among students, and LAT is a more common lifestyle for the better educated, irrespective of age. But LAT also occurs after separation/divorce, with one-fifth of LATs coming from this group. The German evidence suggests that the 'average' LAT lasts about 4 years, with about 45 per cent dissolving, 35 per cent being converted into a cohabiting union and 10 per cent converting into a marriage within 10 years. The British evidence suggests, however, that they may be shorter in duration in Britain, and that the LAT partner usually lives close by.

LAT OVER THE LIFE CYCLE

In the 1998 and 2003 BHPS, all persons who were neither cohabiting nor married were asked, 'Do you have a steady relationship with a male or female friend whom you think of as your "partner", even though you are not living together?' In the SOEP, the following questions were asked, starting in 1991: 'Are you in a serious/permanent relationship?' If that was the case, respondents were also asked 'Does your partner live in the same household?' In our Anglo-German comparisons, we shall compare the British with a sample from the former West Germany (which we refer to throughout as Germany). Table 2.1 shows that the distribution of people across partnership statuses in 2003 was broadly similar in the two countries, with between 20 per cent and 25 per cent of persons aged 16–35 who report being in a 'LAT relationship', compared with 18 per cent in a cohabiting union.

These figures refer to only two broad age groups. How do LAT and other partnerships vary over the life cycle? Combining the 1998 and 2003 British data and German data from 1991–2005, Figure 2.1 plots women's partnership statuses by age. The figure is suggestive of life-cycle patterns. It shows that slightly more than half of women are in some sort of partnership by the age of 19 (Britain: 56 per cent; Germany: 52 per cent). LAT partnerships are most common until the age of about 24, when cohabitation takes over as the modal type of partnership. It remains so until the age of 26, when marriage becomes the modal type of partnership, and about one-half of women aged 28 are married (Britain: 47 per cent, Germany: 50 per cent).

LAT declines in importance over the life cycle, but equally clearly its incidence levels off at around the age of 35 to a very small proportion of all relationships. This reflects the formation of LAT partnerships after separation and divorce. About one-fifth of people in LAT relationships are separated or divorcees, about three-fourths have never been married and 5 per cent are widowed (Britain: 21 per cent separated/divorced; 5 per cent widowed; 72 per cent never married; Germany: 19 per cent separated/divorced; 6 per cent widowed; 75 per cent never married).

British people in LAT relationships were asked about where they saw these relationships going. They were asked which of the following responses 'applies most closely to this relationship': 'I expect we shall get

Table 2.1 Distribution of LAT Partnerships in the UK and Germany, 2003

Year	UK		Germany	
	Age ≤ 35	*Age > 35*	*Age ≤ 35*	*Age > 35*
Married, living together	0.29	0.66	0.27	0.62
Cohabiting	0.18	0.06	0.18	0.06
LAT	0.21	0.04	0.25	0.05
No partner	0.33	0.24	0.31	0.27
Number of observations	2,618	5,389	1,528	3,936

Note: Weighted with cross-sectional weights.

A. British Women, BHPS, 1998 and 2003

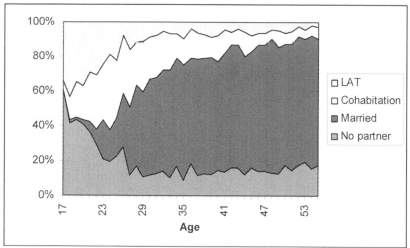

B. West German Women, SOEP, 1991–2005

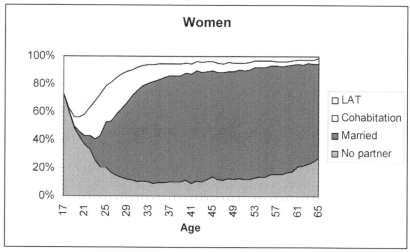

Figure 2.1   Relationship status over the life cycle.

married'; 'I expect we shall live together'; 'I have no plans to live together or get married'. A little over one-half expect to move in together in the future, either in marriage or a cohabiting union. Women were more likely than men to anticipate living together. Among those expecting to move in together, about one-third predicted that they would marry directly, which is above the proportion of first live-in partnerships which are marriages (about 20 per cent). There are, however, substantial age differences. About 20 per cent of LAT people aged 35 and younger expect to marry (40 per cent expect to cohabit) compared to 11 per cent of those aged above 35 (26 per cent expect to cohabit). Comparing women who are mothers of dependent children to those without children, 50 per cent of LAT mothers have no plans to marry or cohabit compared to 38 per cent of LAT women without children in the household. Thus, it appears that a large minority of younger people and a majority of older people have no plans to form a live-in partnership, and so for many the LAT partnership may not be a stepping-stone to a more conventional partnership but a substitute for one.

All persons who were neither cohabiting nor married were also asked to say, 'How likely it is that you will ever get married or remarried to anyone in the future?' Nearly 40 per cent of people in LAT relationships thought it unlikely or very unlikely that they would ever marry, being equally divided between these two categories. There was little difference by sex (male: 37 per cent, compared to female: 41 per cent), but there were big differences by age: for instance, among those aged 35 and under, 22 per cent thought it unlikely or very unlikely that they would ever marry, rising to 79 per cent for persons age over 35. Again, LAT mothers appear less inclined to marry; 63 per cent think that it is unlikely/very unlikely that they will marry in the future compared to 36 per cent of LAT women without children in the household.

People living in cohabiting unions are even less likely to think they will marry in the future. About three-fourths of them thought it unlikely or very unlikely that they would ever marry, with one-third thinking it very unlikely. The proportion is similar among both women and men but increases considerably with age. For instance, 60 per cent of cohabiting people aged 35 and younger think that it is unlikely or very unlikely that they will ever marry. Among cohabiting people aged above 35 the proportion increases to nearly 90 per cent (87.4 percent). From these expectational responses, it would appear that subsequent marriage is an unlikely outcome for a large proportion of the people living in informal unions, particularly those who are older. The next section examines the actual dynamics that are observed.

LAT AND THE DYNAMICS OF PARTNERSHIPS

For both British and German people we can examine how their individual partnership status changed over five years (using the 1998 and 2003 BHPS waves for British and rolling five-year changes for Germans over the period 1991–2005). These are shown in Table 2.2. In both countries,

Table 2.2   Transitions in Partnership Status

A: Transitions in Partnership Status (1998–2003), BHPS

	Married$_{t+5}$	Cohabiting$_{t+5}$	LAT$_{t+5}$	No partner$_{t+5}$
Married$_t$	0.92	0.01	0.01	0.06
Cohabiting$_t$	0.41	0.47	0.05	0.07
LAT$_t$	0.17	0.26	0.32	0.25
No partner$_t$	0.05	0.08	0.14	0.72

Note: 1998 and 2003 BHPS samples.

B: Five-Year Transition Matrix (1991–2005), SOEP

	Married$_{t+5}$	Cohabiting$_{t+5}$	LAT$_{t+5}$	No partner$_{t+5}$
Married$_t$	0.93	0.01	0.01	0.05
Cohabiting$_t$	0.46	0.38	0.06	0.11
LAT$_t$	0.23	0.23	0.32	0.22
No partner$_t$	0.07	0.07	0.16	0.71

Note: West German Sample, rolling 5-year windows.

about one-third of people in a LAT relationship in one year are also in a LAT relationship five years later, although their partners may have changed. The British are more likely than the Germans to be cohabiting or without a partner five years later, while the Germans are more likely to be married. With regard to inflows into LAT relationships, the main sources are people who had no partner five years earlier, followed by those who were cohabiting five years before.

The BHPS permits us to look at duration of LAT relationships in a way that ensures that the LAT partner is the same. Table 2.3 shows that, in both 1998 and 2003, about 40 per cent of the LAT relationships *in progress in that year* had been going on for two or more years. At the other

Table 2.3   Duration of Existing LAT Partnerships, BHPS 1998 and 2003*

Year	*1998*	*2003*
Less than 6 months	0.17	0.17
6 months–1 year	0.19	0.20
1–2 years	0.21	0.23
2–5 years	0.26	0.23
More than 5 years	0.17	0.18
Number of observations	962	1,176

*Weighted responses.

extreme, 17 per cent started less than six months ago. Such figures tend to be an upward-biased estimate of how long a LAT relationship starting today would last, because at a point in time people are more likely to be in a LAT when sampled the longer that they remain in one.

The German panel data allow direct analysis of the dynamics of LATs by following people in LATs from their start. Provided that few people change their LAT partner between years, it should produce unbiased estimates of the duration of LAT relationships, and also information on how a LAT ends: in conversion into a cohabiting union, in marriage or a dissolution of the partnership altogether. Figure 2.2 shows the proportion remaining in a LAT relationship by the number of years since the start of the LAT relationship. Among those starting when aged 16 to 35, a little over one-half remain in their LAT relationship for four years or less. LATs formed after the age of 35 tend to last longer: it takes about five years for one-half to end and about one-quarter are still in the relationship 10 years later. Cohabiting unions can be used as a basis of comparison (not shown in figure). Considering all ages, cohabiting unions last longer: one-half of such unions end after about five years, compared to four years for LATs. To look at this another way, 24 per cent of cohabitations last 10 years compared to 13 per cent for LATs.

How many people subsequently cohabit with their LAT partner? We answer this question by estimating the transition rate into each of the three possible destinations at each year since the LAT started. We then

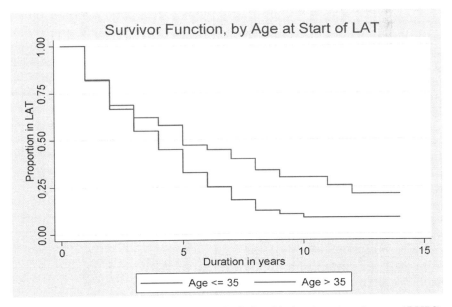

Figure 2.2   Proportion remaining in LAT relationship by time since its start (*BHPS*).

calculate what proportion of people went to each destination in the 10 years subsequent to the start of the LAT. We find that 35 per cent of LAT relationships in Germany end with a cohabiting union, presumably (though not certainly) with their LAT partner of the preceding year. Another 45 per cent dissolve (i.e. terminate in a situation of having no partner) and 11 per cent end in marriage. In contrast, nearly 50 per cent of German cohabiting unions end in marriage, nearly 20 per cent dissolve and about 10 per cent end in a LAT (probably with another partner, but again we cannot be sure). The difference between the dynamics of LAT and cohabiting relationships suggests, as we would expect from Figure 2.1, that LAT and cohabiting unions represent different steps in a person's relationship history, with LAT being a stepping-stone for cohabiting unions for many and the latter being a stepping-stone for marriage. But in both situations there are a large proportion of relationships dissolving, larger in the case of LAT.

WHO LIVES IN A LAT PARTNERSHIP?

This section analyses the type of person who is observed living in a LAT partnership in any particular year. For the purposes of the analysis of persons aged 35 or younger, we restrict the sample to those who are either LAT or in a cohabiting union, because cohabitation is the main partnership alternative for people of this age, and so we compare these two groups. In particular, we estimate a model for the probability of being in a LAT relationship. Table 2.4 shows the 'marginal effect' of a one unit change in a variable (e.g. an additional year of age) or of being in a discrete group (e.g. female) on this probability (summary statistics are shown in Appendix Table 2.1). There are remarkable similarities between Britons and Germans aged 35 and under. Firstly, the probability of LAT declines with age. Given age, women are less likely to be LAT, because at any given age they have 'progressed more' in their partnership life course (from LAT to cohabitation to marriage). Students and those still in school are more likely to be LAT, as are those who have achieved a 'high' level of education. There is one important difference between the countries: people who are not employed are less likely to be LAT in Britain, but more likely in Germany. For Germany, we can also check whether the probability of LAT varies with the population size of the district in which the person lives, which might influence the ease with which LAT relationships can be maintained. There are no significant differences among persons aged 35 and under.

Among persons aged over 35, the analysis sample is restricted to those in a LAT partnership and those who are neither married nor cohabiting, as this appears to be the main alternative for this older group. LAT is less likely for older people and women (given their age), and more likely for

Table 2.4 Relationship Between LAT and Socioeconomic Characteristics[a]

	BHPS		SOEP	
	Age ≤ 35[b]	*Age > 35*[c]	*Age ≤ 35*[b]	*Age > 35*[c]
Age	−0.034	−0.005	−0.035	−0.005
	(12.99)**	(7.86)**	(16.05)**	(7.86)**
Female	−0.046	−0.058	−0.088	−0.067
	(1.95)	(3.69)**	(4.48)**	(4.05)**
Self-employed	0.072	0.066	0.117	0.007
	(1.32)	(2.14)*	(2.70)**	(0.32)
Part-time employed	0.034	0.008	0.061	0.046
	(0.74)	(0.31)	(1.63)	(1.96)
Unemployed	0.031	0.000	0.018	−0.026
	(0.70)	(0.01)	(0.54)	(1.25)
Student	0.347	−0.052	0.215	0.047
	(8.80)**	(0.66)	(10.13)**	(1.16)
Not employed	−0.151	−0.021	0.138	−0.051
	(3.31)**	(0.97)	(5.14)**	(2.51)*
Middle education	0.039	0.020	0.024	0.024
	(1.21)	(0.73)	(1.02)	(1.45)
High education	0.083	0.035	0.082	0.059
	(2.80)**	(2.01)*	(3.50)**	(2.91)**
Still in school	0.254		0.391	
	(2.19)*		(5.71)**	
District size				
2,000–20,000			−0.026	0.021
			(0.54)	(0.78)
20,000–100,000			−0.010	0.052
			(0.22)	(1.79)
100,000 and more			−0.075	0.060
			(1.56)	(2.20)*
Observations	2,405	2,866	9,462	12,266

Note: [a]Estimates are marginal effects from probit equations, with 't-statistics' in parentheses. The reference categories for nonscaled variables are: male, full-time employed, lower educational qualification and district size < 2,000 inhabitants. Regressions also include a dummy for other type of economic activity and other school degree. For the SOEP, regressions also include a maximum set of time dummy variables. *significant at 5%; **significant at 1%.
[b]Aged ≤ 35: Sample of respondents who are either LAT or cohabiting.
[c]Age > 35: Sample of respondents who are either LAT or have no partner.

those with a high educational level (and those with a job in Germany). It appears, therefore, that LAT is a more common lifestyle for the better educated, irrespective of age. For the older group, LAT is also more common in bigger towns (population of 100,000 or more). This may be because the two-residence relationship is easier to manage in bigger towns compared to the two partners living in different small towns.

For Germany we can also test whether LAT has become more important over time by including a set of dichotomous year variables. As a group, these are not significantly different from zero, indicating no significant time trend over the period 1991–2005 in Germany (not shown here).

Taking a more dynamic perspective, we study how these personal characteristics affect the length of time a German person remains in LAT. We do so by studying how they affect the 'exit rate' from LAT, with a higher exit rate implying a shorter time spent in a LAT relationship. Table 2.5 shows that these characteristics have little impact on the exit rate for older people, but for younger people a number are statistically significant. In particular, at each duration of LAT, older young people are more likely to end their LAT relationship, while students and others not employed (other than those seeking work) are less likely to end LAT. There is also evidence that the 'middle' educational group are less likely to terminate their LAT. These results are robust to controlling for persistent unobserved differences between people (unobserved heterogeneity). These patterns explain in part why younger young people (i.e. those aged 35 and under) and students are more likely to be observed in LAT at any particular time (see Table 2.4)— they are less likely to leave a LAT relationship.

SOCIOECONOMIC CHARACTERISTICS OF LAT PARTNERS

Information on the attributes of the person's LAT partner is obviously difficult to obtain in household surveys because he/she does not live in the same household. We make an attempt at this using the BHPS data from 1998 in which information about the three closest friends is provided by the respondent. This attempt relies on making four assumptions. First, the length of LAT partnership must overlap with length of friendship. Second, the friend must be of the opposite sex. While this rules out homosexual LAT relationships, there is no way to distinguish them from other same-sex friendships, which are indeed the predominant ones. Third, they meet most days or at least once a week. This frequency could also be too restrictive, but it is likely to reflect a large proportion of LAT relationships. Fourth, the LAT partner must be the first close friend listed by the LAT person, because a much lower proportion of these friends were of the same sex compared with first-listed friends of people with a partner (50 per cent compared with 80–95 per cent) or with friends listed second and third (50 per cent compared with 70 per cent or more). Clearly we could be 'identifying' more

Table 2.5   Discrete-Time Hazard Rate Models of Exit Rate from LAT (SOEP)

	Logit model without unobserved heterogeneity		Logit model with unobserved heterogeneity	
	Age ≤ 35	Age > 35	Age ≤ 35	Age > 35
Age	0.024	−0.014	0.037	−0.004
	(2.16)*	(1.43)	(2.95)**	(0.38)
Female	0.080	−0.151	0.095	0.174
	(0.85)	(0.86)	(0.94)	(0.80)
Self-employed	0.136	−0.004	0.084	−0.155
	(0.57)	(0.01)	(0.33)	(0.46)
Part-time employed	−0.142	0.415	−0.107	0.099
	(0.58)	(1.58)	(0.42)	(0.32)
Unemployed	−0.131	−0.673	−0.147	−1.043
	(0.61)	(1.70)	(0.65)	(2.26)*
Student	−0.404	0.342	−0.419	0.326
	(3.21)**	(0.54)	(3.16)**	(0.45)
Not employed	−0.384	0.205	−0.397	−0.042
	(2.19)*	(0.74)	(2.16)*	(0.13)
Middle education	−0.270	−0.173	−0.262	−0.119
	(2.29)*	(0.85)	(2.07)*	(0.49)
High education	−0.165	−0.395	−0.127	−0.212
	(1.37)	(1.90)	(0.98)	(0.83)
Still in school	−0.607		−0.589	
	(2.27)*		(2.08)*	
District Size				
2,000–20,000	0.490	−0.467	0.436	−0.562
	(2.07)*	(1.23)	(1.74)	(1.21)
20,000–100,000	0.324	−0.354	0.315	−0.553
	(1.34)	(0.92)	(1.23)	(1.17)
≥ 100,000	0.626	−0.547	0.590	−0.667
	(2.60)**	(1.44)	(2.32)*	(1.44)
Duration-specific dummy variables (11)				
Observations	3,001	1,093	3,001	1,093

Note: The reference categories for nonscaled variables are: male, full-time employed, lower educational qualification and district size < 2,000 inhabitants. Regressions also include a dummy for other type of economic activity and other school degree, and a constant.
*significant at 5%; **significant at 1%.

Table 2.6   Characteristics of LATs, and Their Partner

	LAT	Partners
LAT Women		
Age	32.07	34.78
Distance (%)		
Less than 1 mile		32.53
1–5 miles		27.71
5–50 miles		26.51
Over 50 miles		13.25
Employment (%)		
Full-time employed	58.68	66.87
Part-time employed	12.57	5.42
Unemployed	4.19	8.43
Full-time education	18.56	9.64
LAT Men		
Age	36.70	33.17
Distance (%)		
Less than 1 mile		31.39
1–5 miles		35.04
5–50 miles		21.90
Over 50 miles		11.68
Employment (%)		
Full-time employed	69.34	48.53
Part-time employed	2.92	9.56
Unemployed	4.38	5.15
Full-time education	8.03	19.12

Note: [a]We defined 1st best friend as a LAT partner if (1) opposite sex; (2) they meet most days or at least once a week and (3) if the length of LAT partnership overlaps with length of friendship. According to this definition, 14.25 per cent of LATs' 1st best friend is their LAT partner (aged ≤ 35: 13.19%; > 35: 16.72%).

LAT partners from the friends list if we did not adopt this last criterion, but we believe our procedure is less likely to identify spurious partners. We 'identify' about 14 per cent of first-listed friends as LAT partners on these criteria. A reassuring outcome is that, according to these criteria, a woman's LAT partner is 2.7 years older and a man's LAT partner is 2.5 years younger (see Table 2.6), which corresponds to the common age difference for people with a live-in partner.

Table 2.6 indicates that women in LAT partnerships are more likely to be in full-time education than their partner, and less likely to be employed full-time. This may mainly arise because most LATs involve young people and because of the age difference between partners, with older male partners being more likely to have finished full-time education. About 60 to 65 per cent of LAT partners live within five miles, while only about 12 per cent live 50 miles away or farther. Thus, it appears that LAT relationships usually entail two residences that are relatively near to one another. The small sample of people with 'identified' LAT partners (about 130 in total) precludes more detailed analyses.

CONCLUSIONS

The LAT phenomenon is very similar in Britain and in Germany. It mainly involves young, never married people aged under 25, with the incidence being particularly high among students. But LAT also occurs after separation/divorce, with one-fifth of LATs coming from this group. LAT is a more common lifestyle for the better educated. The German evidence suggests that the 'average' LAT lasts about four years: about one-half of those involving young people (aged 35 and under) remain in their LAT partnership four years or less, with about 45 per cent dissolving, 35 per cent being converted into a cohabiting union and 11 per cent converting into a marriage within 10 years. The British evidence suggests, however, that they may be shorter in duration in Britain, and that the LAT partner usually lives close by.

LAT, along with cohabitation, is part of the substitution of less formal romantic relationships for marriage. The only trend evidence presented here, for Germany, suggests that it was equally prominent in the early 1990s as now. It is, however, attracting more popular attention, possibly because it is more prevalent among the better educated, who write about and comment on society. This chapter has investigated this phenomenon more deeply than some previous studies and put it into the context of the pattern of relationships during people's lives in the early twenty-first century.

NOTE

1. The statistics in this paragraph come from Ermisch (2006).

REFERENCES

Asendorpf, J. B. (2008) Living apart together: Eine eigenständige Lebensform?. *SOEP papers on Multidisciplinary Panel Data Research 78*, Berlin: DIW.

de Jong Gierveld, J. (2004) Remarriage, unmarried cohabitation, living apart together: Partner relationships following bereavement or divorce, *Journal of Marriage and Family*, 66, 236–43.

Ermisch, J. (2000) Personal relationships and marriage expectations: evidence from the 1998 British Household Panel Study. ISER Working Paper 2000–27. Colchester: University of Essex.

Ermisch, J. (2006) Understanding today's families, in *Changing household and family structures and complex living arrangements*, ESRC Seminar Series: Mapping the Public Policy Landscape. Swindon: Economic and Social Research Council.

Haskey, J. (2005) Living arrangements in contemporary Britain: having a partner who usually lives elsewhere and Living Apart Together (LAT), *Population Trends*, 122, 35–45.

Levin, I. (2004) Living apart together: a new family form, *Current Sociology*, 52(2): 223–40.

Milan, A. and Peters, A. (2003) Couples living apart, Statistics Canada, Catalogue no. 11–008.

Schneider, N. F. (1996) Partnerschaften mit getrennten Haushalten in den neuen und alten Bundesländern (Couples with separate households in the former East and West German states), in W. Bien (ed.) *Familie an der Schwelle zum neuen Jahrtausend*. Opladen, Germany: Leske & Budrich, 88–97.

Traub, A. (2005) Neue Liebe in getrennten Haushalten. Zur Bedeutung von living-apart-together Partnerschaften für das Wohlbefinden und Stresserleben allein erziehender Mütter (New love in seperate households. On the importance of living-apart-together partnerships for the well-being and stress perceptions of lone mothers), Berlin: Logos.

Appendix Table 2.1   Summary Statistics, by Age

	BHPS		SOEP	
	Age ≤ 35[f]	*Age > 35[g]*	*Age ≤ 35[f]*	*Age > 35[g]*
Age	25.35	62.35	26.41	61.77
	(5.13)	(16.37)	(4.77)	(16.03)
Female	0.550	0.671	0.535	0.689
Employment status:				
Self-employed	0.046	0.052	0.036	0.052
Full-time employed	0.611	0.245	0.545	0.261
Part-time employed	0.072	0.069	0.047	0.056
Unemployed	0.064	0.025	0.046	0.041
Student, school, training scheme	0.124	0.003	0.223	0.006
Not employed	0.081	0.603	0.074	0.569
Other type of economic activity[a]	0.001	0.001	0.028	0.015
Highest educational qualification:				
Low[b]	0.278	0.541	0.304	0.617
Middle[c]	0.216	0.080	0.309	0.206
High[d]	0.409	0.288	0.350	0.162
Still at school	0.011		0.027	
Other qualification[e]	0.086	0.091	0.010	0.014
District Size				
< 2,000 inhabitants			0.046	0.049
2,000–20,000			0.352	0.300
20,000–100,000			0.260	0.259
≥ 100,000			0.342	0.391
Number of person-year observations	2,405	2,866	9,462	12,266

Note. Figures are means (standard deviations) computed on the number of person-year observations. (BHPS: waves 8 and 13; SOEP: waves 8–22). [a]BHPS: other type of economic activity; SOEP: marginally employed or military/civil service. [b]BHPS: o-levels or lower; SOEP: No school degree or lowest general school degree (Hauptschule). [c]BHPS: A-levels or nursing; SOEP: Middle track school degree (Realschule). [d]BHPS: teaching or higher education; SOEP: Highest school degree (Abitur or Fachhochschulreife); [e]BHPS: commercial, cse, apprenticeship or other; SOEP: other than one of three main school track degrees.
[f]Aged ≤ 35: Sample of respondents who are either LAT or cohabiting.
[g]Age > 35: Sample of respondents who are either LAT or have no partner.

3 Gender Differences in Close Friendship Networks over the Life Cycle

Michèle Belot

INTRODUCTION

Over the last two or three decades, both sociologists and economists have stressed the importance of social ties in life and in particular, in influencing and shaping individual outcomes. Sociologists have long pointed to the transformation of the social environment in modern societies, shifting away from families of fate to families of choice. The new technologies of communication have expanded substantially the set of 'potential' friends, and the popularity of Web-based sites fostering the formation of friendship ties (such as facebook.com, for example) has increased tremendously over the last few years. It is therefore not surprising that economists and sociologists have devoted considerable attention to the role of these *chosen* social ties. Social scientists list different reasons why social networks may be valuable. The most obvious reason is that social relations have an intrinsic value; people enjoy and benefit from interacting with their friends or relatives. But next to that, social networks have also been found to have a valuable instrumental value, by providing access to resources, such as information or material goods (Granovetter 1973). The evidence gathered in many different contexts shows that social networks matter substantially in shaping economic outcomes. For example, there is a growing literature on the role of informal networks in finding a job. Granovetter (2005) stressed the importance of weak ties in the job process, in comparison to strong ties, as they are more likely to provide access to information not available otherwise.

We know a fair amount about the extent to which social ties shape individual behaviour and outcomes, but much less is known about the determinants of social networks, how they differ across people and evolve over the life course. A number of studies, for example, have shown that social networks differ substantially across gender, race or age. This chapter will concentrate on differences across gender. Of particular interest is how these networks vary over the course of life. Sociologists have long argued that because of their position in society, especially their different degrees of engagement in the labour force and child-rearing tasks, women have very different opportunities to make friends than men have. And if social networks play a large role in determining, for example, the position in the labour market, differences in social networks between men and women could possibly provide an explanation for the large differences we observe in terms of occupation or career paths between men and women. It is not the objective of this chapter to establish this type of causal relationship, but we hope to provide a detailed picture of the structure and composition of social networks, which in turn raises a number of questions as to how these could explain differences in economic outcomes.

Until recently, there were no data available to follow the evolution of social networks over time. This has changed, with a number of European household surveys now including questions related to social ties outside the household. Since these surveys typically have a panel component, it has become possible to follow individuals over time and observe how their social ties are affected by different life events. It is important to be able to follow the same individuals over time to be able to distinguish cohort effects from life-cycle effects. For example, widow(er)s may have different social networks from married people because of the status of widowhood itself, but also possibly because, on average, they belong to older cohorts than married people. To understand the effect of life events, such as forming a partnership and raising children, we need to follow the same individuals over time and see how their social networks are affected by those events.

This chapter will describe important differences in the characteristics of friendship networks across gender and over the life course.

GENDER DIFFERENCES IN FRIENDSHIP NETWORKS—REVIEW OF THE LITERATURE

Sociologists have long been interested in gender differences in social networks, both in terms of size and composition. They distinguish between two possible channels through which men's and women's networks could differ (see, for example, Fischer and Oliker 1983 for an early discussion). The first channel is a difference in men's and women's inclinations towards social relations—or what economists would call preferences—whether for biological or cultural reasons. The second channel is a difference in the opportunities to make friends. Because of their different degree of engagement in the labour force and 'home production' tasks, men and women are bound to meet and interact with different sets of people, which in turn should shape their social networks.

One of the most robust findings regarding gender differences in network composition is strong sex segregation. From the preschool age until adulthood, social networks are strongly biased towards same-sex ties. These striking differences in friendship formation at an early age triggered a number of studies in developmental psychology (see Kalmijn 2003 for a review).

Homophily could be part of the explanation—people tend to like people who are like themselves. But also from early on, we observe segregation in social environments such that children have more opportunities to meet children of the same rather than the opposite sex (McPherson et al. 2001).

The second typical finding regarding gender differences in network composition relates to the proportion of relatives in social networks. A number of studies document that the proportion of relatives is larger in women's networks, while men seem to privilege nonkin ties (Fisher and Oliker 1983; Wellman 1985). Moore (1990) argues that the differences in social networks between men and women mainly arise from differences in opportunities to establish social contacts. He shows that the gender differences in network composition fade out once we control for variables related to employment, family and age. But he does find that even after controlling for these variables, women's social networks include more ties to neighbours and relatives and fewer ties to co-workers than men's social networks do. A number of studies focus on the differences in the use of personal ties in the job search process, and in particular in the differences in the identity of the ties used by men and women. Hanson and Pratt (1991) find, for example, that both men and women rely on same-sex personal contacts in finding jobs, and they see this gender bias as more pronounced for men than women. They argue that this perpetuates gender-based occupational segregation, especially for women in female-dominated occupations. More recently, Marmaros and Sacerdote (2002) report results on the effects of peer and social networks on job search using a sample of Dartmouth College seniors. Individuals who were randomly assigned as roommates when freshmen were asked how they use social networking in their job search later on when they reached their senior year. Women were less likely to get fraternity/sorority help, equally likely to get help from relatives, and more likely to use help from professors. Finally, Smith-Lovin and McPherson (1993) describe remarkable differences in the type of voluntary organizations men and women belong to, and argue that these shape the type of 'weak ties' they tend to form. Men tend to belong to large organizations which are related to economic institutions, while women tend to belong to smaller peripheral organizations which focus on domestic and community affairs.

Sociologists have also devoted considerable attention to how social networks change over the course of life and whether these changes are different across gender. Obviously, forming a relationship provides access to a wider social network, almost by definition. Divorce does not necessarily only break up one tie but could be associated with a wider destruction of ties within the network. Sociologists have formulated different arguments regarding how networks could change with the formation of a relationship (see Kalmijn 2003). A first argument is that one has to share time between the spouse and the friends; that is, friends and spouse are direct competitors. People possibly need to reallocate part of the time they used to spend with friends to the more intimate relationship they have just formed. Similarly, the friends of each spouse may also be directly competing with each other. Altogether, competition should decrease the size of social networks. A second argument is the so-called balance principle, which says that triads between people should be transitive. The amount of affection for the partner's friends is expected to grow, and this may eventually lead to an increasing number of common friends. Kalmijn (2003) uses data from a large nationally representative survey in the Netherlands, which include information about the five best friends of each respondent. One attractive feature of the data is that the friends are named, and therefore it is possible to assess how many friends are common between spouses. Kalmijn finds that 58 per cent of people's friends are shared with the partner. Also, 59 per cent of the contacts with friends are joint. Overall, he finds that the number of friends declines over the life course. On the other hand, he does not see any substantial effect of divorce or remarriage on the number of friends.

Hurlbert and Acock (1990) find a slightly different pattern in the US. They use data from the General Social Survey to assess the effects of marital status on the density[1] of the network and the composition of networks (age, mean length of time known, per cent kin and per cent friends). They find that the networks of those divorced or separated are significantly less dense than those of all the other categories (married, widowed or never married). The divorced/separated and the never married also have a lower proportion of kin in their networks in comparison to married people. The networks of widows, on the other hand, resemble the networks of married people in many respects, by being more dense and kin-centred. They find significant gender differences in social networks overall, with female networks more kin-centred than male networks; but they do not find significant gender differences in how marital status affects social networks. Leslie and Grady (1985) study the effects of divorce on social networks on a small sample of women, interviewed at the time of divorce and a year later. Contrary to Hurlbert and Acock, they find that the networks of divorced women become denser and more kin-oriented.

Fischer and Oliker (1983) argue that gender differences in friendship networks emerge more sharply in particular periods of the life course, periods where the opportunities of men and women to meet and interact with other people differ more. They collected data on the size of networks of men and women at different stages of their life. They find that women's networks shrink relative to men's during early marriage and parenthood, while the reverse occurs in the postparental years. Campbell (1988) finds that child rearing decreases women's, but not men's job-related contacts. Munch et al. (1997) argue that the age of the youngest child dictates the time demands of child rearing, and that these demands are different for men and women. They use cross-sectional data (from the first wave of the so-called Ten Towns Study), whereby participants were asked to name people with whom they discuss 'important matters'. They find that having a young child has no statistically significant effect on men's network size, but it has a significant negative effect for women. In particular, women whose youngest child is aged 3 or 4 have significantly smaller networks than do their counterparts with older children. Women's networks are largest when children are infants, reach their minimum when the youngest child is about 3 or 4, and then begin to rebound. However, the composition of men's networks changes dramatically over the child-rearing years; their networks shift towards women and kin relations. This shift seems only temporary though. After children reach school age, the composition of men's networks returns to what it was before the birth of children. Overall, the composition of friendship networks seems to shift towards same-sex friendships over the life course (Kalmijn 2003).

As discussed earlier, most existing studies use cross-sectional data and describe differences in social networks across people. The identification of life-cycle effects is difficult with cross-sectional data because we cannot disentangle life-cycle effects from other sources of heterogeneity. Those who are currently married and have children probably differ from their single counterparts in respects other than their family status, which probably directly influences their social networks as well. It is unclear whether the differences in social networks are due to differences in the stages of life or to other reasons, such as individual sociability, and so on.

By exploiting the panel component of the data, we will be able to describe precisely how social networks change over the life course and in particular with important life events, such as the formation of a partnership, child rearing, divorce, and so on.

EMPIRICAL ANALYSIS

Measures of Friendships

We use data from the British Household Panel Survey (waves 1 to 12). Ideally, we would like to have detailed information about the entire structure of friendship networks of people, but the BHPS only provides information about the *three* closest friends. This truncation presumably encourages the naming of persons 'strongly tied' to the respondent. The information about friendship networks is available in the even waves of the panel (waves 2, 4, 6, 8, 10 and 12).

The truncation may not be as restrictive as it may initially appear. The three named friends are very likely to form part of what Dunbar and Spoors (1995) call the support clique, 'the inner clique of intimates that individuals would normally approach for advice and assistance when in difficulty' (p. 275). They find that the mean size of this support clique is 4.72 in a representative sample of 18- to 65-years-olds in England and Scotland.

We will describe the structure and composition of networks using information from a number of questions. We will present information on the frequency of contacts, the geographical proximity, the gender composition, family orientation and the employment status of the close friendships.

First, for the frequency and geographical distribution of friends, we use the two measures proposed by Belot and Ermisch (2006). The first variable is the number of closest friends living within five miles. The second variable is the number of closest friends with whom the respondent meets at least once a week. Obviously the two variables should be positively correlated as the costs of meeting friends decrease with geographical distance. The information on frequency should also give some idea of the strength of the friendship tie and the intrinsic value of the friendship.

Belot and Ermisch (2006) show that social networks have an important local dimension; that is, those who are nominated as closest friends tend to live close by. When people move, we see a drop in the frequency of meetings and in the number of close friends living nearby. Over time, people's local networks increase again. So it does seem that geographical proximity plays a large role in shaping social networks.

We use three other measures of friendship networks, capturing the characteristics of the closest friends. We will look at the sexual composition of the close friendship network, the family orientation of friendship networks and, finally, the employment status of the close friends, more precisely, the number of close friends who are employed full-time.

Gender Differences in Social Networks: Summary Statistics

We first describe the characteristics of the close friendship network and point to important differences between men and women. At this stage, we pool the whole sample. The next section will examine life-cycle effects in detail.

Table 3.1 shows the distribution of the close friendship network in terms of frequency of meetings and geographical proximity. We look at the number of close friends seen at least once a week and at the number of close friends living within five miles. On average, we find that women see their closest friends slightly more often than men. Of men, 12.7 per cent do not see any of their three closest friends at least once a week, against only 7.4 per cent of women. The difference between men and women is small though. It is quite striking that a substantial share (almost 43 per cent) of both men and women do see all their three closest friends at least once a week. Women tend to have their closest friends in closer proximity, which could explain why they see them more often. But even conditioning on geographical distance, we find that women also tend to see their friends slightly more often than men. Twenty per cent of women do not see any of their friends if their three closest friends live more than five miles away, against 30 per cent of men. So distance seems to be less of an obstacle for women than for men.

Table 3.1   Location of Friends and Frequency of Meetings (per cent)

| Men
Number of close friends
living within 5 miles | Number of close friends seen at least once a week | | | | |
	0	1	2	3	Total
0	29.9	22.6	21.0	26.5	100.0
1	13.6	39.0	23.5	23.8	100.0
2	7.4	16.5	39.9	36.3	100.0
3	4.1	7.7	15.6	72.7	100.0
Total	12.7	20.3	24.5	42.5	100.0

| Women
Number of close friends
living within 5 miles | Number of close friends seen at least once a week | | | | |
	0	1	2	3	Total
0	19.5	27.2	25.6	27.6	100.0
1	8.6	38.9	27.5	25.1	100.0
2	4.6	15.0	43.2	37.2	100.0
3	2.3	8.3	20.5	68.9	100.0
Total	6.8	20.6	29.6	43.0	100.0

We now turn to the composition of social networks in more detail. We first present summary statistics on the gender distribution of the three closest friends. As we mentioned earlier, previous studies have found strong gender segregation in social networks. We confirm this pattern here. Women especially seem to nominate more women as their close friends than men nominate men. Fifty-nine per cent of women have only women among their three closest friends, against a much lower share (39 per cent) of men who only have men among their three closest friends.

Table 3.2   Network Composition: Gender and Kinship

| | Number of friends of same gender (per cent) | | | | |
	0	1	2	3	Total
Men	1.6	14.1	45.0	39.3	100.0
Women	0.3	5.7	35.2	58.9	100.0
	Number of relatives nominated as closest friends (per cent)				
	0	1	2	3	Total
Men	82.50	10.32	4.57	2.60	100.0
Women	74.98	15.40	6.96	2.65	100.0

Another aspect of the composition of social networks is the nature of the relationship, and in particular, whether the close friends are relatives or not. Sociologists have argued that women's friendship networks tend to be more centred on family relations. We constructed a variable measuring the number of relatives nominated among the three closest friends and compared again how these differ between men and women (see Table 3.2). We find that 25 per cent of women report at least one relative as one of their closest friends, against 17.5 per cent of men. This is in line with previous findings indicating that relatives are more present in women's networks than in men's networks.

Finally, we look at the employment status of the three closest friends. Our measure simply counts the number of close friends who are full-time employed. Obviously because of the large differences in the sexual composition between men and women's networks, and because women's attachment to the labour force is weaker on average, we should expect women's friends to be less likely to be full-time employed. Table 3.3 shows the distribution of network composition in terms of employment status, conditional on the gender composition of the network. We see that, indeed, across the board women are much less likely to have full-time employed friends than men are. Thirty-seven per cent of men have all their three closest friends as full-time employed people, against only 12 per cent of women. However, we find that if we compare men and women with the same number of male friends, the gender differences disappear, although men still have a somewhat stronger tendency to be connected to full-time employed people than women do.

Table 3.3 Employment Composition of Networks (per cent)

Men	Number of friends who are full-time employed				
Number of male friends	*0*	*1*	*2*	*3*	*Total*
0	36.0	26.5	19.8	17.7	100.0
1	21.9	30.1	28.2	19.9	100.0
2	14.1	21.1	34.5	30.4	100.0
3	11.9	13.1	23.4	51.6	100.0
Total	14.7	19.3	29.0	37.1	100.0
Women	Number of friends who are full-time employed				
Number of male friends	*0*	*1*	*2*	*3*	*Total*
0	40.7	30.9	19.5	8.9	100.0
1	22.0	33.0	28.4	16.5	100.0
2	13.5	25.2	35.6	25.7	100.0
3	5.5	18.2	29.1	47.3	100.0
Total	32.4	31.3	23.6	12.6	100.0

In conclusion, these descriptive statistics show that the largest differences in social networks between men and women are probably due to the gender segregation of social networks. We do observe small differences in terms of the overall intensity of the network and the presence of relatives in the close friendship network, but these do not compare with the striking and substantial difference in the gender distribution.

We will now investigate in detail how the structure and composition of the close friendship network varies with the life cycle.

Networks and the Life Course

How do friendship networks change over the course of life? We now investigate how different life 'events', such as the formation of a partnership, the birth of children and/or separation and death of a spouse affect friendship networks. Figure 3.1 shows the evolution of the intensity of social networks (measured by the number of friends seen at least once a week) with age, for men and women. We find a similar pattern for both, with a steady decrease in the intensity of social networks up to the late 40s which then stabilises around 2.

We now present estimates of a linear fixed effect model of the determinants of the intensity and composition of social networks, using the measures described previously. The inclusion of a fixed effect enables us

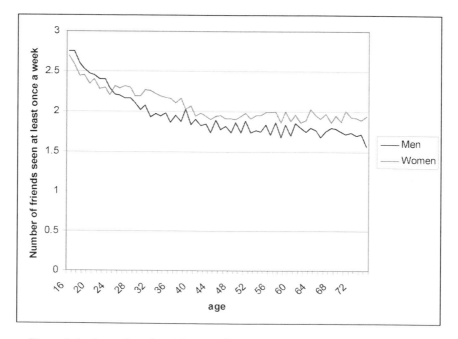

Figure 3.1   Intensity of social networks and age (waves 2–12).

Table 3.4   Life Events and the Size/Intensity of Social Networks

	Number of close friends living within 5 miles		Number of close friends seen at least once a week	
	Men (1)	Women (2)	Men (3)	Women (4)
Age at date of interview	−0.022	−0.025	−0.027	−0.019
	(0.007)**	(0.006)**	(0.007)**	(0.006)**
Age squared	0.000	0.000	0.000	0.000
	(0.000)	(0.000)*	(0.000)**	(0.000)**
No children	—	—	—	—
One child between 0 and 4	0.026	0.053	−0.065	-0.006
	(0.029)	(0.026)*	(0.026)*	(0.023)
One child between 5 and 11	0.018	0.133	0.012	0.127
	(0.027)	(0.022)**	(0.024)	(0.020)**
One child between 12 and 15	0.027	0.101	0.045	0.017
	(0.026)	(0.022)**	(0.023)	(0.020)
One child between 16 and 18	0.030	0.104	0.006	0.034
	(0.045)	(0.037)**	(0.037)	(0.030)
Never in partnership	—	—	—	—
In partnership	−0.094	−0.138	−0.254	−0.209
	(0.047)*	(0.044)**	(0.042)**	(0.038)**
Widow	0.091	0.017	0.157	0.033
	(0.115)	(0.076)	(0.104)	(0.066)
Separated	0.129	−0.012	0.107	0.062
	(0.071)	(0.058)	(0.062)	(0.051)
Living with parents	0.230	0.055	0.008	−0.099
	(0.044)**	(0.042)	(0.039)	(0.037)**
Student	0.124	0.149	0.088	0.170
	(0.054)*	(0.046)**	(0.047)	(0.040)**
Working (part-time or full-time)	0.068	−0.012	−0.023	−0.023
	(0.031)*	(0.022)	(0.027)	(0.019)
Constant	2.386	2.567	2.771	2.496
	(0.163)**	(0.141)**	(0.154)**	(0.133)**
Observations	15,391	18,377	19,244	22,773
Number of cross-wave person identifier	4616	5165	4689	5214
R-squared	0.02	0.02	0.01	0.01

Standard errors in parentheses.
*significant at 5%; **significant at 1%.

to control for unobserved heterogeneity across individuals that is constant over time. Hence, our identification strategy relies on the within-individual time variation in the explanatory variables. We will estimate these determinants separately for men and women.

We start with the determinants of the frequency of meetings with the closest friends and their location of residence. The results are reported in Table 3.4. We find a negative relationship between age and the frequency of contacts with closest friends, both for men and women. Second, being in a partnership has a substantial negative effect on the frequency of contacts with the closest friends, both for men and women. It also seems to be somewhat correlated with the geographical distribution of friends, slightly more so for women than for men. There is no significant difference between the effects of forming a relationship and of dissolving one; overall, being single increases the intensity of social networks.

Next, we find that the arrival of children reshapes the networks of men and women quite substantially: Women's networks become more local, and they tend to see their closest friends more frequently when the children are older (between 5 and 11). Men's networks, on the other hand, are more negatively affected by the presence of children. Fathers of preschool-age children tend to see their closest friends less often. Students see their friends more often; this seems particularly true for girls. Also, when they live with their parents, girls tend to see their friends less often while we find no difference for boys. On the other hand, the social networks of boys are much more local when they live with their parents. Finally, we find that men who work full time are less likely to see their friends, although they are more likely to have local friends (the effect is not significantly different from zero though). We find no strong effect of working for women, maybe somewhat surprisingly.

We now turn to the composition of the network in terms of gender, kinship and employment status. The summary statistics have shown a strong tendency for people to form close friendships with people from the same sex. We now investigate whether and how this tendency changes over time.

Table 3.5 presents the results. We find that the segregation in networks increases with events associated with the formation of a family. First, both men and women see a substantial change in the gender composition of their networks when they form a partnership. Close friendships shift towards friends of the same sex, both for men and women. This could be because some people stop nominating their partner as one of their closest friends once they have formed a partnership (though less than 1 per cent of respondents nominate their partner as one of their three closest friends). Second, the presence of children also shifts men's and women's networks towards homogamous friendships. This is somewhat contradictory to the evidence presented by Munch et al. (1997), which suggested that men's networks tend to become more female with the appearance of children in their lives. However, their analysis relies on a cross-section and therefore does not control for unobserved heterogeneity

Table 3.5 Life Events and Network Composition

	Number of closest friends with same gender		Number of relatives as closest friends		Number of closest friends working full-time	
	Men (1)	Women (2)	Men (3)	Women (4)	Men (5)	Women (6)
Age at date of interview	−0.027	0.004	0.001	0.009	0.119	0.029
	(0.005)**	(0.004)	(0.004)*	(0.004)	(0.006)**	(0.006)**
Age squared	0.000	−0.000	0.000	0.000	−0.001	−0.000
	(0.000)**	(0.000)	(0.000)**	(0.000)**	(0.000)**	(0.000)**
No children	—	—	—	—	—	—
One child between 0 and 4	0.023	0.047	0.035	0.024	−0.058	−0.170
	(0.018)	(0.014)**	(0.014)*	(0.014)	(0.024)*	(0.023)**
One child between 5 and 11	0.039	0.033	0.029	0.031	−0.060	−0.228
	(0.017)*	(0.013)*	(0.013)*	(0.013)*	(0.022)**	(0.021)**
One child between 12 and 15	0.037	0.030	0.004	0.008	−0.084	−0.107
	(0.016)*	(0.012)*	(0.012)	(0.012)	(0.022)**	(0.020)**
One child between 16 and 18	0.086	0.025	−0.033	−0.020	0.011	−0.054
	(0.025)**	(0.019)	(0.017)	(0.018)	(0.034)	(0.031)
Never in partnership	—	—	—	—	—	—
In partnership	0.463	0.421	0.101	0.134	0.078	−0.164
	(0.029)**	(0.024)**	(0.022)**	(0.024)**	(0.038)*	(0.038)**
Widow	0.002	0.368	0.025	0.082	−0.010	−0.088
	(0.076)	(0.043)**	(0.055)	(0.041)*	(0.102)	(0.069)
Separated	−0.055	0.111	0.071	0.092	−0.066	−0.049
	(0.044)	(0.032)**	(0.033)*	(0.032)**	(0.058)	(0.051)
Living with parents	0.111	0.004	−0.107	−0.134	−0.065	−0.068
	(0.027)**	(0.023)	(0.021)**	(0.023)**	(0.036)	(0.037)
Student	0.089	0.041	−0.062	−0.052	−0.718	−0.783
	(0.032)**	(0.025)	(0.024)*	(0.025)*	(0.043)**	(0.040)**
Working (part-time or full-time)	−0.041	0.023	0.041	0.055	−0.294	−0.201
	(0.019)*	(0.012)	(0.014)**	(0.012)**	(0.025)**	(0.020)**
Constant	2.671	2.046	−0.205	−0.445	−0.137	1.111
	(0.107)**	(0.084)**	(0.081)*	(0.082)**	(0.142)	(0.135)**
Observations	17314	20411	38852	44923	17222	20230

(continued)

Table 3.5 (continued)

	Number of closest friends with same gender		Number of relatives as closest friends		Number of closest friends working full-time	
	Men (1)	Women (2)	Men (3)	Women (4)	Men (5)	Women (6)
Number of cross-wave person identifier	4535	5020	5365	5787	4522	5008
R-squared	0.05	0.04	0.01	0.02	0.14	0.08

Standard errors in parentheses.
*significant at 5%; **significant at 1%.

across people, and in particular across people with different family statuses. Next to that, separation and death shift women's networks further towards other women but do not have a large impact on men's networks. Finally, men are more likely to nominate male friends when they live with their parents or are students than otherwise. We find no such effect for women.

The next characteristic of the network we look at is the composition in terms of relatives, and how this composition changes with the life cycle (cols. 3 and 4). We have already mentioned that women are more likely to nominate a relative as one of their closest friends than men are. We actually see a remarkably similar pattern across gender. The events linked with the formation of family shift friendships towards family relatives, both for men and women. It is unclear, though, whether this shift towards family relatives is due to a substitution effect or reflects a reduction in the size of the overall network. One could argue that people who nominate family members as friends may have smaller networks overall since family ties will always survive, while nonfamily ties may be more vulnerable over the life course. In any case, we do not observe any striking difference across gender.

Finally, we look at the employment status of the closest friends. We already know that friendship networks are highly segregated in terms of gender, and we know that this segregation increases with life events associated with the formation of a family, so we expect to find strong differences as well in terms of employment characteristics, since men have a stronger attachment to the labour force than women. If we look at how life events affect the composition of their networks, in columns 5 and 6 of Table 3.5, we find that women are much more affected than men: The number of full-time employed friends decreases substantially when women form partnerships and raise children. Obviously, this pattern goes hand in hand with the change in the gender composition of networks. It may simply reflect the changes in work status that women face on average rather than a change of friends. Since friendships tend to be long-standing, this is a more plausible story.

CONCLUSIONS

We have studied in this chapter how close friendship networks change over the life cycle and whether these changes differ across gender. Most existing studies are based on cross-sectional data, so it is hard to distinguish life-cycle effects from other sources of heterogeneity or from cohort effects. In this study, we use the British Household Panel Survey, which enables us to follow the same individuals over time and investigate how their social networks change with important life events, such as forming or breaking up a partnership and raising children.

The differences we find across gender are in line with previous studies. Social networks are highly segregated across gender; and we find very little differences in terms of the overall size of networks. Women are less likely to have full-time employed friends, but this is essentially due to the gender composition of the networks.

Furthermore, we find that life-cycle events are correlated with important changes in the characteristics of close friendship networks, and these changes differ substantially across gender. For example, women see more of their friends during the child-rearing period, while the opposite is true for men. At the same time, women experience a substantial shift in the composition of their social networks, which become more female, kin-oriented and consequently women are less connected to full-time employed people.

Obviously the analysis focuses on 'strong ties', which may not be of direct relevance for the labour market prospects of women. However, these differences are striking and worth noting. It is hard to assess the consequences of these differences in close friendship networks for the economic and social position of women in comparison to men, but given the large amount of evidence regarding the effects of social networks on behaviour and economic outcomes, it is worthwhile to stress these differences and encourage further research on the subject.

NOTE

1. Density is measured as the mean closeness among alters. The relationship among pairs of alters was coded 1 if especially close, .5 if neither close nor total strangers, and 0 if total strangers.

REFERENCES

Belot and Ermisch (2006) Friendship ties and geographical mobility: evidence from the BHPS, Working Paper Institute for Social and Economic Research Working Papers, paper 2006–33, Colchester, UK: University of Essex.
Campbell (1988) Gender differences in job-related networks, *Work and Occupations*, 15, 179–200.

Dunbar, R.I.M. and Spoors, M. (1998) Social networks, support cliques and kinship, *Human Nature*, 6: 273–90.

Fischer, Claude S. and Oliker, Stacey, J. (1983) A research note on friendship, gender, and the life cycle, *Social Forces*, 62(1): 124–33.

Granovetter, Mark S. (1973) The strength of weak ties, *American Journal of Sociology*, 78(6): 1360–80.

———. (2005) The impact of social structures on economic outcomes, *Journal of Economic Perspectives*, 19(1): 33–50.

Hanson, S. & Pratt, G. (1991) Job search and the occupational segregation of women. *Annals of the Association of American Geographers*, 81: 229–53.

Hurlbert, Jeanne S. and Acock, Alan C. (1990) The effects of marital status on the form and composition of social networks, *Social Science Quarterly*, 71(1): 163–74.

Kalmijn, Matthijs (2003) Shared friendship networks and the life course: an analysis of survey data on married and cohabiting couples, *Social Networks*, 25: 231–49.

Leslie, Leigh and Grady, Katherine (1985) Changes in mothers' social networks and social support following divorce, *Journal of Marriage and the Family*, 47: 663–73.

McPherson, J. Miller and Smith-Lovin, Lynn (1982) Women and weak ties: differences by sex in the size of voluntary organizations, *American Journal of Sociology*, 87 (4): 883–904.

McPherson, J. Miller, Smith-Lovin, Lynn and Cook, James M. (2001) Birds of a feather: homophily in social networks, *Annual Review of Sociology*, 27: 415–44.

Marmaros, David and Sacerdote, Bruce (2002) Peer and social networks in job search, *European Economic Review*, 46(4–5): 870–79.

Moore, Gwen (1990) Structural determinants of men's and women's personal networks, *American Sociological Review*, 55(5): 726–35.

Munch, Alison, McPherson, J. Miller and Smith-Lovin, Lynn (1997) Gender, children, and social contact: the effects of childrearing for men and women, *American Sociological Review*, 62(4): 509–20.

Smith-Lovin, Lynn and McPherson, J. Miller (1993) You are who you know: A network perspective on gender. *In Theory on gender/Feminism on theory*, edited by P. England. New York: Aldine.

Wellman, B. (1985) Domestic work, paid work and net work, in Steve Duck and Daniel Perlman (eds) *Understanding personal relationships*, London: Sage, 159–91.

4   Leaving Home

Maria Iacovou and Lavinia Parisi

INTRODUCTION

At some time during the young adult years, most people progress from being single and living with their parents to living with a partner—and perhaps having children. However, this transition is made in many different ways. Some young people get married, leave the parental home and move in with their husband or wife in such a short space of time that these events may be viewed as essentially contemporaneous. Others move out of the parental home to live with a partner, but do not get married until later, if at all. It is less common for young adults to live with their parents or in-laws as well as a spouse or partner, but it is by no means unknown. And, of course, many young people leave home to live alone or with friends, and do not move in with a spouse or partner until later—possibly much later, or never.

This chapter looks at leaving home and partnership in conjunction with several other transitions which also tend to occur during the young adult years: finishing one's education, finding (or not finding) a job, and starting a family; we also focus on the effect which these transitions have on young people's economic situation.

We take a cross-national perspective, comparing the behaviour of young people across Western Europe. In doing so, we show that there is not just a single pattern of home-leaving and partnership formation, but rather that patterns of behaviour vary according to financial and cultural factors between countries. It shows that the risks associated with home-leaving also vary between countries.

Although we present most of the analysis separately for each country, it is useful for the purposes of discussion and synthesis to think in terms of clusters of countries. We use a typology based on the classification outlined by Esping-Andersen (1990). This consists of:

- The 'social-democratic' regime type, characterised by high levels of state support and an emphasis on the individual rather than the family, typified by the Scandinavian countries and the Netherlands.

- The 'conservative' regime type, characterised by an emphasis on insurance-based benefits providing support for the family rather than the individual, and typified by the continental European states of France, Germany, Austria, Belgium and Luxembourg.
- The 'liberal' group of welfare states typified by a relatively modest level of welfare state provision and a reliance on means-tested benefits, exemplified by the UK and Ireland.

Ferrera (1996) proposes the addition of a fourth category for the southern European countries which were excluded in Esping-Andersen's original typology:

- A 'southern' group of 'residual' welfare states, typified by low levels of welfare provision, and a reliance on the family as a locus of support—typified here by Italy, Spain, Portugal and Greece.

DATA

All the analysis in this chapter is based on data from the European Community Household Panel (ECHP), a set of comparable large-scale longitudinal studies set up and funded by the European Union. The first wave of the ECHP was collected in 1994 for the original countries in the survey: Germany, Denmark, the Netherlands, Belgium, Luxembourg, France, the UK, Ireland, Italy, Greece, Spain and Portugal. Three countries were late joiners to the project: Austria joined in 1995, Finland in 1996 and Sweden in 1997; the final wave of the ECHP was collected in 2001. For technical reasons, we do not analyse data from Sweden or Luxembourg. A fuller discussion of the advantages of the ECHP data, as well as issues arising in its use, may be found in Iacovou and Aassve (2007). The analysis discussed in this chapter focuses on young people aged 16–29, although parts of the analysis look at smaller subgroups of this age range.

AGE AT LEAVING HOME

Leaving the parental home to live independently is a simple concept to define, but not necessarily a simple transition in practice. For some young people, the event is a tidy and straightforward one: they live in their parents' home one day, and move into their own home the following day, never again to return to live with their parents. For other young people, the act of leaving home is much less clear-cut—they may spend protracted periods living partly with their parents and partly elsewhere, or they may leave and return again several times, as the circumstances of their lives (study, jobs, relationships, housing) evolve.

Table 4.1   Age by Which 50% of Young People are Living Away from Home

	Men (1994)	Women (1994)
Finland	21.9	20.0
Denmark	21.4	20.3
Netherlands	23.3	21.2
UK	23.5	21.2
Ireland	26.3	25.2
Belgium	25.8	23.8
France	24.1	22.2
Germany	24.8	21.6
Austria	27.2	23.4
Portugal	28.0	25.2
Spain	28.4	26.6
Italy	29.7	27.1
Greece	28.2	22.9

Source: ECHP (1994), adapted from Iacovou (2002).

We return to this later in the chapter. For now, we note that it creates a problem with measuring the age at leaving home: when looking at large-scale data sets, it is difficult to identify those young people who have left home permanently, as opposed to being in some temporary or transitional arrangement. The proportion of young people living away from home rises with age: in Table 4.1 we report the ages at which half of all young people are observed living away from home, in each country.

In every country, women leave home earlier than men—in most countries, by around two years, except for Greece, where women leave over five years earlier than men. This difference mirrors age differences in relationships: across most of Europe, men are on average two years older than their female partners, except in Greece, where the average age difference in partnerships approaches five years.

Table 4.1 highlights some interesting cross-country differences: the median age at which women leave home ranges from 20 years in Finland to 27 years in Italy, while the age at which men leave home ranges from 21 years in Denmark to almost 30 years in Italy. There is a clear north/south gradient, with home-leaving occurring far later in the southern European countries than in the northern European (and particularly the Scandinavian) countries.

As well as variations in the age at leaving home, we may also observe variations in young people's destinations on leaving home. Figure 4.1 shows the living arrangements of young people who have left home at some time in the past year, and their living arrangements two years afterwards. Four

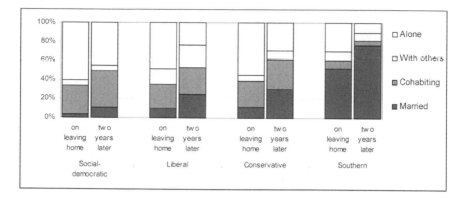

Figure 4.1 Young people's living arrangements, in the year in which they leave home and two years later.
Source: ECHP 1994–2000.

destinations are distinguished: living with a spouse, living with a partner to whom one is not married, living alone, and living with others (i.e., with adults who are not one's parents or grandparents, or partner).[1] This last category is the smallest, and accounts for a sizeable proportion of exits from home only in the Liberal countries. In the UK, young people in this group mainly share homes with people to whom they are not related; in Ireland, and in the southern European countries, a large proportion of people in this group share with siblings and other relatives.

In the social-democratic countries, over 60 per cent of young people live alone after leaving home, around 30 per cent are cohabiting with a partner, and only a small minority are married. Two years on, the proportion living alone has fallen to under half, the proportion cohabiting has risen to almost 40 per cent, and the proportion married has risen to only around 10 per cent. In the southern European countries, the picture is very different. Over half of all young people are married in the same year that they leave home; under 10 per cent are cohabiting, and under a quarter are living alone. Two years after leaving home, the proportion who are married has risen to almost 80 per cent, the proportion cohabiting has fallen, and only 10 per cent live alone.

The liberal and conservative countries occupy an intermediate position, with marriage accounting for only 10 per cent, and cohabitation somewhat under 30 per cent, of exits from the parental home.

This may have its origins in several factors. Most obviously, in the countries where home-leaving takes place particularly early, many young people will not have found a partner with whom they wish to live. However, a more important cause lies in the higher cost of housing in the southern European countries relative to young people's incomes. Where housing is expensive, it is less feasible for a young person to live alone, and it may become culturally embedded for young people to remain in the parental home until they get married and are able to share the cost of independent living with a partner.

These differences in living arrangements, and their effects on the sharing of domestic expenses, have implications for the incidence of poverty and deprivation among young people who have left home. We return to this question later: first, we discuss the factors related to young people's decision to leave the parental home.

FACTORS ASSOCIATED WITH THE DECISION TO LEAVE HOME

There is a sizeable literature on the decision to leave home (Aassve et al. 2003; Ghidoni 2002), and a number of factors underlying the timing of this decision have been identified. Chief among these are economic factors—a young person must have a certain level of financial resources at his or her disposal before leaving home becomes a possibility. These resources do not necessarily come from the young person's own earnings; parents may also contribute towards the cost of their children living independently, and in some countries, relatively generous welfare benefits are available to young people—either in cash or in kind, for example, in the form of subsidised housing. Additionally, young people's expectations of the future may play a role—so that for any given income situation, those in more stable long-term employment may be more likely to leave home than those in less secure employment. Certain factors relating to the family of origin may also be important. For example, young people living in overcrowded or otherwise unsatisfactory conditions may be more likely to leave home early than those living in more comfortable surroundings, as may those living in stepfamilies.

Iacovou (2001), in a study of home-leaving across Europe, finds that in all groups of countries considered, young people's own incomes are positively related to leaving home—as a young person's income rises, so does his or her probability of leaving home. This is consistent with a wish for independence among young people, who, when they have more resources at their disposal, will use these resources to live independently.

However, the effects of parental income vary between groups of countries. Across northern Europe, as parental income rises, the probability of the young person leaving home also rises—but in the southern European countries, the effect is different. For young women in these countries, there is no discernible relationship between parental income and home-leaving, while for young men, the relationship is negative—the probability of a young man leaving home declines as his parents' income increases.

These findings suggest that in the northern European countries, parents have a preference for their young adult children to live independently—and that parents with the appropriate resources are making some of these available to their children when they move out of home. However, in the southern European countries, it appears that parents have a preference for their adult children (particularly their sons) to remain in the parental home, and will use their resources to this end. An interesting corollary of these findings is that while in northern Europe, both young adults and their parents share a preference for independence, there is a disjuncture in southern Europe in the preferences of the two generations, with young people favouring independence, while their parents favour family 'togetherness' more highly.

Manacorda and Moretti (2006), in their study of home-leaving among young men in Italy, also find evidence that Italian parents value family coresidence more highly than their children's independence. They find a strong link between higher parental income and the probability of their offspring staying at home, arguing that Italian parents with higher incomes offer higher income transfers to their children as an incentive to keep them living at home as long as possible.

Although both Manacorda and Moretti (2006) and Iacovou (2001) have hypothesised that the negative relationship between parental income and leaving home in the southern countries is related to parents using their incomes to make transfers to children living at home, or otherwise to encourage their children to remain at home, another explanation is possible. This is that the decision is driven not by parents but by young people's choices—and that young people are more likely to make the decision to leave home if their families are poor. In other words, the decision to leave home is in fact a decision to escape poverty.

Parisi (2008) has investigated this hypothesis using two complementary models—a sample selection model, which models the probability of being poor taking into account that home-leaving rates vary according to poverty status in the family of origin; and a duration modelling approach, allowing for multiple destinations. She confirms that young people from poor families are more likely to leave home at an early age. However, she also observes that young people from poor families are also more likely to end up poor after leaving home—and thus, that early home-leaving is not effective as a strategy for escaping poverty.

LEAVING HOME AND POVERTY

In the previous section, we showed that young people with a certain level of financial resources at their disposal are more likely than other young people to leave home. However, leaving home still carries with it an increased risk of poverty and deprivation. This is driven by two factors, the first being household size. As we saw earlier, young people in several countries, particularly the Nordic countries, are likely to leave home to live by themselves. This means that they alone are responsible for expenses such as rent, utility bills, and so on. Even in southern European countries, where young people tend to leave home to live with a partner, and are extremely unlikely to live alone, household size is smaller for home-leavers than for families where young people are about to leave home (on average halving household size). In all countries, therefore, fewer economies of scale are available in young people's households once they leave home.

The second factor underlying the relationship between leaving home and poverty is the fact that young people's incomes tend to be lower than those of their parents. When young people leave home, they have to rely solely on their own earnings (and possibly those of a partner), which are likely to be substantially lower than their parents' incomes, though this might be mitigated by transfers of money or other resources from the parents.

Figure 4.2 shows poverty rates for two age groups, broken down by country and by whether or not young people have left home. Many features of this figure are completely as expected: for example, poverty rates decline as young people get older, wherever they live. Additionally, poverty rates

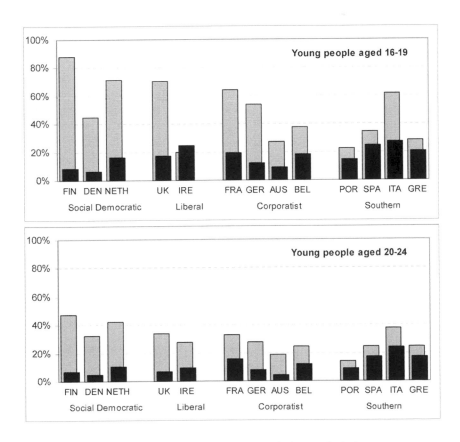

Figure 4.2   Poverty rates, by whether young people live with their parents.
Source: ECHP, adapted from Aassve et al. (2006).

among young people living with their parents vary between countries in a way which we would predict from a knowledge of baseline poverty rates in these countries. In the Scandinavian countries, with their characteristically low poverty rates, the incidence of poverty among young people living with their families is also very low, whereas in the southern European countries, where poverty rates are generally higher, poverty rates are also higher among young people living with their parents.

Poverty rates among young people who do not live with their parents do not follow this general pattern closely. Poverty rates among young people living independently are higher in the social-democratic countries than they are in the southern European countries. This is partly driven by differences in living arrangements. In all countries, we find that young people who leave home to live alone are more likely to be poor than those who leave to form a couple, and in the social-democratic countries, living alone is the dominant living arrangement.

However, analysis in Aassve et al. (2006) shows that while living arrangements are responsible for part of the differences in youth poverty rates between countries, they are not responsible for all of them. Nor are differences in poverty rates attributable to differences in employment status between countries, or the proportion of young people still in education. We suggest that the differences which are not explained by living arrangements are attributable to the age at which young people leave home. In the Scandinavian countries, where home-leaving takes place exceptionally early, many young people leave home without the means to support themselves comfortably—while in the southern European countries, the later age at leaving home means that young people are able to support themselves better once they finally do leave.

This leaves unanswered the question of why young people in the Nordic countries leave home so early, when by doing so they face such a high risk of poverty. Several reasons have been suggested: first, that because early home-leaving is so culturally embedded in these countries, it is an essential element of young people's well-being, even though it renders them vulnerable to a period of poverty. Second, the comprehensive welfare benefits systems in these countries may play a role: young people know they are likely to face a period of poverty on leaving home, but they may be fairly certain that if things turn out badly, they will not face complete destitution. Finally, it has been suggested that although the *incidence* of youth poverty is high in the Nordic countries, the average length of a poverty spell in these countries is low, and many young people are prepared to risk a short spell of poverty in the interests of independence.

INVESTIGATING ISSUES OF CAUSALITY

The analysis in the previous section raises a question of causality: does leaving home *make* young people poor? Or are the two things related, without the relationship being causal? It could be, for example, that young people who are more likely to be poor in the first place are more likely to leave home early. On the other hand, it could be that young people who are at a *lower* risk of poverty are more likely to leave home—in which case, the analysis in the previous section might underestimate the effect of leaving home on youth poverty, with the causal effect being even higher.

Figure 4.3 compares two sets of estimates of the relationship between poverty and leaving home. The first, which we call 'descriptive' estimates, and which do not take into account issues of causality, are based on a sample of young people living with their parents in one year. The extra poverty risk associated with leaving home is calculated by subtracting the poverty rate among those who stay in the parental home the following year from the poverty rate among those who leave home the following year.

The second set of estimates is calculated using a technique known as propensity score matching (PSM). Essentially, this technique (Rosenbaum and Rubin 1983; Caliendo and Kopeinig 2005) compares the poverty outcomes of those people who leave home in a particular year with the outcomes of a group who did not leave home in that year, but who are identical to members of the first group in all observable respects. The PSM estimates are designed to measure the causal effect of leaving home on entering poverty while dealing with the sort of selection effects discussed earlier.

Figure 4.3 displays both sets of estimates for each country, and shows that the two sets of estimates are very similar. Leaving home does make you poor (in fact, in most countries, it makes you even poorer than descriptive esti-

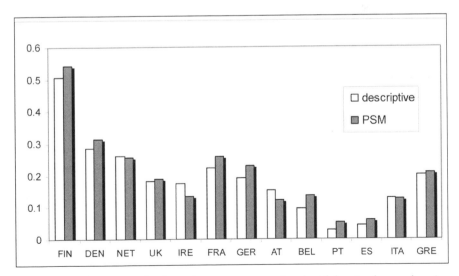

Figure 4.3 The extra risk of entering poverty associated with leaving home: descriptive and PSM estimates.
Source: ECHP, adapted from Aassve et al. (2007).

mates would suggest). It is particularly likely to make a young person poor in Finland, where the extra risk of poverty associated with leaving home is an enormous 54 per cent; the effects are smallest in Portugal and Spain, where leaving home increases the risk of poverty by only around 5 per cent.

We also repeated this analysis using measures of monetary and non-monetary deprivation instead of poverty, and found similar results: leaving home leads to increased levels of deprivation, as well as poverty. These results are reported in Aassve et al. (2007).

ENTERING AND EXITING POVERTY: OTHER FACTORS

Leaving home is not the only factor associated with youth poverty: Iacovou and Aassve (2007) show that other factors are also important, including young people's living arrangements on leaving home (whether they are married or cohabiting, and whether they have children); and their labour market situation (whether they have jobs, or are unemployed, or are studying).

However, it is interesting to note that in most countries, the effect of leaving home on youth poverty is much larger than the effects of the other factors. In the UK, for example, living away from home increases the risk of becoming poor by 12 percentage points—and this risk is increased by an additional 6 percentage points during the year in which the young person leaves home. By contrast, having a baby increases the risk of becoming poor by only 4 percentage points—even in the year in which the baby is born. And being unemployed increases the risk of poverty by only 4 percentage points. The loss of direct parental support is critical.

The only countries in which the effects of living arrangements do not outweigh the effects of other factors are the southern European countries, where the effects of leaving home on poverty are relatively small.

RETURNING HOME: THE 'BOOMERANG BABY' PHENOMENON

As we mentioned in the introduction, leaving home is not necessarily a simple process. Young people retain close links with their parents even after leaving home—and for some of them, these continuing links are manifested by returning to spend one or more spells living in the parental home.

Jones (1995) notes that returns to the parental home are less common in the southern European countries (where home-leaving is late and tends to be contemporaneous with marriage) than in northern European countries (where home-leaving is earlier and tends to be associated with states other than marriage). This is entirely consistent with what we might predict: when northern Europeans leave home, their economic and other circumstances tend to be much less secure than those of their southern counterparts, due to their younger age, and it is entirely intuitive to expect that they would more commonly face the need to return to their parents' home.

However, it is likely that age at leaving home doesn't tell the whole story. We might also expect to observe variations between northern European countries based on factors such as job security in the labour market (with more returns likely in countries with less secure labour markets) and the welfare system (with returns more likely in countries where welfare benefits are less comprehensive for young people).

One problem in analysing returns to the parental home relates to survey attrition—in other words, to the fact that some people who respond to a survey in a particular year subsequently 'disappear'—usually because the interviewing team cannot trace them. Young people are particularly likely to disappear from surveys because they move house frequently; their parents' households are much less prone to attrition. We measure returns to the parental home in two ways. The first uses as its base all young people aged 16–29 observed living away from their parents' homes in year t, and calculates the proportion living away from home in the following year, t + 1. The second uses as its base all parents who have children aged 17–30 who are living away from home in year t, and calculates the proportion of their offspring who return to the parental home in year t + 1. Because attrition among the parental households is much lower, this may present a more reliable estimate of returns home. The disadvantage of this method is that suitable data are not available from all countries, particularly the late joiners to the ECHP.

Figure 4.4 presents estimates of the proportion of young people returning to their parents' home, calculated using first young people, and second the parents of young people, as a base. In almost all countries where both sets of data are available, the figures for returns home are higher when obtained from young people themselves. A likely explanation for this is that young people are relatively likely to leave the sample—but are less likely to disappear from the sample if they return to their parents' homes, if their parents are also sample members.

However, apart from these systematic differences, the ranking between countries appears very similar whether one considers young people themselves or their parents. Under both measures, the UK has by far the highest rate of returns to the parental home, standing at 4 per cent (as measured using young people as a base) and 2 per cent (as measured using parents).

In contrast to the findings reported by Jones (1995), there is little evidence that northern Europeans are systematically more likely than southern Europeans to return to their parents' homes. With the exception of the UK, and to a lesser extent France, there is a relatively low incidence of return to the parental home in northern Europe.

In fact, a lower level of return to the parental home in northern Europe is not inconsistent with intuition, and is quite consistent with the combination of relatively generous welfare-state benefits in these countries, and a

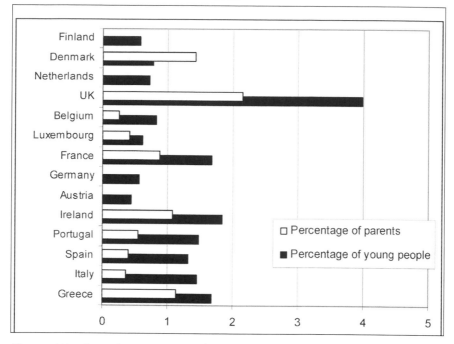

Figure 4.4   Annual percentages of young people and parents experiencing a return home.
Source: ECHP.

culture in which young people and their parents both value independence. In southern European countries, by contrast, few welfare benefits are available to young people in the event of adversity—and coresidence with parents may be more acceptable, to the young people themselves, their parents, and society in general.

Why should the UK have such a high rate of return to the parental home? One possible reason may be that home-leaving in the UK occurs extremely early—the median age at leaving home is similar to the age observed in the Scandinavian countries—but the safety net afforded by the British welfare state is not comparably generous to that available in the Scandinavian countries.

CONCLUSIONS

Leaving home is a crucial stage in the transition to adulthood. It is one of the earliest and most visible transitions on the road to adulthood; we have argued that it is also a transition which requires a certain degree of resources to come about, and which carries with it a not inconsiderable degree of risk. Living away from home is the single most important predictor of youth poverty in nearly every country across Europe, and this risk is at its very highest for young people in their first year after leaving home.

Patterns of home-leaving vary greatly between countries, with home-leaving taking place earliest in the Nordic countries, also relatively early in the northern European countries, and much later across southern Europe. Some of these variations are clearly driven by factors such as social security systems, housing markets and labour markets, which make leaving home at an earlier age easier in northern than in southern Europe. However, we have shown that these factors do not explain the full extent of cross-national differences in home-leaving behaviour. We suggest that these differences are also driven by social and cultural factors—by young people conforming to social norms, and by considerable cross-country differences in the ways in which young people relate to their families of origin.

ACKNOWLEDGEMENTS

Much of the work on which this chapter is based was funded by the Joseph Rowntree Foundation's Ladders out of Poverty programme. Thanks are due to Helen Barnard and Chris Goulden of JRF, who acted as our research liaison officers, and to members of the project's advisory committee: Paul Gregg, Simon Burgess, Jackie Scott, Elaine Squires and Simon Lunn. The ECHP data used in the analysis were produced and made available by Eurostat.

NOTE

1. The category 'living alone' includes lone parents, who live with children but no other adults.

REFERENCES

Aassve, A., Billari, F.C., Mazzuco, S. and Ongaro, F. (2003) Leaving home: a comparative analysis of ECHP data, *Journal of European Social Policy*, 12(4): 259–75.

Aassve, A., Davia, M.A., Iacovou, M. and Mazzuco, S. (2007) Does leaving home make you poor? Evidence from 13 European countries, *European Journal of Population*, 23(3–4): 315–38.

Aassve, A., Iacovou, M., and Mencarini, L. (2006) Youth poverty and transition to adulthood in Europe, *Demographic Research*, 15: 21–40.

Caliendo, M. and Kopeinig, S. (2005), Some practical guidance for the implementation of propensity score matching, IZA working paper, no.1588,. Online. Available HTTP: <http://repec.iza.org/dp1588.pdf>. Accessed on 1 April 2008.

Esping-Andersen, G. (1990) *Three worlds of welfare capitalism*, Cambridge: Policy Press.

Ferrera (1996) The 'southern model' of welfare in social Europe, *Journal of European Social Policy*, 6(1): 179–89.

Ghidoni, Michele (2002) *Determinants of young Europeans' decision to leave the parental household*, unpublished manuscript, UCL, London.

Iacovou, M. (2001) Leaving home in the European Union, working paper of Institute for Social and Economic Research, paper 2001–18 (PDF). Colchester, UK: University of Essex.

Iacovou M. (2002) Regional differences in the transition to adulthood, *Annals of the American Association of Political and Social Science*, 580: 40–69.

Iacovou, M. and Aassve, A. (2007) Youth poverty in Europe, report series of Joseph Rowntree Foundation, York, UK: Joseph Rowntree Foundation.

Jones, G. (1995) *Leaving Home*, Buckingham, UK: Open University Press.

Manacorda, M. and Moretti, E. (2006) Why do most Italian men live with their parents? Intergenerational transfers and household structure, *Journal of the European Economic Association*, 4(4): 800–29.

Parisi, L (2008) *Leaving home and the chances of being poor: the case of young people in southern European Countries*, working paper of the Institute for Social and Economic Research, Colchester, UK: University of Essex.

Poverty and the transition to adulthood: risky situations and risky events, working paper of the Institute for Social and Economic Research, Colchester, UK: University of Essex.

Rosenbaum, P.T. and Rubin, D.B. (1983) Constructing a control group using multivariate matching sampling methods that incorporate the propensity score, *The American Statistician*, 39(1): 33–38.

5 The Social Significance of Homogamy

Malcolm Brynin, Simonetta Longhi and Álvaro Martínez Pérez

INTRODUCTION

Social scientists have for long been concerned to understand the social basis of marriage. This ranges from anthropological interest in kinship patterns (Goode 1964), through sociological analysis of social mobility (Goldthorpe et al. 1987), to economic accounts of the 'marriage market' (Becker 1991). A theme that often recurs in this discussion is the role of homogamy—the idea that 'like marries like'. Why should this be of continuing interest? A compelling reason is that the extent of homogamy tells us something about how open a society might be. If couples become less closely united on the basis of social distinctions such as wealth or education, then social divisions between couples, and between households, become less pronounced. This process would be a complement of other (if sometimes contradictory) evidence of a growth in social mobility. Thus, increasing heterogamy is associated for some analysts with a breaking down of social divisions, and implicitly with the strengthening of an open and democratic society (Hakim 2000; Ultee and Luijkx 1990). Conversely, if homogamy is rising, this suggests some form of social closure, which might also stretch across the generations. Parents who have equally high levels of education, income or wealth can transmit additional benefits to their children through the resultant pooling of resources, whether material, cultural or intellectual (Blossfeld and Timm 2003). This, in Bourdieu's view, would be a compensatory strategy of reproduction that the relatively privileged might use to counteract the equalising effects of increased social mobility (Bourdieu 1976)—the well-off 'close ranks'. Mare speaks of *'barriers* to marriage between persons with unequal amounts of formal schooling' (1991: 30; our emphasis). In this case, homogamy and social mobility have opposite effects.

In the next two sections, before proceeding to our own analysis, we consider two questions. First, is society in fact characterised by decreasing homogamy? Second, if so, can we interpret this as giving rise to greater social openness?

THE MEASUREMENT AND MEANING OF HOMOGAMY

Unfortunately it is not easy to ascertain trends in homogamy. In respect of a frequently analysed dimension, education, the trends are problematic, with some analysts claiming that marriages are becoming more closed (Blossfeld and Timm 2003; Mare 1991; Schwartz and Mare 2005), some more open (Hakim 2000; Ultee and Luijkx 1990—although this latter finding was not conclusive). There are several problems in these comparisons, first of timescale. Hakim's review, for instance, is of a longer period of time than that of some others—the period 1910–1966 in the US. Even though Hakim compares 1949 to 1996 in Britain, for much of that time the spread of higher education was still extremely limited. This means that in the earlier years the marriage market comprised mostly poorly educated people; homogamy was perforce high, and subsequently likely to fall. Further, any decline in homogamy could be the result of increasing choice (there are more educated people for the less educated to choose from, deliberatively) or simply a random result of changes in numbers (the operation of chance, therefore, rather than of choice). These represent two very different processes. Second, trends depend on the methodology used to calculate them. This in turn is partly to do with the unit of measurement. Rough descriptors of education will obscure the level of educational outmarriage as much movement will be across close but nevertheless significant boundaries. For instance, where a junior doctor marries a senior nurse, is this relationship homogamous (by occupation) or not? (Hakim 2000: 208.) Third, there are two related problems where population samples are used: the survival of older couples might not reflect the level of homogamy prevalent when they first married, and with remarriages mixing new and old couples obscures within-sample trends. Ultee and Luijkx (1990) compare population surveys rather than age cohorts (more specifically, restricting to couples recently married), and thus include the full mix of ages. The studies which find increasing homogamy make explicit comparison between cohorts (Mare 1991). They also use log-linear methods to take account of the expansion of education (e.g. the studies in Blossfeld and Timm 2003), though Hakim (2000) uses a different method to take account of time.[1]

Overall, it seems likely that educational homogamy is increasing in several countries. Schwartz and Mare (2005), analysing US data 1940–2003 on newlyweds, find that the 'odds of educational homogamy have been higher since 2000 than in any other decade since 1940' (2005: 641). This is exemplified by intensified polarisation, whereby people at both the top and the bottom of the educational ladder increasingly marry within their groups.

This argument is important because the trends are linked to different views of the nature of social change. We have already mentioned the idea that heterogamy equals social openness. According to Hakim, though, it is also linked to a particular structure of gender relations.

The fact remains that women today continue to prefer marriage to men who have money, status, and power, even when they themselves have achieved high earnings, whereas men continue to prefer young and attractive women, other things being equal. This long established exchange of complementary status and assets has been weakened by the educational equality of women and men, but it has not disappeared completely. (Hakim 2000: 222)

The problem with this statement is the phrase 'other things being equal'. On several significant dimensions, especially education, equality is a fact which is changing how men and women interact. Even if women wish to 'marry up' financially, this does not require them to have a lesser education. In other words, we would expect partners to sort on the basis of education first; *both* partners (not just women) might then seek to ensure that the match is as financially advantageous to themselves as possible.

This assumes a primarily 'cultural' underpinning of relationships where education signals to individuals a range of factors about the broad compatibility of their prospective partners. Kalmijn finds that in partnerships where both partners work, educational matching overrides matching on earnings; he argues that this 'cultural similarity . . . can be understood as an attempt to develop a common lifestyle in marriage' (1994: 448). In Denmark, Nielsen and Svarer demonstrate, if indirectly, that 'joint income . . . show[s] no influence on partner selection' (2006: 25). Educational matches seem more important, suggesting a more cultural basis to marriage.

Such studies do not prove that earnings do not play a role in matching, but their attraction is difficult to distinguish from the attraction of education, on which earnings mostly depend. However, education is probably the more inclusive badge, denoting not only resource outcomes but prestige and lifestyle preferences. It is also of note that education is more equal than in the past, which not only raises women's power relative to men but changes men's perception of the worth of a prospective partner. Men may now gauge the economic value of a marriage in much the same way as do women (Blossfeld and Timm 2003: 341; Brynin and Francesconi 2004; Kalmijn 1998: 399). This is likely not only to create greater equality within couples but to encourage homogamy (Mare 1991: 17; Oppenheimer 1988), thus reducing further the probability of women marrying up.

The idea that marriage is a calculation used to make headway in the social hierarchy rather than to find a compatible partner runs counter to long-standing anthropological and sociological confirmation of the social basis of similarity, and even equality in marriage (e.g. Bourdieu 1976; Kalmijn 1998; Westermarck 1903). Equality is not only a personal preference but often a social prerequisite. What are the forces that would encourage people to cross socially recognised boundaries such as religious prohibition against intermarriage, or even boundaries which are policed less strongly? Like Mare, quoted earlier, Kalmijn argues that 'group identification and group sanctions' (1998: 400) continue to impose social pressure on marriage. In addition, homogamy has a clear emotional underpinning (which Hakim acknowledges), derived from an ability to share problems, beliefs, leisure interests, a sense of humour, and so on (Kalmijn and Bernasco 2001). In Bourdieu's terms, similarity of background ['habitus'] allows a 'spontaneous decoding . . . discouraging socially discordant relationships' and 'induces couples to experience their mutual election as a happy accident' (1984: 243). Material interest itself encourages equality. Goode (1964) explicitly points to the economic loss (to one partner or family) which homogamy prevents, on average, while economists of the family, most notably Becker (1991), build this idea into formal models of marriage markets. Further, Becker argues that homogamy is efficient not only for the partners but for society. On the assumption that one person's education makes the other more productive (on a range of dimensions), where a highly educated person marries someone less educated, neither can gain much (in the former case because the other person has little to offer, in the latter because the other has little on which to build); but where two highly educated people marry, their education has a multiplier effect on productivity. Whether this outcome applies in practice is an empirical question, depending on the distribution of education in marriages, but as education rises it is presumably more likely.

Rising education has the reverse effect to that suggested by Hakim, releasing suppressed social demand for educational equality within couples. As education becomes more equal, this enables greater conformity in terms of mutual rights, expectations, cultural interests, and lifestyles. With the increased pool of female graduates, men who previously married nongraduates need not do so.[2] Certainly choice rises with education, but it works against heterogeneity. Nongraduates can more easily marry graduates than in the past because they are now more available, but by the same token the past did not allow large numbers of graduates to marry each other. This has changed.

THE ROLE OF SOCIAL CHANGE

The argument in favour of a relationship between falling homogamy and increased social openness seems to rest on a simple numerical effect of the rise in education. However, this says nothing about social openness as a value. Our emphasis on the continuity implied by the underlying social and psychological imperatives of homogamy does not mean there are no other pressures for change. We posit here two factors which could be important. First, education itself changes attitudes. In the past, homogamy was extremely high on all dimensions such as ethnicity, religion, wealth and social status (Westermarck 1903). However, while education is correlated with income, beliefs, and so on, the correlation is loose. Trends in educational homogamy, therefore, need not run in parallel to trends in homogamy on other dimensions. Education is also a distinct quality. Higher education especially might encourage liberal views and therefore a desire for social openness and social mixing. Liberal people are more likely than others to marry outside their inherited ethnicity, religion, and so on, and liberalism is related to educational background (Kalmijn 1998: 413). For instance, Lampard finds that higher levels of education are associated with greater political heterogamy, if weakly (1997: 87).

We can posit the effect of a second kind of social change through the growth in cohabitations and in marital breakdown followed by remarriage. Marriage is in decline as a proportion of all unions, and we might expect cohabitations to be less homogamous than marriages: because less is at stake (as the union is not so legally binding), and cohabitation is also the time to experiment. Unless cohabitation itself is strongly associated with education—and we find in the data only a weak association—we should expect rising cohabitation to lead to a decline in homogamy. Interestingly, in his study of political homogamy Lampard finds that heterogamy is stronger amongst couples who are only 'dating', while cohabitees match almost equally to married couples (1997: 87). Nevertheless, this still implies that weaker forms of union join people only weakly matched on their social beliefs. Using German panel data from a sample of young women, Moors' analysis suggests that cohabitation is associated with increased belief in autonomy (2000: 222), and this too implies a reduced tendency towards homogamy.

This should be reinforced by rates of remarriage. Even if heterogamy is a factor in divorce (because homogamy binds couples more strongly: Weiss and Willis 1997; Blossfeld and Müller 2002), there is some evidence that divorce is associated with higher levels of heterogamy in later relationships (Kalmijn 1998: 397). Causes might be that divorce reduces subsequent freedom to choose, for instance, for women with children; the pool of potential spouses or partners is smaller; circumstances might be more constrained; people become less attractive as they age; some people opt out of relationships altogether when a relationship collapses, thus reducing choice yet further. Xu, Hudspeth and Bartowski (2006) find that postdivorce cohabitation is associated with low levels of remarital happiness, which suggests that these relationships are less close than first relationships. Less happy, perhaps, but possibly more free. As an aside, it is worth pointing out that Jane Austen, a precise observer of the value of marriage, suggested that the romance of a first relationship is an impediment to individual freedom. 'Preserve yourself from a first Love & you need not fear a second.'[3] Remarkably, it seems advisable to skip a first relationship. All in all, to return to the point, we would expect marital breakdown and reformation to be associated with declining homogamy.

We have argued that the numerical explanation for a fall in homogamy—that is, simply, that an increase in more highly educated people raises the probability of educationally mixed marriage—is not enough, and also runs counter to what we know about the social basis of marriage. Nevertheless, the nature of relationships is itself changing. In the succeeding analysis we seek to find out whether the factors we believe could be changing patterns of homogamy are indeed having these effects.

ANALYSIS

We test first for trends in homogamy, using census data for England and Wales from the ONS Longitudinal Study (LS), then for the effect of higher education on homogamy, and finally for the effect of cohabitation and repartnership. For the latter analyses we use the BHPS.

Trends

The census data used here to calculate trends derive from the ONS Longitudinal Study, although for this we do not use the longitudinal component. As in many other studies, we construct odds ratios to demonstrate change, though we go further than some in looking at a number of dimensions: not only education but ethnicity and religion. Unfortunately, ethnicity cannot be used to examine trends effectively, as this has been asked only in the last two censuses, while religion, available in these data only in 2001, cannot be used at all. Nevertheless, as we shall see, given the extremely low overall rate of marriage or partnership across ethnic and religious boundaries, trends hardly matter.

This is not the case with education. In 1971 the odds of a nongraduate marrying a graduate, compared to the odds of a graduate marrying a graduate, produced an odds ratio of around 45 to one (i.e. the odds against were very high).[4] This fell to 26 in 1981 and in 1991 slightly further to 23, which we put down to the rising number of female graduates. When the number was extremely small there was a very large pool of male graduates from which to choose, and thus most female graduates were likely, for instance by virtue of encounters at university, to marry a male graduate. In line with Hakim's prediction, therefore, educational expansion reduces homogamy. On the other hand, this changes in the opposite direction when virtual equality in education is achieved. In 2001 the odds are 132.[5]

The trend in the odds is therefore U-shaped, with first a fall in homogamy as a result of greater opportunity, followed by an increase as education approaches equality. Interestingly, this is the same as Schwartz and Mare (2005) find for the US, where educational homogamy decreased from 1940 to 1960 but increased thereafter. In Norway, looking only at people born between 1900 and 1949, Birkelund and Heldal (2003) find an increase in homogamy over the relevant period. It is possible to interpret this trend in purely numerical terms. As any social category becomes relatively large, if choice is random then people in that group have an increased probability of marrying within the group (Kalmijn 1998: 402). However, we prefer the alternative explanation that numerical equality provides the opportunity to partner homogamously, in line with most people's preferences.

It should also be noted that while odds ratios are symmetrical by gender, if we look at percentages instead we might find important differences. With greater female entry into higher education it is easier for male graduates to find an educationally equivalent partner.[6] The proportion of female graduates who married graduates rose from 66 per cent in 1971 to 80 per cent in 2001, but the equivalent rise for men, as more female graduates came 'on stream', was from 15 per cent to 74 per cent.

The ethnicity results (based on the census definition) reveal very little intermarriage. Virtually all intermarriage is between white British and other groups and we therefore base our analysis simply on white against nonwhite. In 1991 the odds ratio was 449; in 2001 it was 454. There is virtually no reaching out across the nonwhite categories. In the case of religion, unfortunately there is no breakdown between Christian denominations in the data. So we compare only Christian, non-Christian, and 'no religion'. There is a difficulty in interpreting the latter (does it mean truly antireligious or just not very bothered?). The most meaningful ratio we can produce is between people stating they are Christian or non-Christian. This odds ratio is 2,401. There is some way to go here before the different religions mix. It would in fact depend on the decline in religion itself. Indeed, the data suggest that people who declare a religion are prepared to live with someone who does not (but who perhaps has a similar religious background). The odds ratio for Christian and 'no religion' is 33, that for non-Christian and 'no religion' is 65—still very high but lower than 2,401.

There will almost certainly be pools of greater social openness in specific regions. The chances of intermarriage in the case of ethnicity, for instance, are virtually nil in many parts of the country where ethnic minorities are not present (though of course this partially reflects the inclinations of ethnic groups, including British white people, who choose to live in their own enclaves, marriage out of which is unlikely). In London especially it is probable that heterogamy is higher than the previous statistic suggests.

Further, we use here the full LS census figures which, as stated earlier, would give different results from analysis of newlyweds. Ideally we would like to know whether new marriages (or partnerships) are increasingly homogamous. But it is not possible to distinguish new marriages in the census. It is of course possible to produce figures by age cohort, but these would have an indeterminate relationship with new marriages (which would include remarriage). However, although our figures are affected by the survival of married couples, which inflates the trend, the figures reflect the balance of homogamy at the 10-year intervals, and the result of this shows that continuing and extensive homogamy is a profound social fact.

New Partnerships

As just noted, the above analysis is of the whole (married) population. We cannot tell from this how closely related people were at the time of marriage. This is unlikely to be an issue in the case of education (generally fixed after a certain point), even less of ethnicity, but is a problem for religion (insofar as people might, for instance, change over a period from Christian to no religion), and even more for occupation and opinions. To examine homogamy in new partnerships we use the British Household Panel Study (BHPS), which, as a panel, enables us to examine closeness of circumstances and values at the time of partnership. An obvious disadvantage is its very small sample size. In the BHPS we have around 150–200 marriages or cohabitations starting each year, though pooling these produces a total of 2,796 new couples (not all of which can in fact be used for the analysis on homogamy because of lack of data on specific characteristics). However, in addition to looking at new partnerships, another advantage of the BHPS is its extensive data on subjective indicators, enabling us to see, for instance, whether homogamy is important in respect of social values.

We have already demonstrated a high degree of homogamy based on LS data. This is repeated in the BHPS data on new marriages, though we do not provide odds ratios but simply percentages. For instance, 64 per cent of couples can be classified as homogamous in terms of education even with fairly refined educational groupings (low education, school-based qualifications, further education and higher education). Seventy per cent of couples have an age gap of no more than three years. Classifying social classes into three groups (professional, managerial and technical; skilled manual and nonmanual; partly skilled and unskilled occupations), we find lower homogamy than in the case of education, by about 10 percentage points. Homogamy on the basis of the social class of the two fathers is lower still, again by about 10 percentage points.[7] In respect of religion, in the BHPS the number of non-Christians is very small and therefore less statistically reliable than in the census. Nevertheless, homogamy on this basis is far higher than we would expect on the basis of chance.

The Effects of Social Change

We hypothesised earlier that two aspects of social change in particular might induce a decrease in homogamy. One was increased education itself, which might encourage greater liberalism and thereby social openness. We test this in Table 5.1, which shows in the first column all new couples; in the second those where both have a degree; in the third, couples where only the man has a degree; and finally those where neither partner has a degree. In each case we show how similar people in couples are to each other on a number of dimensions. If education

Table 5.1   Different Dimensions of Homogamy by Education

Homogamous by:	(1) All	(2) Both degree	(3) Only man has degree	(4) No degrees
Qualification	36.4	—	—	—
Qualification plus/minus one level	64.7	—	—	—
Age (one year difference)	28.6	38.4	27.8	30.4
Age (three years difference)	55.5	70.8	57.3	54.0
Religion	55.0	63.6	47.4	50.1
Social class (grouped)	50.6	76.1	59.2	48.9
Family values	63.1	76.6	76.7	59.0
Political values	50.5	49.7	43.2	51.1

Note: Minimum cell size = 19, maximum = 766, average = 191.

increases social openness, the figures in column 2 should be the lowest. We in fact observe the opposite. Educational homogamy is correlated with other forms of homogamy. While the sample sizes are generally small and sometimes extremely small for the second to fourth columns, ranging from 19 for one cell to 766 for the maximum cell size, not only equal education but equal higher education (that is, comparing the second and fourth columns) seems to be associated with higher levels of homogamy on other indicators. One contributory factor to this might be that more educated people marry later and have more time to find an appropriately homogamous person.

We also hypothesised that cohabitation and repartnership would lower the level of homogamy. Yet our data show that the proportion of educationally homogamous couples is 61 per cent for marriages and 65 per cent for cohabitations (though these percentages would vary with the number of categories used: here we use five); social-class homogamy is slightly higher for cohabiting couples, 50 per cent compared to 46 percent, when we use three broad groups. These figures become 30 per cent and 28 per cent in a more detailed version. Religious homogamy is 53 per cent in both cases. Thus, cohabitation does not after all seem to be associated with greater heterogamy.

We next turn in Table 5.2 to examine the effects of cohabitation and repartnership, now using the entire sample of relationships, on measures of social values. In the upper part of the table we show the percentages of these couples with similar views on gender roles (based on the question 'Do you personally agree or disagree. . . . A husband's job is to earn money; a wife's job is to look after the home and family?'). We distinguish between couples where both partners are egalitarian (agreeing with a 'liberal' view)

Table 5.2   Attitudinal Homogamy Comparing Cohabitation to Marriage and First to Later Unions

	Married	*Cohabiting*	*First union*	*Later union*
Egalitarian	32.9	51.9	30.7	44.0
Traditional	8.3	2.4	9.5	3.7
Neither	9.5	5.8	9.8	7.6
All homogamy *(observations)*	*50.7* *(8,012)*	*60.1* *(1,271)*	*50.0* *(5,996)*	*55.3* *(3,288)*
Labour	31.4	27.6	31.5	30.1
Conservative	25.5	13.1	26.0	20.3
Liberal	5.2	3.7	5.4	4.3
No party	8.4	14.9	8.0	11.5
All homogamy *(observations)*	*70.5* *(15,772)*	*59.3* *(1,559)*	*70.9* *(12,053)*	*66.2* *(5,280)*

Note: The figures are the percentages of each of the four groups who fall into each homogamy pattern.

and those where both are traditional in their views, but we also include here those expressing no clear view either way. Overall, homogamy is greater amongst cohabiting couples. Thus we see, for instance, that 32.9 per cent of all married couples have egalitarian views, compared to 51.9 per cent of cohabiting couples (while 50.7 per cent of married couples and 60.1 per cent of those cohabiting share the same views, whatever these are). We can also see, if less definitively, that people in later unions are more homogamous in their family values than those in first unions.

Both outcomes appear to contradict the hypothesis made earlier that the decline of marriage is likely to be associated with increasing heterogamy. However, we cannot ignore the substantive dimension when we are looking at values and attitudes. In the data, married men are on average aged 50 compared to 34 for their cohabiting counterparts; for women the figures are, respectively, 48 and 32, and younger people are likely to have more liberal views. In addition, the situation of cohabitation is likely to be strongly related to distinctly liberal views. So, cutting across the observed homogamy patterns is a specific distribution of views depending on age and circumstances. Nevertheless, in combination these results suggest that while they are not more heterogamous on the basis of their education, the fluidity of cohabitation and new unions is associated with a tendency for cohabiting individuals to have a specific view of the family, and for cohabiting couples to share this view.

Political homogamy gives a clearer picture as there is no direct relationship between the content of the views and the nature of the relationship. We find that political homogamy is substantially higher in marriages than in cohabitations and, though less so, in first compared to later unions. This therefore accords with the hypothesis of greater homogamy in marriages. Nevertheless, here we get an interesting issue of definition. People may share the same views but also share *not* having a view. Does the latter imply similarity or, somewhat differently, an absence of dissimilarity? Cohabitees are less similar in their views, but sharing the position of no identification with a political party is much more common in this group than in married couples. One reason is again that cohabiting couples tend to be younger and the young have less interest in politics.

Whether because of their age, particular situation or lifestyle, cohabitation can perhaps be seen as the coming together of people who lack a defined view of the world (except perhaps as this world is defined by their own circumstances). We therefore have a clear selection effect. In the remainder of the analysis we try to deal with this, at least indirectly.

Modelling Homogamy

Our method is to regress homogamy on a range of variables, looking first at educational homogamy, and then at homogamy of attitudes to the family (while controlling for educational homogamy). Our aim in both cases is to see whether being in a later union (not the first marriage or partnership) and whether cohabiting rather than being married reduce the probability of homogamy. As we are interested in a view of homogamy across the whole population, we again use the full sample rather than only new relationships.

In respect of educational homogamy we use two methods. In the first, the dependent variable is educational homogamy itself, where this can be at any of five levels (both degree, both other postschool education, both A-level, both GCSE, both lower than this). This is clearly fairly refined; we could not claim that someone with an A-level marrying someone with, say, two GCSEs was carrying educational outmarriage very far. Nevertheless, we have already shown, using census data, that there is a tendency (no more than that) for people to cleave to others in marriage or partnership with a fairly closely related level of education.

For the purpose of this analysis we use logistic regression. As we are modelling homogamy we can think of the unit of analysis as the couple, and can include information about the couple as a unit, such as the length of the relationship, but also about her and/or about him. First we include her own education and her father's social class, whether this class is the same as the social class of the father of the partner (reflecting social-class homogamy, therefore), own age, similarity of age, the length of the partnership, wave, whether in a later union, and whether cohabiting. Through two of these variables—similarity of age and of paternal social class—we control for whether people are in some measure alike. In a variant of this analysis we include his education and father's social class instead of hers. Which—his or her information—contributes most to educational homogamy? We then repeat the analysis, excluding people with degrees, in order to see if the process works differently at lower levels of education.

We should note that although the sample is a panel (the observations are person years, not persons), little actually changes over time. Some people will increase their education, but not many. Some relationships will change—through separation or divorce and repartnership. This is therefore effectively a cross-sectional analysis, only slightly adjusted by time. But we do take account of time. The variables related to this, age and wave, work in different ways. Wave is common across all individuals and therefore shows the effect of time in the aggregate, for instance, as a result of changing attitudes in the population. In addition to this trend factor is the effect of age. This itself works in two ways. Each person is either younger or older than another, so here we have a cohort effect: we would expect different cohorts to have different attitudes and experiences, over and above the trend effect. Each person also ages in the panel by one year, resulting no doubt in incremental change in their attitudes. These three interpretations of time are not easily, if at all, distinguishable, but would be expected to work in similar fashion (though as the dependent variable is largely static over time, the effect of ageing itself is unlikely to be important).

The first results of this analysis are shown in the first two columns of Table 5.3. This uses overall educational homogamy as the dependent variable. The figures show the odds, so that any figure above one denotes a positive impact of the variable on closeness of education within the couple, and less than one shows a negative effect. While the dependent variable shows homogamy at any level of education, which can mean a lot of things, therefore, it is helpful to control for this level for one partner. These effects are shown in the first four rows, where a middling sort of education (A-levels) is the reference category. Homogamy is more likely towards the extremes of the educational hierarchy. It is these extremes, therefore, which tend to be most cohesive through marriage. This seems to confirm the polarisation effect found by Schwartz and Mare (2005), pointed out earlier. Although our result partly reflects the fact that those in between can marry both up or down, the effects are far from marginal. The effect is especially strong where his education is low, while in her case having a degree has a stronger effect. This suggests that a woman with a degree is less likely to 'marry down' than a man with a degree, while a man with very low education is less likely to marry up than the equivalent woman. Father's social class mostly makes little additional difference. However, homogamy is more likely where she has a relatively low paternal social class. This suggests some sort of 'ghetto' rather than polarisation effect: people already disadvantaged match with other disadvantaged people. Finally in respect of class, a similar class background reduces homogamy. This is an extremely interesting finding and suggests that homogamy does not necessarily pass down the generations. It is a free choice.

Being of a similar age (within three years either way) possibly lowers the probability of educational homogamy. This applies to all models, in fact, and is surprising. Length of relationship also reduces the probability of homogamy. Of course it should not have any effect, as subsequent relational survival can hardly have an impact on closeness of education at the time of marriage. Nevertheless, we can assume that a more enduring partnership reflects a closer emotional relationship from the outset, perhaps more likely in homogamous unions, while, as stated previously, less homogamous relationships might also be more likely to break up. In contrast, our results appear to show that longer relationships are less homogamous. It is difficult to see why this should be the case but it implies that homogamy does not guarantee longer relationships.

Older people are slightly more likely to have similar education, and so younger people tend to be more heterogamous. This is reinforced by the trend factor, wave, which reveals reducing homogamy. Thus both the trend (wave) and cohort (age) effects point in the same direction, towards falling homogamy.[8] Later unions have no effect, contrary to the hypothesis mooted earlier. If anything, cohabitation increases rather than reduces homogamy—even more in opposition to the idea that social change in the nature of relationships is reducing the tendency towards homogamy.

In the third and fourth columns of the table we compare homogamy amongst those with a relatively low education (that is, where neither is a graduate). The reference category for education as an explanatory variable is nondegree postschool education. Homogamy is less likely where the woman has lower than postschool education (all the coefficients are below one) but is far more likely where he has a low education. Of course less educated men who marry homogamously must be marrying less educated women. So how come his outcome reflects a 'ghetto' effect but not hers, given that the distributions of education by gender are not dissimilar? Some difference in the distribution accounts for the effect. More important, the probability of homogamy for men at that level is relative to the probability of men at higher levels (specifically, with postschool education) of marrying homogamously, not relative to women. Father's social class also works differently at the nongraduate level, with a polarisation effect in the case of women (which does not happen for female graduates) but a clear tendency for higher paternal class amongst men to promote homogamy. The other variables are much the same as for the first two columns.

While some of these results are slightly puzzling, two outcomes seem clear. First, educational homogamy is polarised amongst those with high and with low levels of education (and in the case of low education, more especially for men). Second, neither later unions nor cohabitation reduce homogamy. In fact, cohabiting couples seem more rather than less likely to match on the basis of education.

The 'ghetto' effect of low education does not mean that escape from the ghetto through marriage is impossible. There is certainly some mobility through marriage and partnership. This is demonstrated in a different form of analysis where we map one partner's education on to the other in order to test the distributional effect of education. The results appear in the final two columns. Here the dependent variable is the wife's education (in five levels) and explanatory variables include her partner's education. We use an ordered logit model which measures the association of the explanatory variables with any increase in the dependent variable, regardless of the size of this increase. The relationship between his and her education does not, therefore, reflect homogamy. What we are interested in seeing is the factors which seem to draw the man to partner a woman with a relatively high level

Table 5.3 Models of Educational Homogamy (logistic regression) and of Relationship Between Partners' Education (ordered logit)

| | Homogamy | | | | Ordered logit | |
| | Same education | | Neither have degree | | | |
	Her education & class	His education & class	Her education & class	His education & class	Her social class	His social class
Degree	6.50***	4.34***	—	—	0.16***	0.15***
Postschool	3.15***	2.39***	—	—	0.84(*)	0.88
A-level	—	—	0.16***	0.25***	—	—
GCSE	1.30	2.09***	0.20***	0.51***	1.34**	1.44***
Low-none	4.71***	8.02***	0.74**	2.05***	2.25***	2.45***
Father class 1	1.08	1.21	1.36*	1.60***	0.40***	0.89
Father class 2	1.05	1.13	1.18	1.17	0.70*	0.98
Father class 3	1.27*	1.07	1.22	0.94	1.05	1.56***
Father class 4	1.52***	1.03	1.38**	0.91	1.44***	1.65***
Father class same	0.88**	0.90*	0.86**	0.90*	0.98	0.97
Similar age	0.83**	0.94	0.83**	0.94	0.93	0.94
Years partnered	0.99*	0.99*	0.99***	0.99***	1.00	1.00
Age	1.02***	1.01***	1.02***	1.01***	1.04***	1.04***
Wave	0.99*	1.00	0.99(*)	1.00	0.93***	0.93***
Later union	1.00	0.99	1.00	0.99	1.05	0.99
Cohabiting	1.16	1.20(*)	1.17	1.16	1.09	1.03
Pseudo R²	.08	.08	.09	.08	.13	.12
Observations	31,291	31,690	27,462	27,852	31,291	31,690

***p <.001; **p <.01; * p <.05; (*)p <.1.
Note: Using her education as explanatory variables in columns 1 and 3; his in columns 2, 4 (and also 5 and 6). Using her father's social class in columns 1, 3 and 5, his in columns 2, 4 and 6. The ordered logit model uses 5 levels of her education as the dependent variable.

of education (whether or not higher than his). Again we present the odds (a figure above one raises the odds and below one reduces them) and again do not present the standard errors, which we exclude for ease of presentation, though the reliability of the differences between the coefficients is more important here.

The dependent variable is always her education and most of the explanatory variables describe her partner, but in the fifth column we include her paternal social class instead of his. These results are very similar. In both cases, marrying a woman with one higher level up the scale of five is more likely the lower his own education. This in fact suggests some sort of marrying-up process, though it does not have to be by much. Where there is marrying up, it is from the lowest levels. Of course, marrying up is more possible from there, but this shows that the process does occur (it need not), and it presumably reduces the tendency towards homogamy. Paternal social class works similarly. Age and wave work in similar fashion, as in columns 1–4, but here the effects imply that marrying up is slightly a thing of the past. Later unions and cohabitation have no noticeable effect. Overall, we can see a tendency for people with low education or paternal social class to marry up educationally. This need not reveal much about preferences but could be the result of frictions: for instance, in specific areas ('marriage markets') those in the diminishing pool of poorly educated people might not be able to find a 'suitable' match. Nevertheless, it shows that some marrying up educationally does occur—for *men*: we do not here test the reverse process.

Homogamy based on attitudes might work differently from that based on more objective measures such as education. We therefore finish with an analysis of similarity of attitudes, using a single variable, the same as in Table 5.2: *Do you personally agree or disagree. . . . A husband's job is to earn money; a wife's job is to look after the home and family?* This is coded to test similarity of a liberal stance. As the battery of questions of which this forms part appears in alternate waves of the BHPS, this considerably reduces the sample in comparison with Table 5.3. We also test relative influence within couples by switching between his and her explanatory variables.

We stated earlier that we would attempt to deal with the problem of selection. We do so here indirectly through controlling for education and for homogamy. However, cohabitation is related to age (on average, younger people cohabit) as is, differently, being in a later union (by construction). Both types of relationships are also increasing over time. Finally, later unions and cohabitations are likely to be shorter than first marriages, which could reduce the sense of commitment not by virtue of the situation itself but simply because time has had less effect. All in all we would expect that the inclusion of the time-related variables, age, wave and length of union would reduce any effect at least of cohabitation and perhaps of later unions. By running models with and without these we help deal further with the selection problem.

The results are shown in Table 5.4. We can see in all four models the positive effect of education on similarity of attitudes (i.e. both are liberal), especially of higher education. Paternal social class has little clear effect, which suggests that similarity of attitudes depends more on education than on the individuals' background. There are three measures of homogamy. Educational homogamy increases the probability of both partners having liberal views, but only clearly when controlling for his education and parental class, though quite substantially. The probability of the couple sharing these views depends on his rather than her education. Similarity of paternal class appears to lower the probability of similar views but not in the full model (though the 'gender' of the controls makes a difference). Age similarity has no noticeable effect. Most important of all, in the first

Table 5.4   Models of Homogamy in Liberal Family Values (logistic regression)

	Her education and father's social class		*His education and father's social class*	
Degree	3.09***	3.72***	2.98***	3.38***
Postschool	1.04	1.32	1.10	1.38(*)
GCSE	0.56***	0.61*	0.93	0.95
Low-none	0.14***	0.22***	0.40***	0.63*
Father class 1	1.15	1.11	0.93	0.94
Father class 2	1.48	1.75(*)	0.64	0.72
Father class 4	1.11	1.17	0.83	0.96
Father class 5	1.10	1.17	0.85	0.97
Same education	1.17	1.16	1.46***	1.45***
Father's class same	0.77*	1.14	0.78*	1.09
Similar age	1.10	1.06	0.95	0.95
Age		0.95***		0.94***
Wave		0.95***		0.97**
Years partnered		0.99		1.00
Later union	1.40***	1.32***	1.30***	1.24***
Cohabiting	2.33***	1.39*	2.20***	1.15
Pseudo R²	*.13*	*.17*	*.08*	*14*
N	*17,608*	*17,608*	*17,827*	*17,827*

***p <.001; **p <.01; *p <.05; (*)p <.1.
Note: The question is: *Do you personally agree or disagree. . . . A husband's job is to earn money; a wife's job is to look after the home and family?* This is coded so that the outcome is 'liberal' (in favour of mother working). The first pair of columns uses her education and paternal class as explanatory variables; the second uses his.

and third columns we can see a positive effect of later unions and a positive, extremely large effect of cohabitation.

When we add the time-related variables, things change. Age itself is unsurprisingly associated with less liberal views; interestingly, so is the trend (denoted by *wave*)—at least the trend within the sample; years partnered appears to have no effect. The changes to the other, key variables are different. No substantial change occurs to the coefficient for later unions but the cohabitation effect falls drastically, though it is still positive. This suggests the probability that some of the relationship between cohabitation and family and gender views is a selection effect—in fact, quite a large part. Cohabitation is in this sense not driving social change. Liberal people are simply more likely to cohabit.

CONCLUSIONS

Our interest is in whether the modern couple is a building block of society in some, functionalist sense, where partners are attracted to each other by their similarity and presumably passing on these characteristics to offspring, or whether, alternatively, society is changing, in particular through the expansion of higher education and changes in marital behaviour. If the latter is true, not only are relationships more fluid than in the past, but the transmission and circulation of social characteristics and of social views are also more fluid. If more educated people have liberal views, the new family relationships they form might serve to break up long-standing social boundaries. If relationships become more flexible, marked by reduced reliance on marriage, then we might expect social similarity within couples to decline.

We find only limited evidence of such effects in the case of objective measures of homogamy, whether of social status, education, religion or ethnicity. Some but not much marrying up (and therefore also marrying down) does occur, but this by no means describes the nature of the modern relationship.

The preceding characteristics, such as ethnicity, mostly do not change with circumstances. Attitudes and social values can change. Attitudinal homogamy remains strong, but it also seems to be affected by the circumstances of the partnership—whether a first or later union, and whether the partners are married or cohabiting. We cannot say for sure how much this reflects the characteristics of people in these situations, but it would appear that the outcome in the case of cohabitation at least is primarily because younger people are more liberal in their views and because such people select into cohabitation. Nevertheless, it seems reasonable that people do change their views to fit their circumstances. Indeed, this might be how social views change in the aggregate anyway. We take this idea further in the next chapter.

Overall, though, we can find no or only very marginal effects of changing education or of new forms of relationship on the degree of homogamy.
The couple relationship continues to be marked by strong social and cultural ties.

ACKNOWLEDGEMENTS

We are very grateful to the Office of National Statistics for permission to use
the Longitudinal Study and for the analytical support of Celsius at University
College London, and in particular to Chris Marshall for his considerable
help in undertaking the analysis. The paper has been cleared for release into
the public domain by ONS with clearance number LS30028A. The authors
alone are responsible for the interpretation of the data. We are also grateful
to Marco Francesconi for his earlier contribution to this work.

NOTES

1. In studies which use log-linear methods to eliminate the effects of changing
   marginal distributions, by very virtue of this fact we can learn nothing of
   the effects on homogamy of the expansion of education. However, Chan and
   Halpin (2003) use event history analysis where they attempt to take explicit
   account of the expansion of the 'opportunity structure' by including this as
   a covariate in their analysis.
2. This selection process is probably also more refined than this suggests. People with the same field of study have a slight tendency to intermarry (Nielsen
   and Svarer 2006: 7–9).
3. Quoted (from an early Austen work *Jack and Alice*), by Ballaster, 1995: x, in
   introduction to *Sense and Sensibility*.
4. 'The odds ratio is defined as the odds that an A-type male marries an A-type
   female (rather than a B-type female), divided by the odds that a B-type male
   marries an A-type female' (Kalmijn 1998: 405). A figure of one would mean
   the odds are equal. In our data, in 1971 0.39% of men without a degree
   married graduates. The remainder, 99.61%, therefore married nongraduates.
   The odds of a nongraduate marrying a graduate are the first figure divided
   by the second, which in this case equals 0.0039. They are therefore virtually
   zero. But this has to be compared to the odds of a male graduate marrying a
   graduate, which may or may not be high. In fact, 14.99% of male graduates
   married a graduate, and so 85.01% did not. This produces odds of a graduate
   marrying a graduate of 14.99 divided by 85.01, which equals 0.176. So the
   odds are not particularly high. However, they are a great deal higher than the
   odds of a nongraduate marrying a graduate. If we divide the two odds, 0.176
   by 0.0039, we get an odds ratio of 45.23. It is much more likely (45 times
   more likely) that a graduate will marry a graduate than will a nongraduate.
5. Unfortunately, the education variable is highly inconsistent across censuses
   and it is only possible to compare at the graduate/nongraduate level across all
   four censuses. However, for more detail we can look at 1971 and 2001, that
   is, at the beginning and end period, as full information is available in these
   years. We find that intermarriage between graduates and those with A-levels

is much more widespread than these figures imply. In 1991 the odds ratio was four, rising to seven (a big change in proportional terms) in 2001. The ratio for degree against a very low education falls, from 133 to 79, but the ratio for A-level against low education rises from 11 to 43. Thus, educational homogamy is more complex than might be inferred solely from the rise of the university. It is also highly graduated. There are barriers to crossing even slight educational boundaries.

6. It should be made clear that homogamy describes couples, so that the odds ratios apply equally to both partners. In contrast, the probability that either a man or a woman marries homogamously need not be equal. This depends on the gender distribution of (in this case) education. Clearly, if, say, 20% of men and 10% of women are graduates, it is harder for men to marry a graduate than it is for women. If the female proportion changes to equal the male proportion, their chances are equal. Whether that gives rise to greater homogamy is, though, an empirical question.

7. If we take women as the unit of analysis, for homogamy to work, women would, when female employment was limited, seek spouses similar to their *father*'s social class. When both men and women are upwardly mobile relative to their fathers it is likely that they seek homogamous relationships on the basis of their own status, not that of their fathers. Otherwise, marriage could return many to the state from which they have progressed. Thus, mobility entails marrying homogamously but at a higher level. While this is similar to Bourdieu's argument, there is one difference. All people seek homogamous marriages but social closure is only effective in the case of upward social mobility.

8. While this is contrary to the preceding LS results, we have here a comparatively very small sample, which cannot be used to describe trends: the interest is instead in the interrelationship between specific variables.

REFERENCES

Ballaster, R. (ed.) (1995) *Sense and Sensibility*, London: Penguin.

Becker, G.S. (1991) *A treatise on the family,* enlarged edition, Cambridge, MA and London: Harvard University Press.

Birkelund, G. and Heldal, J. (2003) Who marries whom? Educational homogamy in Norway, *Demographic Research*, Roctock, Germany: Max Planck Institute.

Blossfeld, H.-P. and Müller, R. (2002) Union disruption in comparative perspective: the role of assortative partner choice and careers of couples, *International Journal of Sociology*, 32(4): 3–35.

Blossfeld, H.-P. and Timm, A. (2003) *Who marries whom?: educational systems as marriage markets in modern societies.* Dordrecht, Netherlands, Boston and London: Kluwer Academic.

Bourdieu, P. (1976) Marriage strategies as strategies of social reproduction, in R. Forster and O. Ranum (eds) *Family and society*, Baltimore: Johns Hopkins University Press.

Bourdieu, P. (1984) *Distinction: a social critique of the judgement of taste*, London: Routledge & Kegan Paul.

Brynin, M. and Francesconi, M. (2004) The material returns to partnership: the effects of educational matching on labour market outcomes and gender equality, *European Sociological Review*, 20: 363–77.

Chan, T.-W. and Halpin, B. (2003) Who marries whom in Great Britain, in H.-P. Blossfeld and A. Timm (eds) *Who marries whom?: educational systems as mar-*

riage markets in modern societies, Dordrecht, Netherlands, Boston and London: Kluwer Academic, 171–94.

Goldthorpe, J.H., Llewellyn, C. and Payne, C. (1987) *Social mobility and class structure in modern Britain,* 2nd edn, Oxford: Clarendon Press.

Goode, W. (1964) *The family.* Englewood Cliffs, NJ: Prentice-Hall.

Hakim, C. (2000) *Work-lifestyle choices in the 21st century: preference theory,* Oxford: Oxford University Press.

Kalmijn, M. (1994) Assortative mating by cultural and economic occupational status, *American Journal of Sociology,* 100: 422–52.

———. (1998) Intermarriage and homogamy: causes, patterns, trends, *Annual Review of Sociology,* 24: 395–421.

Kalmijn, M. and Bernasco, W. (2001) Joint and separated lifestyles in couple relationships, *Journal of Marriage and the Family,* 63(3): 639–54.

Lampard, R. (1997) Party political homogamy in Great Britain, *European Sociological Review,* 13: 79–99.

Mare, R. (1991) Five decades of educational assortative mating, *American Sociological Review,* 56: 15–32.

Moors, G. (2000) Values and living arrangements: a recursive relationship, in L. Waite (ed.) *The ties that bind,* New York: Aldine de Gruyter, 212–26.

Nielsen, H. and Svarer, M. (2006) Educational homogamy: preferences or opportunities? in *IZA Working Papers,* Bonn: Institute for the Study of Labor, p. 34.

Oppenheimer, V. (1988) A theory of marriage timing, *American Journal of Sociology,* 94: 563–91.

Schwartz, C. and Mare, R. (2005) Trends in educational assortative marriage from 1940 to 2003, *Demography,* 42: 621–46.

Ultee, W. and Luijkx, R. (1990) Educational heterogamy and-father-to-son occupational mobility in 23 industrial nations: general societal openness or compensatory strategies of reproduction? *European Sociological Review,* 6: 125–49.

Weiss, Y. and Willis, R. (1997) Match quality, new information, and marital dissolution, *Journal of Labor Economics,* 15: 293–329.

Westermarck, E. A. (1903) *The history of human marriage,* London: Macmillan.

Xu, X., Hudspeth, C. and Bartkowski, J. (2006) The role of cohabitation in remarriage, *Journal of Marriage and the Family,* 68: 261–74.

6 How Close Are Couples?

Malcolm Brynin, Álvaro Martínez Pérez and Simonetta Longhi

INTRODUCTION

In the previous chapter we argued that homogamy is a fundamental building block of social structure. People tend to marry or partner people similar to themselves in terms of social background but also social values or attitudes (and probably more personal, less easily measurable characteristics). We argued that this is a form of social selection and can make society less open. Marriage perhaps has a conservative effect; it is as if the aggregate effects of individual marriage decisions serve to tighten up the transmission of social attitudes over time. However, marriage itself is in decline, with cohabitation substituting for marriage and remarriage following divorce, so we also considered whether the effect of this on the conservation of social values is in decline too. We did not find that this was the case to any significant extent.

It is reasonable to assume that the effect of homogamy intensifies through the process of living together, as partners are likely to influence each other's behaviour, values, and tastes, presumably in the direction of homogeneity of outlook. In this case, *adaptation* reinforces the *selection* effect. But we do not know this is the case. The reverse might even apply. Perhaps the selection effect is so powerful that people can afford to become less like each other after marriage; they go their own ways, because they have over-committed to the cause of solidarity at the outset of their relationship—rather like Victorian bridges that have massively excessive safety margins. Personal bridges can afford to weaken over time, and so the process of living together reduces homogamy.

We consider three questions in this chapter. First, do partners influence each other's views over time? Second, if they do, do they as a result become more similar to each other? Third, do they become different from how they would be if married to someone quite unlike themselves in terms of social background and so on?[1] In general, one might expect people to influence each other within marriage. Such reciprocal influences can be wide-ranging and invisible to either side. For instance, each partner's education might make the other more effective in his or her job (Brynin and

Francesconi 2004). An impact of time of this sort within marriage can be considered equivalent to the experience component of human capital (where this comprises formal education, work experience and motivation). Experience counts. There are transfers of knowledge, understanding, cultural interests, lifestyle preferences, and social values between partners. Individuals in couples are not simply two individuals living together but more than the sum of the parts. The phenomenon of marriage changes people over time. Can we infer from this a basis for social change too?

We argued in the earlier chapter that people are attracted to others similar to themselves, at least on certain characteristics. Many of these are fixed—age (relative to the other person) most obviously, ethnicity, religion (within limits), social class background, and education (which can change after the event, though mostly does not). Other characteristics are subject to change through the fact of emotional and physical proximity to others. This is not only the result of reciprocal influence but of joint experience of external events, for instance, a fall into household poverty. We look in this chapter at opinions and values. These are perhaps the most interesting both for their intrinsic importance and because in principle they are relatively malleable. If there is a gap between partners' attitudes, do they influence each other such that this gap closes?

We analyse all couples, not only newlyweds, focussing on two very different sorts of attitudes. One relates to marriage itself, and is therefore especially interesting. There are six measures of this in the BHPS. We select two which are particularly strong statements: whether a preschool child suffers if the mother works, and whether the husband should work and the wife stay at home. The correlations between partners on these are in fact not that high—between 0.3 and 0.4 for the two values questions. Thus, while people are likely to be married to someone with similar views this is far from being a one-to-one relationship. These beliefs about coupledom give some sense of how the social basis of marriage itself might be changing. For instance, marital 'quality' and stability have been shown to depend on agreement over the gender balance between paid work and family commitments (Greenstein 1995), but by the same token, such beliefs are 'endogenous' to the marriage situation itself. So we cannot be sure whether responses reflect the personal circumstances of each marriage. An additional, more 'objective' indicator is therefore desirable. We choose for this purpose party political support. This is rarely examined in this way. Amongst the studies which do look at the issue, Lampard's analysis (1997) reveals strong political homogamy in Britain, while Zuckerman, Dasović and Fitzgerald[2] find that the 'more years couples live together, the more likely they are to choose the same political party' (2007: 88).

We present our analysis in several stages. First, we address the general issue whether partners influence each other's values over time. Second, we see how far this contributes to homogamy. As just stated, in this analysis we use two different values questions: one concerning family values and the other measuring party political identification. Neither, though, tells us whether the couple is truly close, for instance, emotionally. Third, therefore, and possibly most important of all, we seek to estimate the impact of homogamy on the well-being of the couple itself. At least in the US there is a link between religious homogamy and 'marital quality', though this is in decline as a result of changing beliefs in the family, which are less subject to religious constraints than in the past (Myers 2006).[3] Yet even if the beneficial effect of homogamy might be falling over time it still suggests the continuing importance of reciprocal influence in maintaining marital stability (Weiss and Willis 1997; Blossfeld and Müller 2002). Here we use a measure of psychological stress as our indicator of the potential emotional effects of homogamy.

DO PARTNERS INFLUENCE EACH OTHER'S VIEWS OF THE WORLD?

It is not homogamy itself we are interested in here but within-couple influence. In principle, such influences could make the couple less homogamous over time. The problem in any test of this, though, is that we have no counterfactual: we do not know how much the same individuals would have changed had they married someone else (or indeed not married at all, though we do not test this here). However, the concept of homogamy itself (using education or class as the basis) gives us a means of tackling this. To use education as an example, if partners where both have a degree are more inclined to a particular view of society than the average married individual with a degree, this implies an additional effect of the partnership. While this could be a selection effect, whereby people select partners not only on the basis of their education but of their values, and is therefore an outcome of homogamy, this fineness of selection (as we will show next) seems unlikely. Mutual influence after marriage seems the most probable source of any difference.

For simplicity of presentation we do not show the actual relationship between education or class and the beliefs in question, though it is quite steep in respect of both questions.[4] Kalmijn and Kraaykamp (2007) find a strong relationship in Europe of both higher education and higher social class with egalitarian gender beliefs. Here the question is, in contrast, are men and women in couples who both have a degree more likely to have a liberal family view than the average individual with a degree? And the same for social class. In the first two columns of Table 6.1 we show the relationship between a liberal stance on the first family values question and education and own social class, first for individuals and then for individuals in couples. High education means a degree, and low means nongraduate; high class means the 'service' class (higher managerial or professional, using the Goldthorpe class schema), and low means not in the service class.

Table 6.1   Percentage of Married Individuals Strongly Disagreeing with Conservative Family Values, by own (individual) Education and Social Class and by Joint (couple) Education and Social Class

	Strongly disagrees:					
	Child suffers if mother works		Wife should stay at home, husband work		N	
	Individual	Couple	Individual	Couple	I	C
Graduate (w)	12.2	15.9	41.1	45.2	2,107	1,079
Graduate (m)	6.8	10.9	24.6	33.1	2,422	1,087
Service class (w)	13.3	13.0	36.6	38.5	4,627	2,502
Service class (m)	5.4	7.9	19.1	26.7	6,231	2,426

Note: w = woman, m = man; N is for individual sample (I) in column 5, for couple sample (C) in column 6.

The answer to the preceding question can be seen by comparing the second column to the first, and the fourth to the third. What we are now observing is the percentage of individuals with a conservative view in couples homogamous on the basis of both being a graduate and both being in the service class. The number of observations falls comparing individuals in couples to couples as units because the latter analyses are based on homogamous couples only (so some sample bias is therefore possible). The results are, though, highly consistent. It can be seen that the figures are now almost all higher when we look at homogamous couples—though not always by much. For instance, 12.2 per cent of married women who are graduates have a liberal view on the first question, but 15.9 per cent of women do so where both partners are graduates. For men the figures are 6.8 per cent and 10.9 per cent, respectively. In the case of the second question, for men the difference is much greater. It appears that educational and class homogamy are both associated with a sometimes slight but nearly always distinctive intensification of family values. The sum is greater than the parts.

In the case of political views we find very similar effects. There is a considerable degree of homogamy on this dimension to begin with. For instance, 70 per cent of husbands who support Labour have a wife who does so too; exactly the same applies to Conservative support. Extreme heterogamy, where one partner supports Labour and the other the Conservatives, is especially uncommon, describing only 4.6 per cent of couples. What difference does educational homogamy make to this? The percentage of Labour supporters amongst married individuals with a degree goes up for both men and women when both partners have a degree, though only by 1 percentage point. The percentage of Conservative support declines, by 2 percentage points in the case of women and 7 in the case of men, which shows that two graduates are much more anti-Conservative than one. The relationship with own social class produces strong effects for men in the same direction but not for women, where there is little change either way. Thus, in the case of party support too, partners seem to influence each other.[5] The symmetry of the influence is much the same as reported by Kan and Heath (2006) using the same data to examine the relationship between the balance of views and economic interdependency, but where the symmetry is between each partner's left-right values at one time point and the other's values a number of years later.

We have shown earlier that couples are more than the sum of the parts. Joining together in couples, individuals are more inclined to specific views of society than on average they would be alone. But we still do not know for certain if this is a selection or an adaptation effect. We examine this issue here. To do so we need to use a multivariate analysis, to control as far as possible for as many factors as we can which might be correlated with the original selection decision. The dependent variable is expressed in terms of change over time, showing individuals becoming more liberal in their views. These values questions, based on a five-point Likert scale, appear in the survey every other wave, so change is over a two-year period (which means an individual can of course change views more than once). What factors are associated with such change? In particular, what factors relating to the couple situation influence them?

We show the results in Table 6.2. The level of analysis is the couple, to which we have around 200 to 300 additions every year. These years are pooled and the resulting variable, wave, included as a trend indicator. While our main interest is in the effect of each partner's values and education on the other's values, we also include cohabitation and whether the marriage is a first or later union; as in our earlier chapter we take these to be important indicators of social change. One might expect more liberal views in cohabiting relationships and later unions. We showed in the earlier chapter that this did not reduce homogamy, which remains a strong principle despite the apparently greater flexibility of such arrangements; but that was a selection issue: people who form a nonmarital relationship are not less concerned than married people to partner someone like themselves. Here we produce a different test of this idea: whatever the basis of the selection, do partners in a cohabiting or in a second/later union influence each other more than people in marriages and in first marriages? We would expect not, as marriage implies a closer, more dependent union, but it is possible that the joint investment in a looser relationship reflected in cohabitation might influence cohabiting partners views strongly. In an analysis of young German women, using panel data, Moors suggests that changes in family situation have a causal impact on family values in the direction of belief in autonomy (2000: 224). Presumably this could in turn give rise to complex reciprocal influences within the couple.

We test in the first column factors that are associated with the man acquiring more liberal views on the preceding question and, in the second,

Table 6.2   Factors Associated with Change in Family Values: Whether Agrees Preschool Child Suffers if Mother Works (OLS)

	His views become more liberal	Her views become more liberal	Jointly become more liberal	His views become more liberal relative to hers
Her liberal views	0.11***	−0.46***	−0.35***	0.57***
His liberal views	−0.49***	0.11***	−0.39***	−0.60***
Age	−0.009***	−0.007***	−0.015***	−0.002*
Number children	−0.02**	−0.03***	−0.05***	0.01
Cohabiting	0.06***	−0.01	0.06*	0.07**
Later union	0.02*	0.01	0.03***	0.01
Length of union	0.00	0.00	0.00	0.00
Wave	0.004**	0.001	0.005*	0.003(*)
She is graduate	0.10***	0.04(*)	0.14***	0.07*
He is graduate	−0.03	−0.05*	−0.07*	0.02
She works	0.06***	0.10***	0.16***	−0.05**
He works	−0.04*	−0.06***	−0.10***	0.02
Similar age	0.011	0.032*	0.042*	−0.023
Constant	−1.06***	−0.71***	−1.79***	−0.33***
R squared	*.25*	*.23*	*.19*	*.30*
Observations	*19,106*	*19,312*	*18,912*	*18,912*

with the woman changing her views. Clearly, movement towards more liberal views is more possible from a conservative starting position, and this is what we see in the second row for him and the first for her. The effect of own liberal views is negative (i.e. people with liberal views are less likely to become more liberal). The effect of her liberal views on his change is positive (first row, first column) as is the equivalent effect of his views on her.

So, partners do appear to influence each other (though this could in principle still be a selection effect insofar as that person might have selected a liberal person because, for instance, he or she was in some way predisposed to change his or her own views). Moreover, this exchange is symmetrical. Men and women have equal effects on each other.

As against this, when we look at the effects of education these are asymmetrical, and in fact highly gendered. The effect of her being a graduate on change in both her own and his views (especially his—her own being more likely to be liberal already) is positive. The effect of his being a graduate is negative in both cases, as well as being roughly equal. (It is possible that this is an income effect, with male graduates being able to 'buy out' women from work.) Precisely the same relationships apply to their relative work situations. If she works, the attitudes of both are more liberal; if he works (which perhaps helps to confirm the 'buying-out' hypothesis), they are less so. Overall, the results strongly suggest that her education and work are the driving forces of change in values.

Our other key variables are cohabitation and later unions. Both have an effect on change in his views—far more powerful for cohabitation—but not on hers. It would appear that the family views of men who live in a cohabiting union become more liberal (while the woman perhaps needs less persuasion). Finally, the indicators of time—age, similarity in age, length of union and wave—have different but secondary effects.[6]

The third and fourth columns add no new information but enable an easier view of some of these interrelationships. The third column estimates the effect of the same variables on the sum of the family values in the couple (again coded so that the outcome is greater liberalism). In other words, what factors contribute to couples generally becoming more liberal? The actual figures are simply the sum of the figures in the first two columns, but we can now see more clearly that her education, age similarity, and cohabitation, and, to a lesser extent, later unions as well as time itself (wave) all contribute to greater liberalism in the aggregate.

In the final column, which interestingly has the highest R^2 (even though again no new information is provided), differences in the views of partners are shown. What increases the gap (making change in his views more liberal relative to her change)? This is simply the second column subtracted from the first. Again, we see the power of her views, of cohabitation, of her education and of her work.

Overall, we observe significant reciprocal influences in family values within couples, largely asymmetrical, with the man (implicitly) changing his views as a result of living with a highly educated or working woman. This process is enhanced in unions which are not marriages and not first unions.[7]

We get a 'purer' indication of intracouple influence through an analysis of party political support, which we would not expect to be influenced directly by the family situation itself. We do this by examining switches in party support across two waves. Do differences in views between partners cause these switches? The results are shown in Table 6.3. This compares people who switch party support to those who do not (e.g. those changing from Conservative to Labour compared to those who remain Conservative). The labels in the left-hand column indicate various relationships between partners' views which *precede* the switch. We would expect people who have a partner who supports a party which they do not themselves support to be more likely to switch to that party at a later time. Does this happen?

In the first column we show cases where the woman supports Labour and her husband, either the Tories, Labour, or another party or no party (we combine these two last positions for the sake of simplicity), followed in

Table 6.3   Effects of Partner's Party Support on Changes in Party Support (standard errors in brackets)

	(1) She changes to Conservative	(2) He changes to Conservative	(3) She changes to Labour	(4) He changes to Labour
She is Tory:				
partner Tory			0.122*** (0.020)	0.122*** (0.021)
partner Labour		0.472** (0.129)	0.800 (0.160)	
partner other		2.065*** (0.286)	0.257*** (0.059)	0.640** (0.115)
She is Labour:				
partner Tory	0.409*** (0.118)			0.480*** (0.117)
partner Labour	0.062*** (0.112)	0.077*** (0.115)		
partner other	0.072*** (0.126)	0.052*** (0.083)		1.803*** (0.164)
She is other:				
partner Tory	1.677*** (0.209)		0.661*** (0.091)	0.364*** (0.065)
partner Labour	0.212*** (0.043)	0.220*** (0.041)	1.711*** (0.140)	
partner other	0.455*** (0.053)	0.727** (0.082)	0.905 (0.070)	0.986 (0.079)

the final three rows by cases where she holds the 'other' position while her husband is either Tory, Labour or other. So these combinations represent either matches (e.g. Labour-Labour), weak mismatches (Labour-other) or strong mismatches (Labour-Conservative). Any figure above one indicates a positive effect (raising the odds of the change) while a figure below one is a negative effect. In both of the first two columns the reference category is 'both Tory'.

The first column indicates that if she is Labour she is unlikely to switch to the Tories, but least likely to if her partner is also Labour. If she has a weaker party position (our label 'other'), she is very likely to switch to the Tories if her partner is Tory and unlikely to otherwise. The picture for his switches to the Conservatives is similar. Where she is Tory and he is 'other', the odds of him switching to the Tories are doubled (though, if he is Labour, her being a Tory cannot persuade him to change). All other cases reduce the odds of a switch, but where both partners are other they are reduced the least. Switches to Labour reflect the same patterns.

All in all, one partner's party position seems to predict switches by the other partner. A change to one of the two main parties is more likely where the other partner supports that party, especially where the switch is not from a strongly opposed position. Where both support a party, a switch is least likely. In the case of both family values and party political support, therefore, we observe a relationship between one partner's position and change in the other partner's position over time. Marriage changes the structure of opinions in society.

DO COUPLES BECOME MORE SIMILAR TO EACH OTHER OVER TIME?

The preceding results imply that partners become more similar over time, but do not prove they actually *are* similar at the end of the process. To test this, we remain with the party identification variable. Our focus is couples who do not share a specific political view at one wave and do subsequently (two waves later); that is, one of their views has shifted. What we wish to examine are the factors associated with movement towards this political homogamy. The results are shown in Table 6.4. The dependent variable is in each model a switch from a nonhomogamous position (where partners have different positions towards party identification) to one where they have the same identification.

Our main explanatory variables concern redistribution, the six variables in the BHPS that can be summed to produce a left-wing/right-wing scale. After summing we arbitrarily select a point beyond which we can label 'left-wing', and create a dummy variable to denote this. This is of course endogenous: we are explaining a view of society (identified through party support) through another view of society (opinions on social redistribution).[8] But our aim is not to produce a model of change in individual political affiliation. What we wish to see is whether shared views on redistribution have a greater impact on the probability of shared party support than do individuals views. We accordingly present the results of only these variables plus some others of particular interest.

The first two columns of Table 6.4 show couples in one wave who do not share a Labour ID but who do two waves later (two, because the redistribution questions appear only every other wave). Column one shows cases where it is the husband who adjusts his views to create a politically homogeneous marital pairing. In column two it is the wife who makes the adjustment. In both cases if either has a left-wing view on redistributional issues at any time they are likely to move towards Labour, but there is also some influence from the partner. However, despite the strength of these individual effects, where both partners have a left-wing view, homogamy in party ID is the likeliest outcome.[9]

The other variables shown have some additional effect—not in the case of education in the first column but in the second we can see that the husband is likely to become labour, like his wife, if he is a graduate (though her being a graduate might also contribute), while the effect of their both being a graduate is in fact slightly stronger. Variables not shown are age similarity, whether both work, relative labour incomes, number of children, whether cohabiting, whether in a first or later union, length of union, and wave. We treat these simply as additional controls which have no theoretically interesting relationship to political homogamy, and therefore do not report the results for these.

The final two columns of Table 6.4, showing shifts towards homogamy in support for the Conservative Party, mostly replicate the case for Labour. Joint left-wing views act most to reduce the probability of a shared Conservative ID. In this case, though, education has no significant effect, but the coefficient where both partners are graduates is low (indicating a potentially negative effect).

Overall, it would appear that similarity in social views within a couple induces similarity in political views. This is not just a matter of, for instance, people with left-wing views being likely to support Labour and to live with another person with left-wing views who is also likely to support Labour. We have sought to show a process of adaptation rather than of selection.

Are couples homogamous on one criterion, therefore, homogamous on others? If a woman likes a man with a sense of humour because she has a sense of humour, it is unlikely that this would be enough to bring them together. A funny and highly educated woman is unlikely to be attracted to a poorly educated man simply because he tells good jokes, or vice versa. This is of course partly related to humour itself, which no doubt differs

Table 6.4   Effects of Values and Educational Homogamy on Political Homogamy (logistic regression)

	Shift to Labour		Shift to Conservative:	
	By husband	By wife	By husband	By wife
Husband left-wing	2.74**	1.30*	0.27***	0.65***
Wife left-wing	1.30*	1.85***	0.81	0.30***
Both left-wing	3.36***	2.42***	0.17***	0.25***
Husband graduate	1.25	1.38(*)	1.40	1.19
Wife graduate	0.78	1.33	1.15	0.77
Both graduate	1.07	1.58*	0.93	0.88
Pseudo R²	*.10*	*.06*	*.09*	*.11*
Observations	*3,532*	*3,753*	*2,608*	*2,963*

by education. Nevertheless, even if we assume that people are attracted to others like themselves, on the basis of parental class, own class, income or wealth, education, religion, ethnicity, political and social values, tastes and lifestyles, it is fairly obvious that such multiple selections become increasingly impossible. The correlations attenuate as they multiply. The most selective of aspirants to a perfectly homogamous match would have to wait a very long time to find the ideal partner, only to find that the age gap gets in the way.

Insofar as homogamy is a driving principle, it is likely that people take one criterion as a proxy for others and assume or hope for a high correlation between these. For instance, people select educationally equivalent partners (perhaps also broadly matching by discipline in the case of graduates) because they expect education to be correlated with social status, cultural background, interests and lifestyles. Nevertheless, they cannot be sure these go together.

We demonstrate the relationship between different forms of homogamy in Table 6.5, returning now to family values. We looked at these in respect of homogamy also in Table 5.1, and now it can be seen that the effective sample is even smaller. This is because we are looking not only at partners who both have a degree (or are both in the service class) but who both have liberal family values. It can be seen that 5.5 per cent of graduate couples are equally liberal on the first values issue and 22.2 per cent on the second. In the case of class these figures are 2.9 per cent and 15.5 per cent, respectively. The odds ratios (the probability that a couple homogamous on one dimension will also be homogamous on another) are high, as 5.5 per cent is a lot higher than 0.9 per cent: couples where both are graduates are over five times more likely than where they are not (even where one partner might be a graduate) to share a liberal view on the first issue. In the case of the second issue the relative difference is even larger (22.2 per cent against 3.9 per cent).

Table 6.5 Percentage of Couples Homogamous on Education (both have a degree) or Social Class (both service class), and not Homogamous, where Both Partners Strongly Disagree with Conservative Family Values

	Both partners strongly disagree pre-school child suffers if mother works			Both partners strongly disagree wife should stay at home, husband work		
	Same education or class	Not same education or class	N (liberal couples)	Same education or class	Not same education or class	N (liberal couples)
Education	5.5	0.9	219	22.2	3.9	953
Class	2.9	1.5	195	15.5	5.4	837

Nevertheless, it remains the case that in absolute terms only 5.5 per cent of couples where both have a degree share the first liberal view, and this is much lower than suggested by Table 6.1, which reveals a strong association at the individual level between these views and education (and class). Even though the figures for the second values question, 22.2 per cent, is much higher, matching on education or class does not guarantee a precise match on family values (which need not mean that their values differ greatly).

In the case of party political support, unlike Table 6.5, there is very little difference in the percentage of couples who jointly support Labour between those where both have a degree and those who do not; similarly for class. However, 18 per cent of couples who both have a degree also both support the Conservatives, compared to 10 per cent where they do not both have a degree (though the difference by social class is very slight). Again we get fairly small proportions of couples homogamous on two dimensions.

In this sense, the idea that there is a link between *heterogamy* and greater social openness, as suggested by Hakim (2000), and which we disputed in our earlier chapter, might be true. The complexity of modern life is such that people can match on only a limited number of characteristics. Homogamy is more than the sum of its parts, but the sums themselves are only a small part of the experience of marriage. As Zuckerman, Dasović and Fitzgerald put it in respect of their analysis, 'in most households, both partners do not share more than one or two of the critical variables: social class or religious identity, union membership, high or low levels of religious attendance, maximal levels of political interest' (2007: 90). There is, therefore, a limit to the effects of homogamy. Nevertheless, as a result of the process of adaptation described earlier, with partners influencing each other in the course of their relationship, we would expect a persistent pressure towards homogeneity of views amongst couples.

HOMOGAMY AND HAPPINESS

What does homogamy mean in terms of human happiness? Does it matter if partners are like each other or not? Certainly, in terms of the distribution of resources across the generations, and also of the distribution of social, family or political values across society, it does matter. But whether it does to the individuals themselves is less clear. There is some evidence, albeit disputed, that people who are not similar to each other are more likely to divorce (Weiss and Willis 1997; Blossfeld and Müller 2002). This implies that similarity makes life easier. In reviewing British Social Attitudes data, Lampard (1997: 94) notes that 79 per cent of respondents said having tastes and interests in common was at least fairly important to the success of a marriage. Same social background was deemed equally important in fewer cases (48 per cent of respondents). In contrast, agreement on politics was ranked by only 15 per cent. Yet political homogamy in Lampard's data, as well as our own, is much higher than this suggests. Further, in his own analysis Lampard notes a relationship between extreme political heterogamy (Labour/Conservative) and remarriage: either people with very different views are more prone to split up or, as we argued in our earlier chapter, remarriages may be heterogamous by force of circumstances. But the first explanation is not inconsistent with the latter. People seek similarity where they can and may pay a price when they fail. We have already mentioned research which shows that religious homogamy is linked to higher marital quality and to reduced marital conflict.

We would expect individuals in homogamous relationships to suffer less stress than those who are not. That this is so is demonstrated in Table 6.6, where we regress the General Health Questionnaire score (the 'caseness' version) on educational, age and attitudinal homogamy.[10] It should be noted that the R^2 is low, so there is—unsurprisingly—plenty about the nature of stress that we do not know in a survey like this. But some things seem clear enough. The first two columns look at the effect on the GHQ score of wives (where a higher score indicates more stress), including as a central measure whether she believes that the family suffers if the woman works full time. In the first column her opinion on this is entered as well as his. More traditional women suffer greater stress, even when we control for whether cohabiting or married, education, age, the age similarity between partners, and, though we do not show the results for these controls, for housing tenure, and whether people believe they are either comfortably off financially or in financial difficulties. The husband's family values, though, make no difference. Nevertheless, when we enter the values homogamy indicator (showing the two share the same values) in the second column instead of her husband's values, this is negative. It reduces stress. We find very much the same sort of result (but do not show this) in respect of the other values question we have used previously.

Still looking at wives, the same outcomes do not apply to more objective bases for homogamy. Age similarity makes no difference, and nor does educational similarity. It is of some note, though, that having some form of medium or higher education seems to be associated with greater stress scores, even though, as pointed out earlier, education is also associated with more liberal views. Similarly, cohabitation seems to be linked to greater stress, although our earlier chapter showed that cohabiting couples have more liberal views, which, as we have just shown, are linked to less stress. Using the American General Social Survey 1972–96, Waite (2000: 372–8) shows that cohabiting people, both men and women, score less well on an admittedly fairly simplistic general happiness question than married people (which, though, perhaps because of the relatively small size of the cohabiting group, fails to reach statistical significance). It is possible, of course, that cohabitation is linked to some other factor we have failed to measure or include in our models, so this might not be a direct effect. Yet despite possibly more complex interrelationships, the results suggest that attitudinal homogamy reduces stress.

The picture for men is similar up to a point. One important difference is that cohabitation has no apparent effect. Men do not find living as a

Table 6.6   Factors Associated with Higher Stress Score Using Values Measure: Family Suffers if Woman Works Full Time

	Wives		Husbands	
Wife has traditional values	0.18***	0.18***	−0.01	0.02
Husband has traditional values	−0.01		0.11***	
Couple share same values		−0.10**		−0.04
Cohabiting	0.12(*)	0.12(*)	−0.05	0.06
Age	0.004(*)	0.004(*)	0.002	0.004*
Same age	−0.07	−0.07	−0.07	−0.07
Degree	0.29***	0.29***	0.39***	0.37***
Further education	0.16**	0.16**	0.13**	0.12*
A-level	0.26***	0.26***	0.15*	0.14*
Same education	0.04	0.04	0.12**	0.12**
Constant	0.44**	0.44*	0.41**	0.64***
R^2	.06	.06	.08	.08
Observations	26,828	26,828	26,819	26,819

couple any more stressful than they would if they were married. A more important difference, though, is apparent in that attitudinal homogamy does not reduce stress while educational homogamy increases it. This seems to have little to do with the education of the partner as such. When we enter the education of both partners in the same model, without the homogamy indicator, the wife's education has a slight gradient (higher education going with higher stress), but the coefficient is always small and is nowhere near statistically significant. Thus, even if her having a higher education is materially beneficial to him, this does not reduce his stress levels. It would appear that men do not like their wives to have the same education as themselves. And so, we cannot say that homogamy makes married life more equable; the effects are highly gendered.

CONCLUSIONS

We argued in our earlier chapter that people select a partner partly on the basis of similarity in terms of social background but also of social opinions. There is scope to relax this constraint after marriage. In fact we find the reverse. Marriage increases attitudinal homogamy to an even higher level than at the time of marriage. Further, the reciprocal influences are not always equal. In respect of views about marriage itself, it would seem that the woman's views predominate. However, this does not mean that marriage is a great homogeniser. We also point out that it is difficult for couples to use similarity as a criterion across a wide range of dimensions. They would soon run out of potential partners, and this is the case despite the fact that, as we have shown, living with someone who is similar reduces psychological stress. Even if we would unrealistically expect a preference for perfect homogamy, serendipity, limited information, and errors of judgement would all reduce this. In practice we seem to observe that homogamy across several dimensions falls off quite sharply. So there are strong limits to the homogenising effect of marriage. As a result of chance if not of preferences, variety remains the spice of life.

NOTES

1. Or indeed to no-one at all, though this is not something we consider here, as our interest is in the effects of marriage on homogamy rather than of marriage itself.
2. Who in fact examine the extent of political partisanship in entire families, not just amongst couples.
3. Though Curtis and Ellison (2002) argue that denominational homogamy has no effect, at least on marital conflict; it is disagreement about intensity of belief and observance which counts.
4. There are, though, six family values questions. Such steep gradients do not appear in all six. In the case of one other the gradient is pronounced, but in two the relationship between values and social background is flat and in one even (slightly) in the reverse direction. We choose two of the more extreme views to put people to the test, i.e. to avoid weak, uncommitted responses.
5. There is a further gender asymmetry here. The figure for Labour women with Labour husbands is 76%, and 75% for the Conservative equivalent. Thus, homogamy is always high, but higher if we take the woman as the unit of analysis. (As given earlier, the figure for men as the unit of analysis is 70%.) It is hard to see why, as party support differs little by gender, but it implies that men who support either Labour or the Conservatives are more willing to live with a partner who does not than are the equivalent women.
6. There is a trend factor (wave) in favour of men becoming more liberal. Age works the other way for both men and women. Similarity of age has an effect in her case, encouraging greater liberalism, though not in his. Length of union makes no difference.
7. We have only shown results for the first values question, in order to save space. The story in respect of the second is broadly similar in most aspects. In particular, the effects of each other's values on change in the partner's values remain virtually the same. However, the impact of cohabitation is smaller in respect of change in his values, and is now of the opposite sign in respect of hers—though the coefficient only borders on statistical significance, and the man is now much more likely to become more liberal if he is a graduate. In addition, her being in work changes his views more positively towards the liberal position than with the other values question. Overall we find a lesser

impact of marital status but a stronger effect of education and of work. It remains the case that her education appears to influence his views more than his influences hers.

8. That this is the case is clear enough from the very low pseudo R^2 that we obtain when we run the models without the left-wing variable.

9. Though the differences between these effects are weaker if we take into account the uncertainty surrounding the estimates in the specific sample, as indicated by the standard errors, which for simplicity of presentation we do not show.

10. This variable converts the valid answers to a battery of twelve Likert-type questions dealing with subjective well-being into a single 12-point scale

REFERENCES

Blossfeld, H.P. and Müller, R. (2002) Union disruption in comparative perspective: the role of assortative partner choice and careers of couples, *International Journal of Sociology*, 32(4): 3–35.

Brynin, M. and Francesconi, M. (2004) The material returns to partnership: the effects of educational matching on labour market outcomes and gender equality, *European Sociological Review*, 20: 363–77.

Greenstein, T. (1995) Gender ideology, marital disruption, and the employment of married women, *Journal of Marriage and the Family*, 57: 31–42.

Hakim, C. (2000) *Work-Lifestyle choices in the 21st century*, Oxford: Oxford University Press.

Kalmijn, M. and Kraaykamp, G. (2007) Social stratification and attitudes: a comparative analysis of the effects of class and education in Europe, *British Journal of Sociology*, 58: 547–76.

Kan, M.-Y. and Heath, A. (2006) The political values and choices of husbands and wives, *Journal of Marriage and the Family*, 68: 70–86.

Lampard, R. (1997) Party political homogamy in Great Britain, *European Sociological Review*, 13: 79–99.

Moors, G. (2000) Values and living arrangements: a recursive relationships in L. Waite (ed) *The ties that bind*, Hawthorne, New York: Aldine de Gruyter, 212–26.

Myers, S. (2006) Religious homogamy and marital quality: historical and generational patterns, 1980–1997, *Journal of Marriage and the Family*, 68: 292–304.

Curtis, T. and Ellison, C. (2002) Religious heterogamy and marital conflict: findings from the national survey of families and households, *Journal of Family Issues*, 23: 551–76.

Waite, L. (ed) (2000) *The ties that bind*, Hawthore, New York: Aldine de Gruyter.

Weiss, Y. and Willis, R. (1997) Match quality, new information, and marital dissolution, *Journal of Labor Economics*, 15: 293–329.

Zuckerman, A., Dasović, J. and Fitzgerald, J. (2007) *Partisan families: the social logic of bounded partisanship in Germany and Britain*, New York and Cambridge: Cambridge University Press.

Part II

Relationships and
Social Welfare

7 Young Child-Parent Relationships

John Ermisch

The mother-child relationship is the first that we have, and it is at the core of kinship networks. From the literature on the psychological relationship between mothers and children we know that mothers have a powerful long-term effect on the well-being of their children. But when does the mother's influence on her child's development start to manifest itself? In this chapter I show that it not only occurs very early but that this early influence has a continuing, long-term effect.

There is growing evidence that differences in children's intellectual, emotional and personal development by, for example, parents' socioeconomic status or educational attainment, emerge at early ages and that these differences cast a long shadow over subsequent achievements. For instance, Leon Feinstein's (2003) analysis of British children born in 1970 (from the British Cohort Study 1970) shows that differences in an index of child development by parents' socioeconomic status (or education) emerged by 22 months of age. There are similar gaps at 42 and 60 months. In turn, the child's position in the development index distribution at 42 months was found to be strongly related to the child's educational and vocational achievements at the age of 26. Using the Aberdeen Children of the 1950s cohort study, Raymond Illsley (2002) demonstrates large social-class differences in height at age 5 and in performance on a picture intelligence test at age 6/7. These social class differences persisted in achievement tests at ages 9 and 12. Cunha and Heckman (2007, including Web appendices) find large differences in American children's scores on the Peabody Individual Achievement Test–Math by parents' 'permanent' income at age 5 throughout the range of income.[1] These differences persist as schooling proceeds over the next nine years. Carneiro and Heckman (2002) show that the PIAT–Math test score (at age 12) and long-run average family income (over the entire childhood, from birth to age 18) have strong effects on the probability of college enrolment. Also, studies of the early childhood intervention programmes in the United States, such as Head Start, have indicated the long-run effects of these early interventions (Currie and Thomas 1995; Currie et al. 2002).

Children living in poverty may have nutritional deficits owing to their low income, which in turn affect their development. But the developmental differences are not just between the poor and nonpoor—for instance, the difference in average PIAT–Math test scores between the third and highest income quartiles in the US is large (Cunha and Heckman 2007). What lies behind these differences throughout the income distribution?

Do the socioeconomic differences in these examples mainly reflect genetic differences in cognitive ability between groups?[2] Despite the fact that cognitive ability is one of the most heritable behavioural traits, the 'heritability' calculation is population-specific.[3] It tells us nothing about the contribution of the environment to between-group differences or changes over time. Causes of individual differences have no necessary implications for the causes of differences between groups. Furthermore, gene expression interacts in important ways with family environment, making it difficult to partition the two effects (Rutter 2006). Height, for example, is a highly heritable trait (90 per cent of the individual variance attributable to genetic inheritance), but the average height of a population of a given country can increase dramatically over a generation because of better nutrition and other improvements in living standards (i.e. large changes in the environment).

General cognitive ability is also not immutable but can be altered by the environment. Other evidence also points to an important environmental role: In an analysis of the Peabody Individual Achievement Test (PIAT) reading and maths scores of offspring of members of the National Child Development Study (1958 British birth cohort), Galindo-Rueda and Vignoles (2002; Table 9) find that the social class of the mother significantly affects these scores after controlling for the mother's cognitive ability measured at ages 7 and 11. Thus, the socioeconomic differences in cognitive ability at preschool ages are unlikely to reflect genetic differences to any large degree: average genetic differences between groups are small compared with individual differences within groups (Plomin 1999), although between-group differences may be larger when groups are defined by parents' education or income than, for example, ethnic groups.

From this evidence it is natural to pose the following question: What do 'better-off' parents do to improve their children's preschool environment, and as a consequence their achievements in education? The answer to this would enhance our understanding of intergenerational mobility enormously because of the strong relationship between educational achievements and lifetime income. It also has important implications for appropriate interventions in the lives of disadvantaged young children. In other words, what types of parent-child interactions and parental behaviour during children's preschool years are conducive to later educational and economic success, and how are they correlated with parents' income, education or socioeconomic group? In addition to such longer term consequences, child-parent interactions are likely to have direct effects on children's well-being during childhood.

This chapter develops some measures of young child-parent interactions and suggests some partial answers to the questions posed earlier, thereby opening the 'black box' containing the mechanisms that produce associations between socioeconomic status and children's cognitive development. It uses the first two sweeps of the Millennium Cohort Study (MCS). The sample population for the MCS was drawn from all live births in the UK over 12 months from 1 September 2000 in England and Wales and from 1 December 2000 in Scotland and Northern Ireland. The survey for the first sweep occurred between June 2001 and January 2003 when children were aged about 9 months, gathering information from the parents of 18,819 babies, about themselves and the babies (e.g. problems during pregnancy, birth weight). The second sweep took place when the children were around 3 years of age, and the third sweep took place during 2006, when the survey child entered primary school, at age 5. Measures of parent-child educational interactions, such as reading to the child and teaching the alphabet, mother-child interactions like scolding, and indicators of parenting style such as whether there are regular meal- and bedtimes and regulation of the number of hours that the child watches TV per day, were collected when the child was aged 3. Physical measurements, such as height and weight, and two cognitive assessments were also made at age 3. The latter are the British Ability Scales Naming Vocabulary scale (BAS) and the Bracken School Readiness Assessment (BSRA).

The next section documents the socioeconomic differences in these two cognitive assessments at age 3, and confirms in broad terms the results from the analysis of the 1970 birth cohort, namely, that large differences emerge by the cohort member's third birthday. In the second section, measures of parent-child interactions are constructed. It examines how these differ by socioeconomic group, and the next section relates them to the cognitive assessments at age 3. In the fourth section, the nature and implications of child-parent interactions among children aged 5–15 are analysed using the British Household Panel Study.

SOCIOECONOMIC DIFFERENCES IN COGNITIVE OUTCOMES AT AGE 3

The British Ability Scales Naming Vocabulary scale (BAS) assesses the spoken vocabulary of young children; the test consists of a booklet of coloured pictures of items that the child is asked to name (see Hansen 2006: 41–3 for further details). The Bracken School Readiness Assessment (BSRA) is used to assess basic concept development in young children; the concepts assessed are argued to be directly related to early childhood education and to predict readiness for more formal education (Hansen 2006: 44–6). In both cases, the percentiles of the distribution of the normative (standardised) scores are used as the cognitive measure.[4]

The two measures of cognitive assessment are relatively strongly correlated, with a correlation coefficient of 0.575, suggesting that they are measuring some common phenomena. Girls do significantly better than boys, scoring on average nearly 9 percentile points higher for each assessment.

The primary indicator of socioeconomic position used in the analysis is the mother's educational qualifications when the child was aged 9 months (i.e. at the first interview with the parents). Higher educated women tend to have better educated partners, and this reinforces the income gap between these and less educated women.[5] Differences in the distribution of cognitive assessments by mother's educational qualifications are shown in Figure 7.1. There is a clear gradient, with better educated mothers having 3-year-olds who are ranked higher in terms of cognitive ability. Children of mothers with a first degree have about a 30 percentile point higher mean ranking than children whose mothers have no qualifications. Note that there is no presumption that differences in mother's educational attainment 'caused' the differences in cognitive assessment that we observe; education is only used as a convenient grouping variable, reflecting many differences in women's family background and individual orientation and lifestyles. For comparison, Figure 7.1 also shows mean percentiles of child's birth weight by mother's education. The birth-weight gradient is much shallower than that associated with the cognitive assessments, although it is statistically significant.[6] Children of mothers who had a partner present at the time that they were first interviewed score much better in terms of cognitive assessment rankings (11–15 percentile points higher) and birth weight (7 percentile points higher).

Large differences also emerge if the means of the cognitive assessments are compared across current income groups—about 20–30 percentile points between the lowest and highest income group. Thus, the MCS data confirm the patterns in the previous studies mentioned at the outset of the chapter. That is, large differences in cognitive development by socioeconomic group

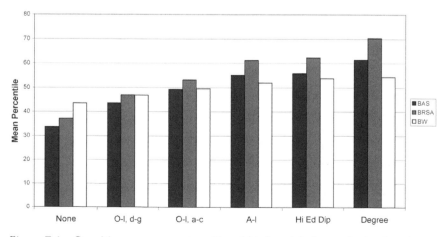

Figure 7.1   Cognitive assessments (age 3) and birth weight by mother's education.

are already evident at age 3. As the patterns are similar for the two cognitive measures, in the subsequent analysis we take a simple average of them as our indicator of cognitive ability at age 3.

PARENT-CHILD INTERACTIONS AND PARENTING STYLE

What do more educated parents do during the child's first 3 years that is conducive to higher cognitive assessments? To address this query, two sets of questions from Module B: Parenting Activities are used to extract measures of 'latent variables' that I call 'educational activities' and 'parenting style'. The former uses questions about *how often* someone at home reads to the child, teaches the alphabet, teaches counting, teaches songs, poems and nursery rhymes and how often the child paints or draws at home.[7] These five activities are reduced into a common 'factor' using principal components analysis. There is evidence of only one factor, which 'loads' positively on all five activities, suggesting that it has a clear interpretation as an indicator of parents' educational activities.[8] Figure 7.2 shows how its mean varies by mother's educational attainments (note that the factors have zero mean and unit standard deviation by construction).

Better educated mothers clearly are more frequently involved in educational activities with their children. Comparing means, the no-qualification group and the degree-qualification group differ by 0.45 of a standard deviation in the educational activities factor. Another question asks whether or not 'anyone at home ever takes [the child] to the library'. Figure 7.2 also shows that the proportion answering 'yes' rises with the mother's educational group.

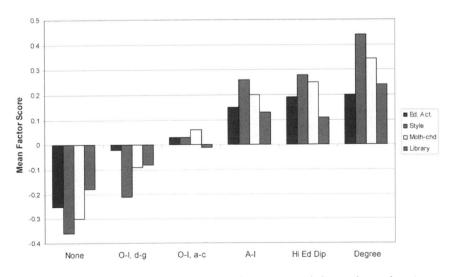

Figure 7.2 Parents' educational activities and parenting style by mother's education.

The measure of 'parenting style' draws on six questions: are there 'lots of rules' in the family, are rules strictly enforced, does the child have meals at regular times, does the child go to bed at regular times, how many hours a day does the child watch television or videos, and how important do you think it is for a family to eat meals together? There is evidence of only one factor, which loads positively on all responses other than the amount of television viewing.[9] Thus, higher values on this factor can be interpreted as 'more structured' parenting. Comparing mean parenting style scores in Figure 7.2, the no-qualification group and the degree-qualification group differ by 0.8 of a standard deviation in the parenting style factor.

A third measure of child-parent interactions concerns the relationship between the mother and the child at the interview when the child was aged 3. It is based on the interviewer's observations on whether: (a) the mother introduced the interviewer to the child; (b) the mother did not scold the child; (c) the mother answered the child's questions verbally; (d) the mother praised the child spontaneously more than once. Given the dichotomous nature of all of the responses, a factor analysis is not appropriate. The simple sum of the 'yes' responses is used as an indicator, with a larger sum indicating better child-mother interactions; 60.5 per cent of mothers score 4, 29.5 per cent score 3, 7.5 per cent score 2 and 2.5 per cent score 0 or 1. Figure 7.2 shows that better educated women have better scores (standardised to be mean 0 and variance 1) on this indicator, with the difference between the no-qualification group and the degree-qualification group being 0.65 of a standard deviation.

What do these factors actually measure? They could reflect unobserved traits of the parents, or indeed the way in which they respond to survey questions like those used to derive the factors. One way to explore this possibility is to see whether they are associated with fetal growth (birth weight divided by length of gestation), which is affected by antenatal inputs of the mother, such as antenatal care. The idea is that parents' behaviour after the child's birth cannot have a causal impact on fetal growth. I regress fetal growth on these factors, parents' education and other controls (e.g. a child's sex and ethnic group). The coefficients of variables relating to educational activities (including 'reading to' and 'taking to library'), parenting style and mother-child interaction factors are statistically insignificant as a group. Individually, the only one of these that is statistically significant is 'taking to library', with a p-value of 0.017. Although hardly conclusive, this exercise suggests that the significant effects of educational activities, parenting style and mother-child interaction factors on cognitive development found in the following section are not driven only by unobserved traits of the parents that improve their parenting at all stages, including during the antenatal period. There appears to be a direct relationship between parents' actual behaviour and the early cognitive development of the child. Of course, all of these data on parenting, being based on mother's responses and interviewer observations, are subject to measurement error.

PARENTS' BEHAVIOUR AND COGNITIVE OUTCOMES

Children scoring better on parents' educational activities and mother-child interactions (and perhaps parenting style) may directly benefit in terms of their well-being during childhood. As noted at the outset of the paper, they might also fare better over the longer term if these parental behaviours affect their cognitive and emotional development. This section estimates a series of multivariate regressions with the average of the two cognitive assessment variables at age 3 (in percentiles) as the dependent variable.

A key explanatory variable is educational activities. Compared to the other elements of the educational activities factor discussed previously, the frequency of reading to the child is more concentrated in the top three categories ('every day' (57 per cent), 'several times a week' (19 per cent) and 'once or twice a week' (16 per cent).[10] 'Reading to' is, therefore, split off into a categorical variable and the remaining four activities are combined into a factor like before.[11] This new educational activities factor varies less with mother's education than the comparable factor shown in Figure 7.2 (the difference between the top and bottom education categories is 0.24 of a standard deviation). The frequency of reading to the child varies considerably with mother's education; for instance, the pattern for the proportion reading to their child daily looks very similar to the proportion ever taking their child to the library in Figure 7.2.

It is important to control for ethnic differences that could confound the analysis. There are large differences among ethnic groups in the means of cognitive assessment percentile scores at age 3, the scores for parents' educational activities, parenting style, mother-child interactions and birth weight. For example, the 'other Asian' group, which is dominated by Bangladeshis, records the lowest mean assessments and the lowest mean scores for parents' educational activities and parenting style, while the Indian group is much closer to Whites in these respects. Children from Pakistani, other Asian and Afro-Caribbean backgrounds score significantly more poorly than whites on the mother-child interactions. Why the minority ethnic groups record poorer average cognitive assessments than whites and why these differ amongst the main ethnic groups is a subject for future study. For example, do the very low scores for Pakistani and Bangladeshi children reflect less use of English in the home amongst these groups?

It is also important to control for 'fetal growth'.[12] Epidemiological research has demonstrated that fetal growth is strongly related to the nutritional environment (caloric intake) *in utero*, which affects brain growth and the health of the child. There is evidence that it continues to affect health status in middle age through its impact on important chronic conditions like coronary heart disease and diabetes—see Barker's (1995) 'fetal origins hypothesis' and Case et al. (2005) for recent British evidence consistent with it. Studies of twins indicate that a child's fetal growth affects short-term outcomes like infant health and mortality rates and long-run ones like educational attainment, earnings, adult height and health. There is, however, some controversy about the size of these effects and where in the distribution the effects are largest. For instance, Almond et al. (2005) finds small effects of birth weight on the health status of the infant at birth or shortly thereafter. Other studies suggest that the small short-run effects may be misleading, because larger-birth-weight babies have better long-run outcomes (Behrman and Rosenzweig 2004; Black et al. 2005; Royer 2005), although there is no consensus on the size of these effects. These associations may reflect direct causal influences (e.g. of nutrition *in utero*), or they may reflect interaction between postnatal investments by parents and fetal growth. In either case, fetal growth may be related to early cognitive development.

All of the regressions control for the child's sex, exact age in days, ethnic group and fetal growth. The results are shown in Table 7.1. In the first column, there are no socioeconomic controls; in the second, socioeconomic controls are added to the sample of all mothers and the third column includes these controls for a sample of mothers who had a partner present when the child was aged 9 months; in this case mother's and father's education are entered in nine combinations: for each education group of the mother, dichotomous variables indicate whether the father has same level, a higher level or a lower level. The frequency of reading to the child, whether or not parents ever take him or her to the library, and the mother-child interaction score have relatively powerful effects on cognitive assessments. The factors for parents' other educational activities' and parenting style have smaller effects.

Addition of the socioeconomic controls reduces the impacts of the parenting variables, although parents' educational activities and mother-child interaction still have strong and precisely estimated associations with cognitive assessments. Similarly, the gradients in cognitive assessment with respect to mother's education are flatter when we take parent-child interactions and other socioeconomic indicators into account. For instance, if column (2) of Table 7.1 only contained the mother's education groups, then their coefficients would be 11.1, 18.6 and 25.5 percentile points, respectively, in comparison with 3.5, 6.2 and 9.2 in Table 7.1.

The impact of fetal growth indicates that prenatal investments are also important for cognitive development. Taking the model in column (2), the coefficient of the square root of fetal growth indicates that a standard deviation higher fetal growth increases cognitive assessments by 2 percentile points. Only-children and children from larger families fare less well in terms of their cognitive assessments at age 3. In particular, compared to a child with one sibling, an only-child scores 4.8 percentile points lower, and one with two siblings scores 5.5 percentile points lower. The combination of age (positive) and age squared (negative) tells us that cognitive assessments increase with the mother's age until she is around age 37. Children of mothers having an unemployed partner or no partner (when the child was

Table 7.1 Linear Regression Coefficients for Cognitive Percentile Scores*

	(1)	(2)	(3)
Reading to child: (reference: 'Never')			
Every day	22.9	15.8	16.3
	(2.2)	(2.2)	(2.3)
Several times per week	17.0	12.8	13.6
	(2.3)	(2.3)	(2.4)
Once or twice per week	10.6	9.3	10.0
	(2.2)	(2.2)	(2.3)
Once or twice per month	9.6	8.6	9.4
	(2.8)	2.7)	(2.8)
Less often	6.6	7.1	8.6
	(2.8)	(2.9)	(3.0)
Takes child to library	5.2	3.6	3.2
	(0.6)	(0.6)	(0.6)
Other parent education activity	1.86	2.08	2.13
	(0.31)	(0.30)	(0.31)
Mother-child interaction (reference: sum equal 0 or 1)			
Sum = 2	8.9	7.7	7.6
	(2.4)	(2.2)	(2.2)
Sum = 3	14.7	11.1	11.1
	(2.1)	(1.9)	(1.8)
Sum = 4	22.7	16.5	16.4
	(2.2)	(2.0)	(1.9)
Parenting Style	1.63	0.42	0.23
	(0.29)	(0.29)	(0.33)
Square root of fetal growth	14.06	12.70	12.28
	(2.35)	(2.38)	(2.53)
Age mother	—	2.03	1.64
		(0.47)	(0.52)
Age mother squared	—	-0.028	-0.022
	—	(0.008)	(0.008)
Mother's educ.**			
O-level/GCSE, grades a–c	—	3.5	***
		(0.8)	

(continued)

Table 7.1 *(continued)*

	(1)	*(2)*	*(3)*
A-level/high. ed. diploma		6.2	***
		(0.9)	
First degree or higher	—	9.2	***
		(1.0)	
No partner when child aged 9 months	—	−3.0 (1.1)	—
Partner no job when child aged 9 months	—	−2.5 (1.0)	−2.7 (1.0)
Partnership break, 9 months to 3 years	—	−2.3 (1.1)	−2.2 (1.3)
Only-child	—	−4.8	−5.5
		(1.5)	(1.5)
Square root of the number of siblings	—	−11.05 (1.20)	−11.33 (1.26)
R^2	0.212	0.292	0.294
N	9,612	8,819	7,543

*Average of BAS and BRSA scores. All equations control for ethnic group, child's age in days, child's sex. Standard errors are in parentheses.
(1) All mothers; no other controls.
(2) All mothers; also controls for household income category.
(3) Mothers with partner when child aged 9 months; also controls for household income category.
**Education reference group: no qualifications or O-level/GCSE, grades d–g.
***Combinations of parents' education levels: for each group of the mother, whether father has same level, a higher level or a lower level; 9 combinations in all.

aged 9 months) or experiencing a partnership break between the child's age of 9 months and 3 years have, on average, cognitive assessments 2–3 percentile points lower.

With regard to the control variables not shown in Table 7.1, girls obtain higher scores on the cognitive assessments (about 7 percentile points higher). A pattern of assessment scores by ethnic group remains after controlling for parenting behaviour and the socioeconomic attributes of the parents. Among the minorities, Pakistanis and other Asians (mainly Bangladeshis) score worst, followed by Indians, Afro-Caribbean and 'other ethnics'.

Of the parenting factors investigated, educational activities, particularly reading to the child, and mother-child interactions are of greater importance. If we attribute causal links between these and cognitive assessments, it is clear that differences in parents' educational activities and mother-child interactions, at least as measured by the questions in the MCS, can account for some of the large socioeconomic differentials in cognitive achievements at age 3. Thus, this analysis has opened the 'black box' a little. We still do not know why, after controlling for some apparently important aspects of parenting, better educated mothers, those with partners when the child was aged between 9 months and 3 years, and those with a partner in a job have children who reach a more advanced stage of cognitive development by age 3. The impacts of family size and mother's age on cognitive development also merit further investigation.

CHILD-PARENT INTERACTIONS WITH OLDER CHILDREN

So far we have focussed on parental interactions with very young children, and their association with cognitive development; that is as far as the Millennium Cohort will currently take us. To go further we use the British Household Panel Survey (BHPS) (which, though, has the relative disadvantage of a much smaller sample size). In this section responses to questions in the 2002 BHPS are used to characterise parental interactions with children aged 5–15. These questions were addressed to parents of children aged under 16 living in household, and their responses are specific to each child. Here we focus on mothers' responses to these questions. The analyses are undertaken for two age groups: 5–10 and 11–15. For children aged 5–10 there are 1,053 mothers with 1,378 children, while for children aged 11–15 there are 944 mothers with 1,235 children.

Parents were asked 'How often does CHILD (name) quarrel with you?' They were also asked 'How often does CHILD talk to you about things that matter?' For mothers of children aged 5–10, arguments with their child decreased with both the child's and mother's age but their frequency did not vary with the mother's educational qualifications (results not shown). 'Talking about things that matter' was more frequent for girls and for mothers with higher educational qualifications, and it declined in frequency with the child's age. Parents were also asked about the frequency of their help with homework. Help was more frequent among mothers with an A-level or higher qualification, and it declined as the child aged.

Among mothers of children aged 11–15, arguments occurred less often for mothers with at least an A-level qualification. Their frequency declined with the mother's age, and quarrels were more frequent for girls than boys. 'Talking about things that matter' was also more frequent for girls, and it declined in frequency with the child's age. Better educated mothers helped with their adolescent children's homework more often, but help declined with the child's age.

The answers to four questions about parents' behaviour toward their children—How often do you yell at CHILD? How often do you spank or slap CHILD? How often do you cuddle or hug CHILD? How often do you praise CHILD?—form a consistent pattern. The first principal component based on answers to these four questions can be identified with 'supportive behaviour' by the mother: it loads negatively on responses to the first two questions (yelling and spanking) and positively on responses to the last two questions (hugging and praising).

In both age groups, the indicator of mother's 'supportive behaviour' increases steeply with the mother's educational qualifications. In a multivariate analysis (results not shown) that allows for a mother-specific residual influence that is uncorrelated with her educational qualifications or age, supportive behaviour increases with the mother's age and her qualifications; it decreases with the age of the child and is higher for girls than boys. Variation among children within families is important: it accounts for about 50 to 60 per cent of the variance in the indicator of mother's supportive behaviour; the rest of the variance is specific to the mother.

Is this behaviour associated with the children's subsequent educational attainments? For children aged 10–15 in 2002 (born 1987–1992), we calculate the average value of the supportive behaviour indicator for each mother. We then match these values to mothers of young people (aged 11–15) in the British Youth Panel 1994–2003 (born 1979–1992), who are followed into the BHPS proper (i.e. when aged 16 and older). The maximum educational qualification achieved by 2003 is calculated for each child and classified into three groups: 'GCSE grades d–g', 'GCSE grades a–c' and 'A-level and above'. Note that most of these children in the matched sample are not the same children as observed aged 10–15 in 2002, but they have the same mother. That is, we will be relating the average supportive behaviour of mother with adolescent children to the educational outcomes of their older brothers and sisters.

Table 7.2 reports an 'ordered logit' analysis for child's educational attainments. This model has the property that the logarithm of the odds[13] of the child being in an educational attainment category higher than any particular one depends linearly on the explanatory variables, with the impact being the same irrespective of the particular category under consideration. That is, an estimated coefficient of the model measures the proportionate impact of a variable on the odds ratio associated with any particular category. For instance, the estimates in the first column of Table 7.2 indicate that the odds of being in a higher education category are about 25 per cent higher when the value of the supportive behaviour scale is one standard deviation higher. The first two columns use all the matched children and include the maximum age observed as a control variable; the second two columns confine the sample to children who were observed at age 18 or older, because it is usually not possible to take A-level examinations before the age of 18. The standard errors of the parameter estimates are adjusted for multiple children having the same mother.

The analysis indicates that in all four sets of parameter estimates, the scale for mother's supportive behaviour is positively and significantly associated

Table 7.2 Impacts of Mother's Support Behaviour and Education on the Odds of Higher Qualifications for her Children*

	Children aged 16 or older		Children aged 18 or older	
	(1)	(2)	(3)	(4)
Maximum age of child	0.43	0.44	—	—
	(0.07)	(0.08)		
Sex of child	0.39	0.48	0.80	0.95
	(0.17)	(0.17)	(0.32)	(0.34)
Supportive behaviour scale	0.25	0.18	0.34	0.27
	(0.08)	(0.08)	(0.13)	(0.13)
Mother's highest qualification:				
O-level/GCSE	—	0.68	—	0.79
		(0.28)		(0.47)
A-level	—	0.41	—	0.20
		(0.34)		(0.48)
Other higher	—	1.10	—	1.16
		(0.30)		(0.53)
Degree or higher	—	1.43	—	3.09
		(0.32)		(1.04)
N	543	543	190	190

Asymptotic standard errors in parentheses; standard errors adjusted for clustering by mother.

with child's highest educational qualification achieved so far. The estimated impacts of the scale are smaller when we control for mother's educational attainments. This is expected because it has been shown that better educated mothers score higher on the supportive behaviour scale. Nevertheless, like the analysis of 3-year-olds' cognitive assessments, this evidence is consistent with certain types of child-parent interactions being conducive to children's better educational achievement. It is also likely to be the case that children whose parents behave more supportively toward them are better off during their childhood (i.e. experience higher well-being).

CONCLUSIONS

The chapter has demonstrated considerable variation across families in how parents interact with their children. Some of this variation is systematic. In particular, better educated mothers tend to 'score higher' on educational activities and better child-mother interactions with their young children. Such behaviour is likely to enhance the well-being of children during childhood. It also is associated with better cognitive development during the preschool years. Supportive behaviour toward older children is also more evident among better educated mothers, and this behaviour is associated with better educational attainments for their children.

One of the core relationships that we have during our life—that with our parents and our mother in particular—has been shown to have important influences on how we develop during the early years of childhood and on the adults that we become. These influences work in part through what mothers do in terms of educational activities with their children and the supportiveness of their parenting. While most of us instinctively know this, the measurement of the long-term effects of maternal care is beset with problems. We hope that the research presented provides some indications of ways of doing this as well as the value of the data sets used for future research in this area.

NOTES

1. In the Web appendices, they also demonstrate that large differences by income in scores on the Peabody Picture Vocabulary Test emerge at age 3 and persist over the next 11 years. Further, differences by income in an index of antisocial behaviour are evident at age 4 and persist through age 12, particularly between the lowest three income quartiles.
2. The correlation in cognitive assessments at age 3 between twins from the Millennium Cohort Study is 0.8, but this represents both genetic and environmental similarities.
3. 'Heritability' is the proportion of observed variance in general cognitive ability that can be accounted for by genetic differences among individuals *in a particular population at a particular* time (e.g. see Plomin et al. 1997). For example, there is some evidence that 'heritability' may be larger in better educated (socially advantaged) families (Rowe et al. 1999; Turkheimer et al. 2003).
4. The MCS sample is clustered geographically and disproportionately stratified to overrepresent areas with higher proportions of: (1) ethnic minorities in England; (2) areas of high child poverty; and (3) the three smaller countries in the UK: Wales, Scotland and Northern Ireland. The clustered sample design and nonresponse at the first sweep is taken into account in all of the statistical calculations in the chapter, and so the statistics presented should be representative for UK births during the sampling period. The analyses only include singleton births, thereby dropping the 246 sets of twins and 10 sets of triplets in the data.
5. For example, there is a strong relationship between (banded) household income at the first interview and the mother's educational attainment.
6. The percentile points of the child's birth-weight distribution were created by using the weighted distribution of birth weights in the sample at the first sweep. Mean percentiles were calculated using weighting based on the clustered sample design, as was the case for the cognitive assessments.

7. There are eight categories of frequency for these responses with the exception of 'reading to', which has six.
8. The factor loadings are 0.46, 0.65, 0.77, 0.73 and 0.52, respectively.
9. The factor loadings are 0.45, 0.49, 0.68, 0.70,−0.33 and 0.47, respectively.
10. Furthermore, there are only six categories of response in the 'reading to' variable, the remaining three (and their incidence) being 'once or twice a month' (3%), 'less often' (2%) and 'never' (3%), compared to eight categories for the other elements.
11. The factor loadings for this new factor are 0.68 (alphabet), 0.80 (counting), 0.73 (songs) and 0.54 (drawing).
12. In terms of proximate causes, variation in birth weight primarily reflects variation in length of gestation and fetal growth at a given gestation length. The regressions below include the square root of fetal growth, which imposes a declining marginal effect of fetal growth as it increases.
13. The odds of being in a given category is the probability of being in that category divided by the probability of not being in it.

REFERENCES

Almond, D., Chay, K. and Lee, D. (2005) The costs of low birth weight, *Quarterly Journal of Economics*, 120: 1031–83.

Barker, D. (1995) Fetal origins of coronary heart disease, *British Medical Journal*, 311: 171–74.

Behrman, J. and Rosenzweig, M. (2004) Returns to birthweight, *The Review of Economics and Statistics*, 86: 586–601.

Black, S., Devereux, P. and Salvanes, K. (2005) *From the cradle to the grave? The effect of birth weight on adult outcomes of children*, Los Angeles: University of California.

Carniero, P. and Heckman, J.J. (2002) The evidence on credit constraints in postsecondary schooling, *The Economic Journal*, 112: 705–34.

Case, A., Fertig, A. and Paxson, C. (2005) The lasting impact of childhood health and circumstance, *Journal of Health Economics*, 24: 365–89.

Cunha, F. and Heckman, J.J. (2007) The technology of skill formation, *American Economic Review*, 97 (Papers and Proceeding): 97: 31–47.

Currie, J., Garces, E. and Thomas, D. (2002) Longer term effects of Head Start, *American Economic Review*, 92: 999–1012.

Currie, J. and Thomas, D. (1995) Does Head Start make a difference? *American Economic Review*, 85: 341–64.

Feinstein, L. (2003) Inequality in the early cognitive development of British children in the 1970 cohort, *Economica*, 70: 73–98.

Galindo-Rueda, F. and Vignoles, A. (2002) Class ridden or meritocratic? An economic analysis of recent changes in Britain, IZA Discussion Paper No. 677, Bonn, Germany: Institute for the Study of Labor.

Hansen, K. (2006) *Millennium cohort study first and second surveys. A guide to the datasets*, 1st edn (July), London: Centre for Longitudinal Studies, Institute of Education, University of London.

Illsley, R. (2002) A city's schools: from inequality of input to inequality of outcome, *Oxford Review of Education*, 28: 427–45.

Plomin, R. (1999) Genetics and general cognitive ability, *Nature*, 402: C25–C29.

Plomin, R., Defries, J.C.. McClearn, G.E, and Rutter, M. (1997) *Behavioral genetics*, New York: W.H. Freeman and Co.

Rowe, D.C., Jacobson, K.C. and Van den Oord, E.J. (1999) Genetic and environmental influences on vocabulary IQ: parental education as moderator, *Child Development*, 70: 1151–62.

Royer, H. (2005) Separated at girth: estimating the long-run intergenerational effects of birthweight using twins, Ann Arbor: School of Public Health, University of Michigan.

Rutter, M. (2006) *Genes and behavior: nature-nurture interplay explained*, Oxford: Blackwell.

Turkheimer, E., Haley, A., D'Onofrio, B., Waldron, M., and Gottesman, I.I. (2003) Socioeconomic status modified heritability of IQ in young children, *Psychological Science*, 14: 623–28.

8   Adult Child-Parent Relationships

John Ermisch

The continuing relationship between adult children and their parents, once the former have left home, is likely to affect both children's and parents' welfare. Their well-being may, for instance, be enhanced if they keep in contact with one another and receive help from each other. This chapter analyses how help and contact between generations varies with the socio-economic and demographic characteristics of the two generations, and it uses this analysis to shed light on the validity of a number of theories of intergenerational family relations, including altruism, exchange, reciprocity, gender and evolutionary theories. It also considers how these relations contribute to inequality across individuals and between generations. In particular, do those with more economic resources also benefit from more contact and help, or do more contact and help compensate for lower levels of economic resources?

Most empirical studies of intergenerational family relations have used American data, primarily because other countries, like Britain, have been hampered by lack of suitable data. However, in the 2001 wave of the British Household Panel Survey, information about frequency of contact with each parent, help provided by parents and help given to parents, was collected from respondents who had a living parent not residing with them. These respondents were also asked how long it would take to travel to each parent's residence. Similar questions were asked of parents who had adult children living elsewhere.

FAMILY CONSTITUTIONS

In advanced economies like Great Britain, older parents are often observed making financial transfers to their adult children. Financial transfers in the opposite direction are rare, but other types of transfers from children to parents are important. In particular, parents' contact with their adult children, as well as help from them, is usually valued by parents, and can be viewed as particular examples of *service*s from children to their parents that do not have clear market substitutes (Cox, 1987). While provision of these may initially increase the child's well-being as well as that of the parents, at the margin they are provided at some cost to the adult child if they undermine his or her independence and use scarce time.

It is important to our understanding of relationships no longer based on coresidence to know whether the maintenance of reciprocity (whether equal or not) is based on an exchange calculus, or altruism, or some combination of these. Richard Smith (1996) suggests that there is no compelling evidence from English history, even going back to medieval times, that people have generally assumed automatic responsibility for their elderly parents. He believes that it

> seems possible to argue with conviction that reciprocal exchange on the basis of mutual advantage is the essence of support between kin, making the family a group whose relationships are founded on material considerations and not solely glued together by what Janet Finch calls "moral imperatives and ties of affection". (p. 44)

Our central question, therefore, is whether we can describe what appears to be the outcome of mutual affection, giving resources or help, can be viewed as underpinned by some sort of exchange idea—effectively an implicit contract. Might there be reciprocal intergenerational exchange over the life cycle that could be motivated by selfish material considerations? Cigno (1993, 2000) presents a theory in which everyone could be better off in an extended family network of transfers of money and 'services' covering three generations at different stages of life. We can refer to this as a 'family constitution' that arranges transfers to its young members from its middle-aged ones and enforces repayment later when the young 'borrowers' have become middle-aged and the middle-aged have become old. It specifies the minimum amount of money and services that each middle-aged adult transfers to the children and the minimum amount expected back, subject to the provision that a person will receive nothing when old without having transferred in middle age the prescribed amount to her parents. It is a *self-enforcing* family constitution in the sense that it is in the best interests of every family member to obey it and to have it obeyed. If people are purely self-interested, then they would only transfer the minimum amounts specified, but this could nevertheless be interpreted as adult children's 'moral duty', which is fulfilled because the constitution is self-enforcing.[1]

One immediate implication of this simple theory is that each *family dynasty* (i.e. a series of generations) could specify different constitutions— different 'moral duties'. It also suggests that transfers of services from selfish adult children to older parents should be *larger* for parents who are better off financially. This could happen for two reasons. First, when parents are richer, monetary transfers from children are worth less to parents than services. Second, family dynasties with more resources would prescribe larger transfers of services. The relationship between the transfer of services from children and parents' material resources is therefore important for assessing the relevance of a family constitution binding selfish people, and it forms the basis of our analysis. If we should find that higher parents' resources are associated with *less* help from or contact with their adult children, this would not be consistent with the family constitution model when people are selfish.

The constitution may contain a simple rule that children are allowed to pay less than the prescribed amount to their parents if the children's income falls below a particular level (Cigno, forthcoming). In this case, we would find that service transfers would increase with the child's income among those adult children who are unable to pay the prescribed amount, but we would still expect that richer parents would receive more of such services. In addition, with a family constitution binding selfish people, there would be no services from (permanently) childless adult children to their parents, because they cannot benefit from the family constitution when they are older (and cannot be punished by their children for deviating from it). Thus, we would expect that the absence of a grandchild would be associated with less contact with parents and less help being given to them.

Extrafamily institutions that support elderly parents, like the old Poor Laws or the current welfare state, might lead to substitution by adult children of nonfinancial support (i.e. services) for financial support. This may account for the fact that in the seventeenth to eighteenth centuries it was not uncommon for elderly parents to be receiving Poor Law support while their children lived in the same parish (Smith 1996), and it may partly account for today's low level of financial transfers from adult children to parents.

So far we have assumed that everyone is selfish, but the strength of emotional ties can also be important. Yet other motivations are not ruled out by a family constitution. For instance, under altruism (caring for the level of welfare of others) it is possible to give to parents more than the minimum amount prescribed by the constitution. However, the constitution will still be needed as a defence against the possible appearance in one generation of a 'black sheep' who does not even do the minimum (Cigno, forthcoming). So what motives best account for variation in services provided by adult children to their parents that are *above the minimum amount*?

If altruism does not undermine this model, it complicates it. For instance, under altruism, where the child has higher resources (a good income) this might increase the gift of nonmaterial help or of contact simply because more resources are generally available. But at the same time these resources increase the child's bargaining power in family decisions, and this might reduce the help and contact (Cox 1987; Ermisch 2003, Ch. 9). The net effect of altruism cum bargaining on the relationship between child's income and services to parents is, therefore, unclear. On the other hand, because higher parents' resources increase their bargaining power in family decisions, these should unambiguously encourage help and contact from their adult children.

An alternative hypothesis that might account for the transfer of money from parents to adult children and of help/contact from them to parents (above the minima prescribed by the family constitution) is that it reflects a concern for 'fairness'. The basic idea is as follows. Assume that adult children try to avoid outcomes in which they are much better off than their parents—they have an aversion to inequity between parents and children. One way that they can do this is by keeping in contact with and providing help to their parents, because such services enhance the well-being of their parents. As these services cannot be obtained in the market, parents can even encourage their children to supply more of them by transferring money to them, knowing that their children will respond in providing more services to reduce inequity in well-being between parents and children. This reasoning implies that it is *possible* for higher parents' resources to reduce such services because a higher parent's income decreases the need to use services to reduce inequity. This prediction differs from the family constitution theory *when people are selfish* (so that the transfers of money and services prescribed by the constitution are binding), and it also differs from that derived from a theory of transfers (above the minimum prescribed in the constitution) based on altruism and bargaining, which the preceding paragraph has shown to imply that higher parents' resources *increase* services received from children.

In sum, we contrast two different types of theory about the motivation for cross-generational transfers. Each of them has as its foundation the idea of a family constitution, whereby people are encouraged to give in the expectation of return—not, however, from those to whom they give but from the next generation. In one theory people are either selfish or altruistic, and if altruistic they make transfers above the minimum prescribed by the constitution on the basis of bargaining. In the second theory, transfers above the minimum are motivated by the desire to reduce unfairness across generations—a model therefore based on aversion to inequity rather than on selfishness or altruism. These models lead to different empirical predictions. The first suggests, contrary to intuition, that well-off parents receive more resources from their children than do less-well-off parents (though usually through the provision of services rather than of money). In addition, when people are selfish, the older parents will receive nothing (or very little) from their children (the middle generation) where there are no grandchildren, however well-off the former are. Looking at the reverse direction, older parents make no transfers to their children when they are selfish. The fairness principle instead implies that both high-income parents and high-income children receive less and give more, with the existence of grandchildren making no difference. The remainder of the paper examines these associations, also taking into account the effect of distance between parents and children, which can clearly affect the probability of transfers of services.

DATA AND METHODS

In the eleventh annual wave of the British Household Panel Survey in 2001, information about frequency of contact with each parent was collected from respondents who had a living parent not residing with them. They were also asked about help given to and received from parents, and how long it would take to travel to the parents' residence. Similar questions about contact were asked of parents who had adult children living elsewhere (about the one with whom they had most contact if more than one adult child was living apart from them), and they were also asked about help given to and received from children not living with them. In terms of the dimensions of 'intergenerational solidarity' identified by the latent class analysis in Silverstein and Bengtson (1997), measures of contact and help based on these questions reflect 'opportunity structure' (geographic proximity and frequency of contact) and 'functional exchange' (providing and receiving assistance).

In order to focus on parents who are in the latter part of their life cycle, the parents' sample is restricted to those aged 60 and over, and the children's sample is restricted to those with at least one living parent aged 60 or older. The average age of the parent responding to the questions about contact and help is 72, and 56 per cent are female.[2] The average age of the adult child respondent is 44, while his/her mother's average age is 72, and 54 per cent of the adult children are women.[3]

Table 8.1 shows the frequency of the parent's contact with the adult child (with whom the parent has most contact if there is more than one living elsewhere), and also the frequency of contact with their mother (as reported by the adult children). Table 8.2 shows the types of help that parents report receiving *regularly or frequently* from children living elsewhere (they may receive more than one type), and also the children's reports of the types of help given regularly or frequently to their parents. Receiving lifts in their child's car, shopping and home maintenance and improvement are the most popular forms of help received by parents, but about one-half of parents receive no regular or frequent help from their children (according to either parents' or children's responses). It is rare for children to provide regular or frequent financial help to their parents. Table 8.3 shows that contact with and help provided to parents decline with distance from parents.

With respect to financial transfers from parents to children, each parent is asked whether or not he or she provides *frequent or regular* financial help to adult children not living with them, and each child is asked if he or she receives such help. Overall, 17 per cent of parents say they provide such help, and 11 per cent of adult children say they receive it.[4]

The analysis will measure the association of economic resources of either the child or parent with frequency of contact and help. Three measures of economic resources are used in the analysis, each of which is an imperfect indicator of resources available to parents or adult children. One is the logarithm of current equivalent household income, which is defined here as the monthly household income (in the month preceding the interview) of a person's household divided by the square root of household size. Another is current net financial wealth, which is financial assets less debts (other than mortgages) of the tax/benefit unit in which the person lived in 2000, as estimated from the BHPS wealth data by Banks et al. (2002).[5] The third is the value of the person's house in 2001 for owner-occupiers, with tenants' value being set to zero. As expected, persons with higher current equivalent household income tend to have higher net financial wealth and higher house values, and house value is positively correlated with net financial wealth.[6] As an alternative to house value, it is possible to use housing equity (obtained by subtracting mortgage debt from house value), but house value appears to be a better indicator of longer-term resources than housing equity, particularly for the adult children.

These three measures of resources are combined into one indicator of economic resources using *principal components analysis*, which finds mutually uncorrelated linear combinations of the three measures that have maximal variance. The first principal component, which accounts for the largest proportion of the variance, is taken as our indicator of economic resources.[7] This indicator has unit variance by construction, and so a unit change is interpreted as a one standard deviation change in economic resources. While related to economic resources, educational attainments and homeownership may have separate impacts from resources, because, for example, they may affect the geographic location of the adult child relative to his/her parents, and so they are also included as explanatory variables in the analysis.

Frequency of contact is an 'ordered response', with the categories given in Table 8.1. As any particular aggregation of categories may be arbitrary, frequency of contact is analyzed using an ordered logit model. This model has the property that the logarithm of the odds[8] of being in a frequency-of-contact category larger than any particular one depends linearly on the explanatory variables, with the impact being the same irrespective of the particular category under consideration. That is, an estimated coefficient of the model measures the proportionate impact of a variable on the odds ratio associated with any particular category. Distance between parent and child is modelled in the same way, and the categories are those given in Table 8.3. The other variables analyzed are dichotomous: whether or not a parent receives regular or frequent in-kind help from an adult child, and whether or not a parent provides regular or frequent financial help, childcare or other in-kind help to adult children. In these cases the appropriate method is a binomial logit model.

Table 8.1   Frequency that Child Sees His/Her Mother or Father, Parents Aged 60 and Over

Frequency	Parent's Response[a]	Child's Response (Sees Mother)
Daily	20.9%	11.4%
At least once a week	48.6	41.1
At least once a month	14.2	18.3
Several times a year	11.6	19.8
Less often	3.9	7.5
Never	0.8	2.0
Total	100	100
Unweighted N[b]	1,586	2,927

[a]Child with whom parent has most contact if more than one living elsewhere.
[b]The sample includes only original panel members interviewed in 2001 and temporary sample members living with them, not members of the ECHP and Scottish and Wales booster samples. Weighted using cross-section weights.

Table 8.2   Regular or Frequent Help from Children, Parents Aged 60 and Over

Per cent Reporting:	Parent's Responses	Child's Responses
Getting lifts in their car	36.6	28.5
Shopping for you	25.2	22.2
Providing or cooking meals	15.1	10.5
Help with personal needs like dressing, eating, bathing	1.6	3.1
Washing, ironing or cleaning	6.7	7.2
Dealing with personal affairs like paying bills, etc.	10.7	15.6
Decorating, gardening, repairs	18.8	22.0
Financial help	3.1	6.0
None of these	45.5	49.7
Unweighted N*	1,586	2,927

*Sample and weights as in Table 8.1.

Table 8.3   Distance to Child's Residence and Contact With/Help Regularly or Frequently Provided to Parent, Parents Aged 60 and Over

	% Who See Child at Least Weekly*	% Who Telephone Daily*	% Who Receive In-kind Help**
Less than 15 minutes	93.5	36.8	64.1
(N = 1416)			
Between 15 and 30 min.	82.6	32.0	63.5
(N = 636)			
30–60 minutes	62.8	19.5	60.0
(N = 355)			
More than one hour	11.9	14.0	22.8
(N = 796)			
Total	69.6	28.9	54.2
Unweighted N[a]	1577	1577	1577

*Child with whom the parent has most contact.
**Regularly or frequently.
[a]Sample and weights as in Table 8.1.

PARENTS' RESOURCES AND TRANSFERS

This section reports how frequency of contact with adult children, in-kind help received from children, and financial transfers to children vary with parents' economic resources and the presence of a grandchild. Table 8.4 shows the logit coefficients for the economic resources variable and the impact of having a grandchild; the other variables included in the model are indicated in the notes to Table 8.4. For example, the coefficient on parents' resources in the first row indicates that the odds of receiving in-kind help are 23 per cent lower when the parents' resources are one standard deviation higher. The standard errors of the parameter estimates are adjusted for multiple respondents from the same household, because, for example, spouses' decisions about contact with parents may be correlated.

Parents' Receipt of In-kind Help From and Contact With Adult Children

Among parents aged 60 and over with an adult child living apart from them, about one-half receive *regular or frequent* in-kind help from an adult child (i.e. at least one of the types of help listed in Table 8.2 other than financial help), according to the parent's or child's report. The first row of Table 8.4, which does not condition on distance from their adult child

Table 8.4   Impacts of Economic Resources and Grandchildren on the Odds of Regular or Frequent In-kind Help from Adult Children to Parent and Frequency of Contact, BHPS 2001**

Dependent Variable	Economic Resources	Has Grandchild
Parents' variables[a]		
1. Parent's receipt of in-kind help	−0.23	0.07
	(0.07)	(0.23)
2. Parent's receipt of in-kind help, distance controls	−0.15	−0.13
	(0.08)	(0.25)
3. Parent's frequency of seeing child*	−0.21	0.52
	(0.06)	(0.21)
4. Frequency of seeing child*, distance controls	−0.06	0.13
	(0.06)	(0.21)
5. Distance from child	0.23	−0.46
	(0.08)	(0.23)
Child's variables[b]		
6. Parent's receipt of in-kind help	−0.16	0.27
	(0.050)	(0.13)
7. Parent's receipt of in-kind help, distance controls	−0.02	0.19
	(0.05)	(0.13)
8. Frequency of seeing mother	−0.26	0.27
	(0.05)	(0.12)
9. Frequency of seeing mother, distance controls	−0.02	0.00
	(0.04)	(0.12)
10. Distance from parent	0.38	−0.33
	(0.05)	(0.12)

*Contact with child with whom the parent has most contact.
**Asymptotic standard errors in parentheses; standard errors adjusted for clustering in households.
[a]Model includes the following other variables: Parent's sex; age and age-squared; highest educational qualification; whether or not he/she is an owner-occupier; the parent's marital status (married, cohabiting other); whether or not the parent lives alone; whether or not there is only one child living outside the household; whether or not the child is an only-child; the logarithm of the number of children living elsewhere; the logarithm of the number of living grandchildren; whether or not the parent's health limits his/her daily activities; and whether or not the parent is retired.
[b]Models include the following other variables: Child's sex; age and age-squared; highest educational qualification; whether or not he/she is an owner-occupier; the child's marital status (married, cohabiting other); mother's age (or father's if mother is not alive); the number of dependent children; whether or not the child is an only living child; and the logarithm of the number of living siblings.

with whom they have most contact, shows that parents with more economic resources are less likely to receive regular or frequent in-kind help from their adult children. The second row shows that, after controlling for how far the parent lives from her adult son or daughter, the impact of economic resources is smaller, and not statistically significant at the 0.05 level, although it is so at the 0.10 level. The fifth row indicates why the effect of economic resources on regular or frequent in-kind help declines when controlling for distance. It shows that a parent with more economic resources lives farther from the adult child with whom he/she is in most contact. Living closer substantially increases the probability of receiving regular or frequent in-kind help; for instance, the model in row 2 indicates that, compared to living an hour or more away, living within 15 minutes increases the odds of receiving regular or frequent help by a multiple of 6.5 (coefficient not shown in table). Row 10 shows that children with more economic resources live farther from their parents.

The negative effect of parents' economic resources on receipt of regular or frequent in-kind help, perhaps even after controlling for distance, is not consistent with the binding family constitution model (i.e. when the self-enforcement constraints are binding), nor is it consistent with altruism cum bargaining governing transfers above the minima prescribed in the constitution. It may reflect the availability of imperfect market substitutes for many of these types of in-kind help, which richer parents substitute for their children's help. It may also reflect, in part, statistical bias from omitting a measure of child resources if higher children's resources reduce help. Row 7 indicates, however, that the negative effect of child's resources disappears when we control for distance, suggesting that the impact of omitted variable bias on the estimated effect of parents' resources is small.

But is it correct to control for distance? Other theories contend that distance between parent and child is chosen with possible provision of help to and contact with parents in mind (Konrad et al. 2002; Rainer and Siedler 2005). Also, in the family constitution model, distance is not an 'excuse' for failing to transfer the prescribed services to older parents unless financial transfers compensate. But there is no evidence that compensation takes place—only 3 per cent of parents receive regular or frequent financial transfers from their adult children and almost all (91 per cent) of parents who receive financial help also receive in-kind help. If, for these reasons, distance is endogenous, it should be excluded from the in-kind help and contact equations.

Higher parents' economic resources also reduce the frequency that the parent sees the child, the estimated impact being statistically significant in row 3 of Table 8.4, but not significantly different from zero when distance is controlled (row 4). If, as suggested earlier, we should not condition on distance, the negative effect in row 3 is not consistent with either the binding family constitution or with altruism cum bargaining models governing payments above the minima. In the case of child-parent contact, the imperfect market substitute rationale for a negative effect is not compelling. The evidence in row 8 of a negative effect of child's income on contact with his/her mother suggests that omitted variable bias may overstate the negative impact of parents' resources in row 3, but this bias is unlikely to be large enough to turn a positive effect into a negative one. Another possibility is that more affluent parents spend more time seeing friends and neighbours. In the BHPS, people were asked how often they talked to their neighbours and how often they meet friends or relatives not living with them. Similar analysis of these responses indicated that more affluent parents spoke *less* frequently with their neighbours than less affluent ones and met with friends and relatives as frequently.

The negative impacts of parents' economic resources on receipt of regular or frequent in-kind help and frequency of contact also are not consistent with predictions of the 'strategic bequest theory' of Bernheim et al. (1985). In that theory, parents threaten their child with disinheritance if he or she does not provide them with sufficient attention and help. The disinheritance threat may not be credible if there is only one child, because the parents are assumed to care for their child's well-being. But among families with two or more children the threat may be credible, and we expect contact and help to increase with 'bequeathable' wealth. That is not what is found when we construct a measure of total net wealth, which is the sum of net financial wealth and housing equity, and substitute it and current equivalent income for the economic resources variable. When the sample is confined to parents with two or more children, total net wealth has a significant negative effect on receipt of in-kind help, even after controlling for distance, and no significant impact on frequency of contact. The failure of the strategic bequest prediction may arise because, as Cigno (forthcoming) points out, the children can counter the parents' strategy by agreeing to redistribute the bequests amongst themselves.

It is, however, possible to explain the negative effects of parents' resources on frequency of seeing their adult child and in-kind help received by children's aversion to inequity between them and their parents. That is, higher parents' resources reduce help from and contact with their child because they reduce inequality between parents and adult children, thereby reducing the need to provide services in order to reduce inequity in well-being. While, as noted above, richer parents need help from their children less because they can buy services, contact with children is likely to have few market substitutes.

The family constitution model predicts that selfish adult offspring who do not have children themselves would opt out of the constitution, because they would not benefit from in-kind or financial transfers in their old age. They would not provide help to their parents, neither in-kind nor financial, nor contact. Table 8.4 shows that, using either the parents' or children's responses (see rows 3 and 8), when we do not control for distance, frequency of contact between parents and their children increases significantly if there is a grandchild. According to the children's responses (but not the parents'—see rows 1 and 6), adult children who have a child themselves are also more likely to provide in-kind help to their parents. Thus, this evidence is consistent with the family constitution model with predominantly selfish children, although it is more likely to reflect the provision of childcare by parents, which must involve contact and could be coupled with an exchange of childcare for help. The virtual absence of a 'grandchild effect' on either contact or help after controlling for distance reflects the tendency for parents with a grandchild to live closer to their children (see rows 5 and 10). This suggests adjustment in location by either parents or children when a grandchild arrives.

Other Influences on Help From and Contact With Adult Children

Existing evidence indicates that women are more involved in kin networks and may control men's access to kin (e.g. see Hagestad 1986; Silverstein and Bengtson 1997). In the context of the theory of family constitutions, women may take the responsibility for fulfilling its transfer prescriptions, even for their partner's parents. This would make it more likely that women are observed being in contact with their parents and helping them. Further, women's greater provision of services to their own children may give them greater access to support when they are old. Analysis of the BHPS data confirms that women are more involved in these interactions. Mothers are more likely to receive regular or frequent in-kind help and to see their children more frequently than fathers. Daughters are more likely to provide in-kind help and to see their parents more often than sons.

Parents who live closer to their child, who live alone, who have more living children or whose health limits their daily activities are more likely to receive regular or frequent in-kind help. Frequency of contact declines with the parents' age and distance from their children and increases with the number of children they have had. Parents with health limitations tend to live closer to their children.

From the children's perspective, those who have a partner or who have more siblings see their parents less frequently and are less likely to provide regular or frequent in-kind help. Help is also less likely when there are more dependent grandchildren. It also appears that frequency of contact and help increases with the age gap between parents and adult children, suggesting that within a family more help and contact is provided by later born children (i.e. higher birth order).

FINANCIAL TRANSFERS FROM PARENTS TO ADULT CHILDREN

In the family constitution model *with selfish parents*, older parents would not make transfers to their children. Either parental altruism or people's aversion to inequity between parents and children would lead us to expect

Table 8.5   Impacts of Economic Resources and Grandchildren on the Odds of Regular or Frequent Financial Transfers from Parent to Adult Children, BHPS 2001*

	Economic Resources	*Has Grandchild*
1. *Parents' variables*[a]	0.32	0.15
	(0.08)	(0.28)
2. *Parents' variables,*[a] *distance controls*	0.34	0.13
	(0.08)	(0.28)
3. *Child's variables*[b]	−0.36	0.49
	(0.12)	(0.22)
4. *Child's variables,*[b] *distance controls*	−0.31	0.42
	(0.12)	(0.22)

Asymptotic standard errors in parentheses; standard errors adjusted for clustering in households.
[a]See corresponding footnote in Table 8.4.
[b]See corresponding footnote in Table 8.4.

that financial transfers increase with the parents' resources and decline with the child's resources. To examine this, whether or not parents give (children receive) frequent or regular financial help is the dependent variable in two analyses, one using the parents' responses, the other the children's.[9] As noted previously, 17 per cent of parents report giving regular or frequent financial help to their adult children, and 11 per cent of children report receiving such help. The estimated impacts of the parents' economic resources and the presence of a grandchild on regular or frequent financial help are shown in the first two rows of Table 8.5, and the estimated impacts of child's economic resources and a grandchild are shown in the third and fourth rows.[10] As expected from the altruism cum bargaining and inequity aversion theories, the estimates show that parents with more economic resources are more likely to provide regular or frequent financial help, and more affluent children are less likely to receive such help. Controlling for distance has little effect on the impacts of the parent's or child's economic resources on the probability of receipt (cf. rows 1 and 2, and 3 and 4). Consistent with evolutionary theory, Table 8.5 indicates that the presence of a grandchild makes it significantly more likely that adult children receive financial help from their parents according to the children's responses. But this is not confirmed by the parents' responses.

The analysis also indicates that fathers are more likely to provide regular or frequent financial help than mothers, and the probability of financial help increases with the number of adult children. Analysis from the children's perspective shows that sons, those in a partnership and those with more siblings are less likely to receive regular or frequent financial help.

The last association may arise because the more siblings one has the more competition there is for financial help from parents. The probability of such help increases with the number of dependent grandchildren and with the age gap between parents and adult child.

LOCATION AND THE IMPACT OF PARENTS' RESOURCES

We have seen that parents' resources are negatively related to frequency of contact with their adult children and with the odds of receiving in-kind help from them, but these effects diminish (and disappear in the case of contact) when we control for distance between parents and adult children. This is because adult children with more affluent parents live farther away from them. Thus, the effects of parents' resources on contact and in-kind help operate through their effect on the children's location relative to their parents. The following analysis begins to address this issue by examining how parental income affects the distance that children move when they leave their parental home. A sample of young people who move away from their parents below the age of 30 in the first 12 waves of the BHPS is selected. The distance (in kilometres) of their move is related to income in their parental home other than their own income (mainly that of their parents), as well as their age and sex. Table 8.6 shows that young people who leave higher-income parental homes move farther away. Children from higher-income families are more likely to move away to become full-time students in higher education, and many of these return to their parental home temporarily. But the strong effect of parental income on distance moved is still there when we control for whether or not they are full-time students in the first year after leaving home (column 2), and when the sample is confined to those who were not full-time students in the first year after leaving home (col. 3). In the latter two specifications, the income effect is smaller, but still relatively large—a 10 per cent higher income increases distance by about 3.5 per cent. This suggests that parents' economic resources affect a person's location relative to their parents very early in their adult life.[11]

Where children live relative to their parents when their parents are aged 60 and over also depends, of course, on the extent of subsequent movement by both parents and children. The BHPS data indicate that each year 1.7 per cent of people aged 18–50 (who have left their parents' home) move 60 kilometres or more. Furthermore, those who move such distances in the past are more likely to do so again. For instance, among those who moved 60 or more kilometres in the previous year, 17.2 per cent do so again in the current year, compared with 1.5 per cent among those who did not move 60 or more kilometres in the previous year.[12] Longer-distance geographic mobility declines with age. For instance, among persons aged 60 and over, only 0.4 percent move 60 or more kilometres each year, and the corresponding movement rates for those aged 18–30, 30–40 and 40–50 are 4.5

Table 8.6 Distance Moved Upon Leaving the Parental Home, BHPS 1992–2002, not Controlling for Being Full-time Student (model 1), Controlling for Being Student (model 2) and Excluding Students (model 3)*

Variable	Dep. Var. Ln(distance) 1	Dep. Var. Ln(distance) 2	Dep. Var. Ln(distance) 3
Log parental income$_{t-1}$ [a]	0.605	0.338	0.367
	(0.071)	(0.064)	(0.068)
Age	−0.392	0.428	0.534
	(0.215)	(0.204)	(0.234)
Age-squared	0.0052	−0.0102	−0.0122
	(0.0047)	(0.0045)	(0.0051)
Female	−0.125	−0.107	−0.072
	(0.102)	(0.090)	(0.107)
Household size$_{t-1}$	−0.288	−0.195	−0.232
	(0.045)	(0.040)	(0.045)
Living in Scotland or Wales	−0.447	−0.267	−0.130
	(0.149)	(0.150)	(0.153)
Full-time Student$_t$	—	2.136	—
		(0.119)	
Constant	5.545	−3.870	−5.381
	(2.433)	(2.288)	(2.645)
N	1,281	1,281	974
R^2	0.149	0.324	0.051

*Standard errors in parentheses; standard errors adjusted for multiple observations on some people:
N *of people* = 1137 in columns 1 and 2; 906 in column 3.
[a]Household income other than young person's income.

per cent, 1.2 per cent and 0.7 per cent. Thus, a significant proportion of the British population appear to be sufficiently mobile to adjust their relative locations later. This might be undertaken by either the parents or the adult children, but particularly by the latter. As evidence of such adjustment, the presence of a grandchild is associated with a smaller distance between parent and child, and consequently more frequent intergenerational contact. Nevertheless, the more distant departure for young people from wealthier homes may have long-lasting impacts. They may be sufficiently 'forward looking' about their supply of future contact with and help to their parents in response to the parents' expected resources. In this case, the reason that higher parents' resources reduce help from and contact with their child is that they reduce inequality between parents and adult children, which reduces the need to provide help/contact in order to reduce inequity in well-being. Alternatively, their first move may initiate a dynamic process that affects their location relative to parents in the longer term.

CONCLUSIONS

The chapter uncovers a number of important associations concerned with flows of contact and help between parents aged 60 and over and their adult children. In particular, more affluent parents are more likely to provide regular or frequent financial help to their adult children and more affluent children are less likely to receive it, as either altruism or inequity aversion theories would suggest. Also, more affluent children see their mother or father less frequently and are less likely to provide them regular or frequent in-kind help, and more affluent parents see their adult sons and daughters less frequently and are less likely to receive regular or frequent in-kind help. An explanation for these associations with parents' resources is that adult children provide more frequent contact and in-kind help to reduce the inequity in well-being if their parents are worse off than they, and higher parental resources reduce the need to make such 'service transfers'. That is, while family constitutions may operate, there are a sufficient proportion of people making transfers in excess of the minima prescribed by them and these transfers are motivated by inequity aversion rather than altruism.

But these associations concerning contact and in-kind help primarily reflect a tendency for more affluent children and parents to live farther apart, with greater distance reducing contact and in-kind help. Thus, an important part of the story about intergenerational relations concerns parents' and children's location decisions relative to each other.

In light of the importance of this 'family geography', the chapter also investigates how parental income is associated with the distance that children move when they leave their parental home. It finds that young people who leave higher-income parental homes move farther away. Where children live relative to their parents when their parents are aged 60 and over also depends, of course, on the extent of subsequent movement by both parents and children. A significant proportion of the British population appears to be sufficiently mobile to adjust their location later, particularly the adult children. As evidence of such adjustment, the presence of a grandchild is associated with a smaller distance between parent and child, and consequently more frequent intergenerational contact. Nevertheless, the more distant departure among young people from wealthier homes appears to have long-lasting impacts. Children may be sufficiently 'forward looking' about their supply of future contact with and help to their parents in response to the parents' expected resources, or their first move may initiate a dynamic process that affects their location relative to parents in the longer term. This deserves further investigation.

There are also significant gender patterns, perhaps because women put more effort into maintaining kin networks. Daughters have more frequent contact with their mother or father than sons, particularly if they have a dependent child, and daughters are more likely to receive regular or frequent help from parents: financial, childcare or other in-kind help. Mothers are more likely to receive regular or frequent in-kind help from an adult child and see them more frequently than fathers. Fathers are more likely than mothers to provide financial help to their adult children. Family size also affects intergenerational relations: adult offspring with more brothers and sisters have less frequent contact with their parents, and they are less likely to receive financial, in-kind or childcare help from their parents. Children also respond to particular parental needs: parents whose health limits their daily activities are more likely to receive regular or frequent in-kind help from and see their adult children more frequently. These effects also operate through distance: parents whose health limits their daily activities tend to live closer to their children.

NOTES

1. Binmore (2005: 87) suggests a similar intergenerational contract that can be sustained by selfish people.
2. Also, 88% have grandchildren, 64% are married, 30% live alone, 76% are owner-occupiers, 22% have educational qualifications beyond 'A-level', 82% are retired, for 32% their health limits their daily activities and 20% have just one child living outside the parents' household.
3. Seventy-one per cent of these adult children are married, another 13% cohabit; 81% have at least one child and they average 0.9 dependent children (i.e. aged less than 16). One-half have a qualification above 'A-level', 83% are owner-occupiers and in 35% of the cases their mother lives alone. Eighty-seven percent have a living sibling, and among these the average number of brothers and sisters is 2.5.
4. Note that this does not imply that 83% (89%) of parents will never make financial transfers; they may do so in the future or did in the past, or their transfers may be irregular and infrequent.
5. These data are available from the UK Data Archive, University of Essex.
6. For instance, in the BHPS 2000 wealth data, homeowners have a mean net financial wealth of £17,500 compared with £3,100 for tenants. Other data also indicate that owner-occupiers are much more likely to have other financial assets, particularly riskier investments, and they also have higher average levels of wealth (Banks and Tanner 1999, Tables 5.2 and 5.5).
7. That it is sufficient, in this particular case, to use only the first component is suggested by the fact that the second and third characteristic roots of the correlation matrix are less than unity and close to one another. A factor analysis approach, which makes weaker assumptions about the decomposition of the correlation matrix of the three variables, finds only one positive characteristic root, which indicates the presence of one factor in this set of three variables. The factor score associated with it is correlated with the first principal

component with a correlation coefficient of virtually one. The factor scoring coefficients (loadings) combining the income, net financial wealth and house value indicators are estimated separately for the adult child and parent samples, but in each case they are, to the first decimal place, 0.4, 0.4, 0.5, respectively.

8. The odds of being in a given category is the probability of being in that category divided by the probability of not being in it.

9. Again, because we only have data on one side of the transfer-service arrangement in each analysis, the estimated impact of parents' economic resources on the probability of providing regular or frequent financial help would be biased downwards if higher child's resources reduce transfers. Similarly, the estimated impact of child's resources would be biased upward if higher parents' resources increase transfers.

10. The standard errors of the parameter estimates are adjusted for correlation between respondents from the same household (e.g. two parents may be reporting financial help to the same child).

11. We can examine how the distance at first departure from parents relates to how far they live from their parents at the 2001 wave of the BHPS. This sample is, of course, still quite young and many have only left the parental home a few years earlier. In any case, the coefficient (std. error) of log distance at the time of leaving home in an ordered logit for distance from a person's mother in 2001 (using the same categories as in Table 8.3) is 1.01 (0.05).

12. Comparing those who moved 60 or more kilometres two years ago with those who did not, the movement rates are 13.7% and 1.5%. Also, the marginal effects (standard errors) in a simple probit equation for the probability of moving 60 or more kilometres associated with movement this distance in the previous year and two years ago are 0.128 (0.012) and 0.088 (0.011).

REFERENCES

Banks, J., Smith, Z. and Wakefield, M. (2002) The distribution of financial wealth in the UK: evidence from the 2000 BHPS data, London: Institute for Fiscal Studies Working paper WP02/21.

Banks, J. and Tanner, S. (1999) *Household saving in the UK*, London: The Institute for Fiscal Studies.

Bernheim, B.D., Schleifer, A. and Summers, L.H. (1985) The strategic bequest motive, *Journal of Political Economy*, 93: 1045–76.

Binmore, K. (2005) *Natural justice*, Oxford: Oxford University Press.

Cigno, A. (1993) Intergenerational transfers without altruism: family, market and state, *European Journal of Political Economy*, 9: 505–18.

———. (2000) Self-enforcing family constitutions, in A. Mason and G. Tapinos (eds) *Sharing the wealth: intergenerational economic relations and demographic change*, Oxford: Oxford University Press.

———. (forthcoming) The political economy of intergenerational cooperation, in S.C. Kolm and J. Mercier Yther (eds) *The handbook of giving, reciprocity and altruism*, Amsterdam: North Holland.

Cox, D. (1987) Motives for private income transfers, *Journal of Political Economy*, 95: 508–46.

Ermisch, J.F. (2003) *An economic analysis of the family*, Princeton, NJ: Princeton University Press.

Hagestad, G.O. (1986) The family: women and grandparents as kinkeepers, in A. Pifer and L. Bronte (eds) *Our aging society*, New York: Norton, 141–60.

Konrad, K., H. Kunemund, K.I. Lommerud and J. Robeldo (2002) Geography of the family, *American Economic Review*, 92: 991–98.

Rainer, H. and Siedler, T. (2005) The geography of the family re-examined, University of Essex: ISER.

Silverstein, M. and Bengtson, V.L. (1997) Intergenerational solidarity and the structure of adult child-parent relationships in American families, *The American Journal of Sociology*, 103: 429–60.

Smith, Richard (1996) Charity, self-interest and welfare: reflections from demographic and family history, in M. Daunton (ed.) *Charity, self-interest and welfare in the English past*, London: UCL Press.

9 Gender and Time Use over the Life Course

Man Yee Kan and Jonathan Gershuny

INTRODUCTION

Since the introduction of the Equal Pay Act in 1970 in the UK, the gender wage gap has been falling. The figure was 37 per cent in 1973 (comparing the hourly wage of female full-time workers with that of male full-time workers), but it appears to have bottomed out at 18 per cent in 1999 (EOC, 2002). The differential in women's and men's human capital (in the forms of educational skills and labour market experience) is one common explanation for the earnings gap by gender (e.g. Mincer and Polachek 1974). Similarly, it has been argued that women's domestic responsibilities also reduce their acquisition of human capital (Becker 1965, 1991[1981]; Dolton and Makepeace 1990). This chapter focuses on the time use of married and cohabiting men and women and examines the impacts of the division of domestic labour on their respective potential labour market earnings. While there is a huge literature on the effects of family responsibilities on women's careers, within both sociology and economics, this is usually treated as a single-step event. In this chapter we show, instead, that the process is incremental and continuous. In terms of relationships, this means that whether they like it or not, and in spite of slowly changing ideologies over women, the family, and work at the societal level, men and women increasingly get locked into the positions they find themselves in.

Women in the UK and other developed countries undertake the bulk of housework regardless of their employment statuses (Gershuny 1992; Kan 2008; Layte 1999). This gendered division of labour might partly be due to an initial difference in human capital between partners (Becker 1991[1981]), and is also likely to be related to family circumstances (e.g. whether dependent children are coresident or not). Differential specialization of men and women at a particular life stage, in one or other tasks, especially in paid and unpaid work, has implications for their future options for participation in these activities. Therefore, the differences in the daily time-use practices between men and women should result in differentiation in their rates of accumulation of human capital, and can help explain the persistence of gender inequalities in the macrosocial structures, and in particular, the gender gap in labour market earnings.

This chapter tests the hypothesis that the gendered division of labour is intensified over the life course, with men and women becoming more specialized in paid work and unpaid domestic work, respectively. We argue that the gendered division of labour and the differentials in partners' potential earnings reinforce each other over time. The initial gap between partners' human capital levels induces a gendered division of labour. Focussing more on domestic work rather than paid work, women are at a more disadvantaged position in the accumulation of human capital than men, which reinforces the gender differential in labour market earnings. The chapter contributes to the field of study by adopting both a time-budget analysis (i.e. of how individuals allocate their time to major categories of daily activities) and a life-cycle perspective (i.e. how changes in time-use practices are initiated after major life-cycle events). Investigations will be based on longitudinal time-use data collected from the same individuals. It will demonstrate how changes in family circumstances, such as getting a partner, having a child, and the child growing up, influence men's and women's time-use practices.

DATA AND METHODS

To investigate individuals' time budgets from a life-course perspective, we need high-quality longitudinal data on time use. Ideally, these time-use data should be collected at different life-cycle stages of the same individuals. There are two main types of time-use data. The first, which are generally referred to as 'stylised' estimates, are based on responses to questions about the amounts of time devoted to various classes of activity in a 'normal' week in survey interviews. The second type of time use information is calculated from entries in a time-use diary, in which the respondent is requested to keep a detailed record of activities throughout the day. Diary data are usually more accurate and cover all types of activities during a day. But the diary method also usually yields a low response rate and is impractical for a large-scale panel survey. Thus diary-based time use estimates are not available in large national panel surveys or cohort studies in the UK.

Data Calibration

We employ a method to combine the strengths of a large national panel survey, which collects detailed longitudinal information about family circumstances from respondents, and a diary study, which contains high-quality time budget information. We calibrate a set of time-use variables for a long-running panel survey, the British Household Panel Survey (BHPS 1994–2005) with evidence derived from a smaller scale panel survey that collected time-use information by both the questionnaire method and the diary method from the same respondents (the Home On-line Study, HoL,

1999–2001). The questionnaire part of the HoL shares very similar questionnaire-derived time-use predictor variables with the BHPS. These questions include respondents' usual hours of routine housework and paid work, the frequencies at which they participated in various forms of leisure activities (including doing sports, eating or drinking out, seeing a film or play, or attending a social club), and whether or not they were responsible for common types of household work (including cleaning, cooking, childcare, and grocery shopping). We regress diary-based time-use estimates in HoL on its stylised time-use estimates, and then multiply the resulting regression coefficients with the same stylised predictor variables in the BHPS. Thus, we obtain a calibrated measure of time-use patterns. This covers all five major daily activities: (1) paid work/study; (2) routine housework; (3) care and other domestic work; (4) consumption and leisure; and (5) sleep, rest and personal care.[1] The BHPS does not contain direct measures of the time spent on activities (3), (4) and (5). For the time spent on paid work and routine housework, we replace a nominal estimate with a real figure. We should note that these calibrated time-use estimates inevitably contain a degree of error.

The Life Course

We hence have a strong panel of data from BHPS with a calibrated index of time use for the respondents. In order to investigate the effect of changes in family stage, we adopt a frequently used panel analysis technique of pooling pairs of successive years; that is, we add pairs of successive years from the same individuals to increase the number of transitions. The pooled file derived from the 1994–2005 samples contains eleven successive pairs of observations. For simplicity's sake, we present cases from the pooled sample as a "pseudo-panel" to illustrate the common form of the family life cycle. We examine transitions such as forming a new partnership over these pairs of years. We also create separate pooled samples to trace changes in time-use practices the year before and five years after having the first child. Our analysis of time-use change over the life cycle, which we show in graphical form, is restricted to cases where respondents were aged between 19 and 40 before the family transition, because most of the major life-cycle events occur within this range, while change in time-use practices among the older age group in the wake of life-cycle events is not substantial (Gershuny 2003).

Multivariate Analysis

Multivariate analyses will be conducted to test the relationship between the domestic division of labour and potential labour market hourly wages.[2] First, Ordinary Least Squares regression (OLS) models will be applied to the sample for depicting time-use changes after childbirth. Then OLS and individual-level fixed-effect models will be employed for a sample of married and cohabiting men and women aged between 16 and 60 regardless of their parental status. The aim is to test the precise effect of domestic work on the potential wage loss stemming from the gap in work experience between men and women.

FINDINGS

Time Use Practices over the Conventional Family Life Cycle

Figures 9.1 and 9.2 illustrate changes in men and women's time spent on paid work, routine housework, other domestic work, sleep and rest, and consumption and leisure throughout the conventional course of family formation.

The overall time-use changes for static family circumstances (in terms of partnership and the presence of children) were small. For example, for men and women who had stayed partnered with no child in two successive years, there was only a small increase in paid work time. Women who had acquired a partner did not change their paid work time significantly, with a minor reduction from 396 to 378 minutes per day. The corresponding change in men's paid work time was not significant (from 445 to 447 minutes). Major changes in paid work time occurred after having a child: both women and men reduced their paid work time significantly (from 363 to 234 minutes and from 442 to 407 minutes, respectively). Women's reduction in paid work time was therefore significantly larger than men's (the proportions being 36 per cent and 8 per cent, respectively). Moreover, women's paid work time continued to decrease until the child left home or

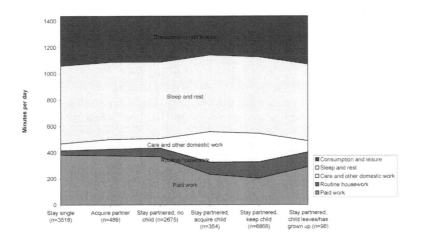

Figure 9.1 Time use practices over the lifecourse, women aged 19–40.

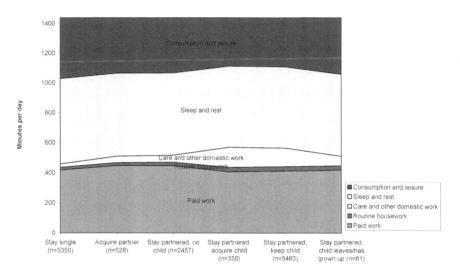

Figure 9.2   Time use practices over the lifecourse, men aged 19–40.

was aged over 16, but hardly reached the level before childbirth. Men's paid work time, on the other hand, remained more or less stable after the birth of the child.

The pattern of changes in time spent on routine housework mirrors that of paid work-time changes. However, single women already undertook more housework (32 minutes) than single men (17 minutes). Time on routine housework was relatively stable in the period where there was no observed change in family status. Significant increases in routine housework time were observed in the period where individuals had acquired partners, but the change was more substantial in the case of women: their housework time almost doubled (from 27 to 50 minutes). Having a child brought a substantial rise in routine housework time for women (from 66 to 94 minutes) and a much smaller absolute increase for men (from 22 to 30 minutes). Women's routine housework time continued to increase over the life course and did not drop much even after the child grew older or left home. Men's routine housework time, however, remained more or less stable.

Time spent on care for family members and other nonroutine types of domestic work (e.g. shopping, gardening, and household repairs) revealed somewhat different patterns from those of routine housework time. Single women's time was still longer than single men's (54 vs. 22 minutes). But both men and women increased their time on these activities significantly after forming a partnership, and after childbirth. Their times peaked at 134 and 232 minutes, respectively, in the year just after the birth. Men increased their time by more than 185 per cent and women by

218 per cent. These findings concur with recent research which suggests that men are more willing to undertake childcare responsibilities than other traditionally feminine household work, such as cleaning and cooking (Gershuny 2000; Robinson and Godbey 1997). Women's and men's time spent on childcare and nonroutine domestic tasks reduced gradually as the child grew up or left home, but still stayed at a level higher than before having children.

Men's consumption and leisure time was longer than women's at all stages of the family life cycle. Both men's and women's figures dropped after partnership formation and also after the birth of a child—by about 50 minutes per day in the latter case. Their time on these activities hardly recovered when the child remained coresident with them, but increased significantly when the child was old enough to leave home. Time on sleep and rest reduced slightly over the life cycle. Women spent longer on sleep, rest and personal care than men (which in fact probably reflects more time on personal care than men).

The total work time (paid work time and unpaid domestic work time) of single women was slightly longer than that of single men. Nevertheless, both men's and women's total work time increased after getting a partner and peaked after having a child.

Time-use Practices Before and After Childbirth

In what follows, we examine time-use changes five years after having a child, which, as shown earlier, is a major life-cycle event that initiates changes in time-use practices. In order to examine how the gendered divi-

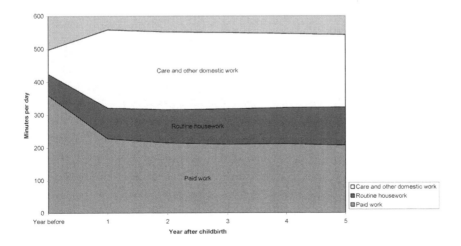

Figure 9.3   Time spent on paid work and unpaid domestic work before and after the birth of first child, women aged 19–40 (n = 747).

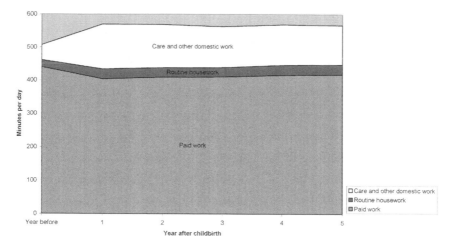

Figure 9.4　Time spent on paid work and unpaid domestic work before and after the birth of first child, men aged 19–40 (n = 671).

sion of labour is reinforced over time, we focus on the time spent on paid work and unpaid domestic work.

Figures 9.3 and 9.4 indicate changes in women's and men's time use practices in the year before and five years after the birth of a child. Since many women left employment or changed from full-time to part-time employment after having a child, their paid work time naturally fell—from 359 to 228 minutes in the year just after the birth of their children. Their paid work time continued to fall in the next four years. In the case of men, their paid work time dropped only by a modest level from 440 to 403 minutes in the year just after the childbirth, and bounced back gradually in the following few years. As for routine housework, women's time increased by about 50 per cent, from 65 to 93 minutes in the year after childbirth. Men, on the other hand, did not increase their time on routine housework significantly. The main change in their contribution to domestic work was on childcare and nonroutine types of housework. This went up by nearly 200 per cent, from 46 to 136 minutes in the year after childbirth, and decreased gradually as the child grew older. As for women's time spent on these activities, it increased even more dramatically, by 220 per cent, from 74 to 237 minutes in the year after childbirth and also went down to some extent when the child grew older. Concomitantly, women's and men's time on consumption and leisure dropped after childbirth and recovered gradually when the child grew older.

The Reinforcement of the Gendered Division of Labour After Childbirth

In Figures 9.5 to 9.7, we classify women and men into three groups according to the female partner's self-reported employment statuses before

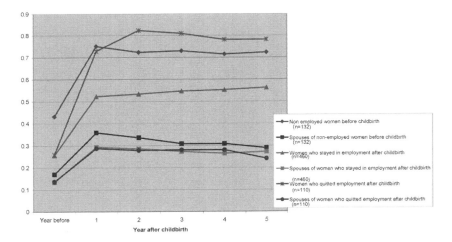

Figure 9.5   Proportion of unpaid domestic work to all work after the birth of first child.

and after childbirth: (1) the female partner was not employed in the year before childbirth; (2) the female partner was employed in the year before and the year after childbirth; and (3) the female partner was employed in the year before childbirth but quitted employment in the following year.

Considering the proportion of domestic work to all work (paid work and unpaid housework) in Figure 9.5, time-use practices of the three groups of men display a somewhat similar pattern; the proportion increased to the highest in the year after childbirth (to 36 per cent in the case of spouses of nonemployed women and 29 per cent in the other two groups) and continued to fall in the years after. In the case of women, the three groups behave differently. Women who had stayed in employment still spent a high proportion of their work time on unpaid domestic work: the figure jumped from about 26 per cent to 52 per cent in the year just after childbirth and increased steadily by 4 per cent in the next four years. Women who had quitted employment had the highest ratio of domestic work to all work after childbirth: the figure rose from 26 per cent to 73 per cent in the first year after childbirth and reached a maximum of 82 per cent in the second year; then it dropped only to some extent in the next few years. Women who were not employed before childbirth spent about 75 per cent of their work time on unpaid domestic work in the year just after childbirth (the figure was 43 per cent before the birth). The figure fell slightly, by 3 per cent, in the next few years. It is interesting to note that the proportion of domestic work to all work for nonemployed women did not equal 100 per cent, which perhaps reflects the possibility that women's self-perceived employment status is affected by their labour market strategies (e.g. employed women planning to leave their jobs just before or after childbirth might have considered themselves to be not employed). Similarly, some women

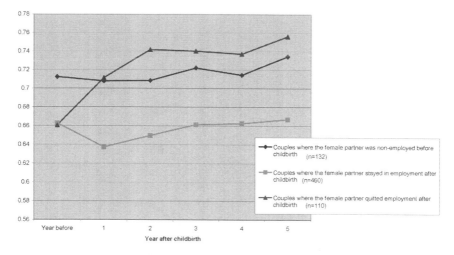

Figure 9.6   Proportion of domestic work done by women after the birth of first child.

who undertook a small proportion of paid work (e.g. for a temporary job or a part-time job) probably did not consider themselves to be in employment. To sum up, the gendered division of labour is much intensified after childbirth regardless of women's employment strategies in relation to childcare, with men's paid work time being roughly stable but women devoting a higher proportion of their work time to unpaid domestic work.

Figure 9.6 illustrates the ratio of domestic work done by women to total domestic work undertaken by both partners before and after the birth of the first child. The overall trend of all the three groups is that the domestic division of labour is increasingly gendered in the five years after childbirth. The proportion of women's domestic work time grew at the fastest rate, from 66 per cent in the year before the childbirth to 76 per cent five years later in the case where the female partner had moved out of employment. The proportion increased to a mild extent in the other two groups, by 2 per cent from 72 per cent to 74 percent, in the period of observation in the case of nonemployed women before childbirth, and by 1 per cent, from 66 per cent to 67 per cent, in the case of women who had stayed in employment. In fact, in the latter case, the proportion dropped to some extent by 2 per cent in the first year after childbirth and then rose thereafter.

IMPLICATIONS FOR FUTURE EARNINGS

Women are in a less advantaged position compared with men in terms of accumulation of human capital, since they become more specialized in

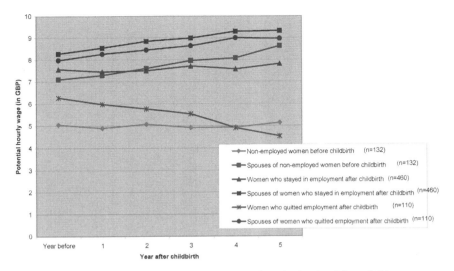

Figure 9.7 Potential hourly wage before and after the birth of first child.

domestic work and less specialized in paid work after having a child. In Figure 9.7 it can be seen that men's potential earnings rose steadily after the birth of the first child, while only women who had remained in employment after having a child managed some increase in their potential earnings, though this was modest. Potential earnings of women who were nonemployed before childbirth wobbled and hardly rose in the years after. Women who had left employment even experienced a significant fall in their potential wage in the five years after having a child.

MULTIVARIATE ANALYSIS RESULTS

Table 9.1 presents OLS models of the association of potential wages with the domestic division of labour, which are based on the same samples as used in Figures 9.5 and 9.6. We regress women's and men's potential wages separately in order to examine if there are any substantial differences between their associations with the share of domestic work and both partners' domestic work time. We see that the results are consistent with those of Figure 9.7: for both men and women, their potential labour market income is negatively associated with their share of domestic work in the sum of both partners' domestic work, when years after childbirth, number of children, last year's and partner's potential wages are taken into account. It can also be observed that the association is stronger for women than for men (the coefficients being–3.641 and–1.805, respectively). In the second set of models, the share of domestic work is replaced with both partners' domestic work time. For both men and women, their potential wage is

Table 9.1 OLS Models of the Associations Between Domestic Work Participation and Potential Wage After Childbirth

	Women				Men			
	B	Robust SE	B	Robust SE	B	Robust SE	B	Robust SE
Share of domestic work	−3.641***	0.552			−1.805**	0.612		
Weekly domestic work time/100	0.550***	0.001			−0.286**	0.001		
Partner's weekly domestic work time/100	0.222**	0.001			0.144*	0.001		
Number of children	−0.219*	0.093	−0.027	0.086	0.284**	0.097	0.270**	0.100
Years since the birth of first child	0.055*	0.025	0.017	0.024	0.165***	0.026	0.166***	0.027
Last year's potential wage	0.803***	0.025	0.768***	0.025	0.872***	0.021	0.871***	0.021
Partner's potential wage	0.068***	0.019	0.064**	0.018	0.109***	0.025	0.113***	0.025
Constant	3.222***	0.446	2.383***	0.301	0.778**	0.286	0.161	0.326
R^2		0.766		0.776		0.768		0.763

Note: Data from the British Household Panel Survey, 1994–2005. N = 2,997 couples.
In the OLS models, standard errors take account of multiple observations of individuals.
*p < .05. **p < .01. ***p < .001.

Table 9.2 OLS and Fixed Effect Models of the Associations Between Domestic Work Participation and Potential Wage—Married and Cohabiting Men and Women

	Women						Men					
	OLS Model		OLS Model		FE Model		OLS Model		OLS Model		FE Model	
	B	Robust SE	B	Robust SE	B	Robust SE	B	Robust SE	B	Robust SE	B	Robust SE
Share of domestic work	−5.030***	0.361	—	—	−0.185	0.115	−5.780***	0.440	—	—	−0.224	0.148
Weekly domestic work time/100	—	—	−1.111***	0.000	—	—	—	—	−1.189***	0.001	—	—
Partner's weekly domestic work time/100	—	—	0.233***	0.001	—	—	—	—	0.254***	0.001	—	—
Number of adults	−0.252***	0.041	−0.228***	0.039	0.089***	0.019	0.053	0.065	0.069	0.064	0.268***	0.025
Number of children	−0.246***	0.034	0.228***	0.040	−0.142***	0.019	0.010	0.047	0.139*	0.058	0.302***	0.023
Partner's potential wage	0.349***	0.013	0.307***	0.013	0.129***	0.006	0.567***	0.020	0.542***	0.020	0.206***	0.009
Constant	7.234***	0.269	6.476***	0.187	5.254***	0.100	6.253***	0.260	5.217***	0.255	6.157***	0.106
R²/ Between groups R²	0.243		0.298		0.215		0.212		0.218		0.145	

Note: Data from the British Household Panel Survey, 1994–2005. N = 22,858 for women, and 21,425 for men. The OLS models include dummies for year; standard errors take account of multiple observations of individuals.
*p < .05. **p < .01. ***p < .001.

associated negatively with their own domestic work time but positively with their partners' domestic work time. This result suggests that individuals' potential wage would benefit from their partners' domestic work participation but would be hampered by their own participation.

The models in Table 9.2 aim to establish further the association between the domestic division of labour and potential labour market earnings using a full sample of married and cohabiting men and women aged between 16 and 60 regardless of their parental status. The results for women and men concerning the domestic division of labour appear to be rather symmetrical: their potential labour market earnings are negatively associated with their share of domestic work (see the first set of models); they are also associated negatively with their own domestic work time and positively with their partners' domestic work time. What is more, the coefficients in the women's and the men's models concerning domestic work participation are of similar size. Nevertheless, we should note that the coefficients concerning the share of domestic work in the fixed-effect models (which control for unobserved and unchanged characteristics of individuals) are negative but not significant. This result suggests that the hypothesized causal effect of the domestic division of labour on potential wage may operate through some unobserved characteristics within individuals, for example, their work orientation.

DISCUSSION AND CONCLUSION

This chapter has attempted to provide a moving picture of how men and women allocate their time to different activities in the course of the family life cycle. It has combined different types of data not only to confirm the well-known gender gap in work experience and the domestic division of labour, but also to show the continuity of this gap over time. It is not a one-off effect. There are significant changes in partners' time-use practices in the wake of life-cycle events. In particular, the changes in association with family transitions are more substantial for women than for men. Compared with men's time-use pattern, women's time on paid work, housework and other unpaid domestic work is associated to a greater extent with the presence of a dependent child. Nevertheless, there is still a significant increase in men's time spent on domestic work after a child is born, although this consists mainly of childcare and other types of nonroutine domestic work. These increases in domestic work time are concomitant with decreases in their time spent on consumption and leisure activities.

We have found that the division of labour between partners becomes more gendered when men and women move across the family life-cycle stages. At the initial stage, the differences in time use between men and women are relatively small, with men undertaking slightly more paid work and women slightly more unpaid domestic work. But the gender differentials in time use become more pronounced after partnership, especially after the birth of the first child. Interestingly, total work time (paid work and unpaid domestic work) is slightly longer in the case of women before a partnership starts, but women and men undertake roughly similar amounts of work at later stages of the family life cycle.

The abovementioned observations concur well with the contentions that we have outlined at the beginning of this chapter. Whereas an initial difference in human capital induces a gendered division of labour, this difference is reinforced over the life course: men and women become more specialized in paid work and domestic work, respectively, while domestic work participation is in turn negatively associated with potential labour market earnings. Therefore, despite the fact that the total amount of work (including paid work and domestic work) tends approximately to equalize for men and women at the later stages of the family life cycle, an important issue regarding gender equality arises: women and men accumulate different levels of human capital over time. Having been more specialized in paid work than women, men acquire a higher level of human capital than women. Women's potential labour market earnings fall significantly after having a child, as women allocate considerable amounts of time on domestic work at the expense of their investment in paid work. The only exception is women who stay in employment after childbirth. Their potential earnings continue to rise, although at a slower rate than men's. This is not just a matter of immediate welfare, which depends in part on how money is allocated in the household. Individuals' potential labour market income is a powerful determinant of their life chances in society (such as health and life expectancy). It also influences significantly bargaining power within marriage.

NOTES

1. For more details of the data calibration exercise, see Kan and Gershuny (2006a). We calibrate time use estimates from wave 4 (1994) of the BHPS, the first wave when major stylised time-use variables were collected.
2. Potential wage is estimated by the Essex Score, which is calculated based on respondents' educational qualifications, their most recent occupation, and labour-market statuses in the 48 months prior to the interview. It has been shown to be a valid indicator of social position and a significant predictor of earnings in the labour market (see Kan and Gershuny 2006b).

REFERENCES

Becker, G.S. (1965) A theory of the allocation of time. *Economic Journal, 75*: 493–517.
Becker, G.S. (1991 [1981]) *A treatise on the family* (enl. ed.), Cambridge, MA: Harvard University Press.

Dolton, P.J. and Makepeace, G.H. (1990) The earnings of economics graduates, *The Economic Journal, 100*(399): 237–50.

EOC (Equal Opportunities Commission) (2002) *Facts about women and men in Great Britain*, Manchester: Equal Opportunities Commission.

Gershuny, J. (1992) The domestic labour revolution: a process of lagged adaptation? in N. Abercrombie and A. Warde (eds) *Social change in contemporary Britain*, Cambridge: Polity Press.

———. (2000) *Changing times: work and leisure in postindustrial society*, Oxford: Oxford University Press.

———. (2003) Time, through the life course, in the family. In J. Scott, J. Treas, and R. Martin (eds) *The Blackwell companion to sociology of families*, Oxford: Blackwell.

Kan, M.Y. (2008) Does gender trump money? Housework hours of husbands and wives in Britain. *Work, Employment and Society, 22*(1): 45–66.

Kan, M.Y. and Gershuny, J. (2006a) Infusing time diary evidence into panel data: an exercise on calibrating time-use estimates for the BHPS, *Working Paper of the Institute for Social and Economic Research Paper 2006–19*, Colchester, UK: University of Essex.

———. (2006b) Human capital and social position in Britain: creating a measure of wage earning potential from BHPS data, in *Institute for Social and Economic Research Working Paper 2006–3*, Colchester, UK: University of Essex.

Layte, R. (1999) *Divided time: gender, paid employment and domestic labour*, Aldershot, UK: Ashgate.

Mincer, J. and Polachek, S. (1974) Family investments in human capital: earnings of women, *Journal of Political Economy, 82*: S76–S108.

Robinson, J.P. and Godbey, G. (1997) *Time for life: the surprising ways Americans use their time*, University Park: Pennsylvania State University Press.

10 Residential Mobility, Mobility Preferences and Psychological Health

Priscila Ferreira and Mark Taylor

INTRODUCTION

Moving home is a major event in people's lives, the result of an often drawn-out and difficult decision which has effects that are not easily predicted. These include direct economic impacts (perhaps from a change in job if that triggered the move, but also the costs of the move and of the new home itself) and indirect welfare effects associated with, for example, attempts to establish new or maintain old social networks. When two people jointly consider a decision to move, these issues are inevitably more complex. In this chapter, we study the extent to which relationships matter both in determining residential mobility behaviour and the impact of residential mobility on psychological health.

Evidence suggests that about 10 per cent of individuals and 8 per cent of couples in Britain move house each year and the majority of moves are of short distance, while the young, the highly educated, those in high-level occupations, private tenants and higher income households have the largest migration propensities.[1] We extend and complement existing studies in a number of ways. Firstly, we examine the extent to which mobility rates vary across family types, particularly in relation to children. It is well known that married individuals have lower rates of residential mobility than single people, but how do these vary with the age of children?[2] Secondly, we examine residential mobility in the context of the mobility preferences and subjective evaluations of local area quality of adults within the family, taking into account the preferences of both partners. Thirdly, we relate mobility outcomes conditional on preferences to measures of individual mental well-being to examine whether and how moving home affects psychological health, again considering the relationship: is the impact equal for both partners?

The intuitive explanation used to explain residential mobility and choice of location is the household life cycle.[3] The housing needs of households change due to either changes in circumstances or in housing market conditions (Kan 1999). For instance, when the household enters the childbearing and childrearing stages of the life cycle, both the current neighbourhood and the current accommodation may be judged on new standards (Lee et al. 1994). In this way, residential mobility allows adjustments in housing consumption in response to changes in either demand (changes in household size, structure, or in socioeconomic status) or supply (in the local urban or economic environment). The decision to move can be seen as a function of pushes from the original dwelling or area and pulls toward the new one (Rossi 1955; Bolan 1997).

Most residential mobility is related to family, accommodation or job, but the ordering of preferences is less obvious and rarely known.[4] The unsuitability of current housing is in fact the most common reason for moving, in particular the desire for more space, tenure change, and for cheaper dwellings. However, a significant proportion of mobility is associated with household and family characteristics (and expected changes therein). Although many individuals express dissatisfaction with their neighbourhood, area characteristics actually explain a small proportion of residential mobility (Clark and Onaka 1983; Böheim and Taylor 2002). Subjective measures of neighbourhood quality influence mobility behaviour indirectly through influencing mobility preferences, but the direct effects of local area quality measures are weak (Lee et al. 1994). Expected or unexpected changes in circumstances or in housing market conditions result in residential dissatisfaction which may be translated into desires to move and more specific expectations to change residence (Kan 1999). For instance, some households may not be able to move because of the costs involved or the inability to locate a suitable alternative residence. Other households may move suddenly and unexpectedly due to financial, employment or household structure shocks.

As a result of the preceding process, some households are in disequilibrium with regards to their housing consumption. For Britain, Böheim and Taylor (2002) show that more than 40 per cent of individuals express a preference for moving (the majority for area or housing reasons), and while the propensity to move is three times greater for those expressing a preference for moving than for those who do not, this still leaves substantial unsatisfied demand. Kan (1999) finds that socioeconomic circumstances (e.g. retirement) have almost no impact on actual mobility once expectations are taken into account. Unpredictable events such as unemployment force households to change their mobility plans.

What are the effects of a household move? Numerous studies show that family migration typically has negative impacts on labour market outcomes for women in terms of employment and wages, although these may be sensitive to the reasons for migration.[5] In contrast, given that many moves relate to men's employment needs, there is evidence of positive returns to migration among men (Bartel 1979; Yankow 2003; Böheim and Taylor 2007). There is a history of research indicating that psychological health is affected by unsustainable housing commitments, housing type and quality.[6] Brett (1980) finds that residential mobility may involve changes in routines, roles and identities, and therefore can be expected to affect mental well-being. Brett (1980), Gullotta and Donohue (1983) and Weissman and Paykel (1972) have found negative psychological effects of residential moves for women. This may be because traditionally women spend more time in the house than men and are more likely to develop social ties to a location, and are therefore more affected by any move (Blair and Lichter 1991; Turner and Marino 1994). Women are also more likely to be a tied mover and are more likely to have to adapt their career plans to the needs of their spouses (Bielby and Bielby 1992; Shihadeh 1991; Taylor 2007).

The earlier discussion not only implies that relationships matter, both in terms of determining mobility outcomes and in terms of the impact of mobility on mental health, but that we should also be concerned with the balance of effects within relationships. Next we test both for migration effects and for the equality of these effects within couples.

DATA

Panel data are required to accurately assess the impact of mobility preferences at a particular point in time to mobility outcomes in the subsequent period $t + 1$, and to examine the impact of mobility on psychological well-being. By tracing how an individual's mental well-being changes following a residential move, we are able to identify whether or not the individual benefits or suffers. Our analyses use the first 14 years of the British Household Panel Survey (BHPS), covering the period 1991–2004 (the latest year of data currently available). As part of maintaining the panel sample, information is collected on the migration behaviour of BHPS respondents, identifying those that move house and attempting to follow all migrants who remain in Britain. Although attrition rates among migrants are higher than among nonmigrants, Buck (2000) reports that almost 75 per cent of actual movers between 1991 and 1992 were traced (compared to an overall response rate of 90 per cent), while over the years of available panel data, an interview was possible with at least one household member in almost 80 per cent of moving households.

We identify migrants from responses to the question "Can I just check, have you yourself been living in this (house/flat) for more than a year?" In addition, at each date of interview respondents are asked "If you could choose, would you stay here in your present home or would you prefer to move somewhere else?" From responses to these questions we can identify both individuals who are unhappy in their current residence and those who subsequently experience a residential move. By matching responses across husbands and wives we can identify couples in which both partners agree about their mobility preferences and in which partners disagree. Intuition suggests that single persons are more able to meet their mobility preferences than married persons, that individuals whose mobility preferences are met enjoy welfare gains, and those whose mobility preferences are not met suffer welfare losses. We measure these welfare gains and losses through psychological well-being.

The 12-item General Health Questionnaire (GHQ) has been used in all waves of the BHPS and is a reliable and widely applied self-completion assessment measure of minor psychiatric morbidity in the UK (Argyle 1989; McCabe et al. 1996). The items take the form of responses to the following questions:

"Have you recently:

1. Been able to concentrate on whatever you are doing?*
2. Lost much sleep over worry?
3. Felt that you are playing a useful part in things?*
4. Felt capable of making decisions about things?*
5. Felt constantly under strain?
6. Felt you couldn't overcome your difficulties?
7. Been able to enjoy your normal day to day activities?*
8. Been able to face up to your problems?*
9. Been feeling unhappy and depressed?
10. Been losing confidence in yourself?
11. Been thinking of yourself as a worthless person?
12. Been feeling reasonably happy all things considered?*"

Answers are coded on a four-point scale running from 'disagree strongly' (coded 0) to 'agree strongly' (coded 3—asterisked questions are coded in reverse), and added together provide a total GHQ score of mental distress ranging from 0 to 36. High scores correspond to low feelings of well-being (high levels of stress) and vice versa. This is sometimes known as a Likert scale.[7] The GHQ in the BHPS has been shown to be robust to retest effects making it a suitable longitudinal instrument (Pevalin 2000).

We focus explicitly on men aged 16 to 64 and women aged 16 to 59 who were interviewed for at least two consecutive dates of interview. We use an unbalanced panel in the sense that individuals enter and leave our sample as they enter and leave the relevant age range, or enter or leave the sample over time. Removing individuals who have missing information on any variables used in the analysis results in a sample size of 15,025 individuals contributing 87,409 person year observations.[8]

DESCRIPTIVE FINDINGS

Table 10.1 illustrates residential mobility among the selected sample. Of the sample, 10.3 percent move house each year, 8.4 per cent move within

Table 10.1   Residential Mobility and Partnership Status: BHPS 1991–2004

Partnership status t-1	% move t—1 to t	% move within regions t—1 to t	% move between regions t—1 to t	N
Single	14.28	11.59	2.69	24,782
Partnership:	8.78	7.17	1.60	62,627
No children	*8.90*	*7.23*	*1.67*	*29,260*
All children age < 5	*14.69*	*11.89*	*2.80*	*7,871*
All children age > = 5	*5.72*	*4.75*	*0.97*	*20,187*
Children of both ages	*10.96*	*9.08*	*1.88*	*5,309*
Total	10.34	8.43	1.91	87,409

a standard geographical region while 1.9 per cent move between regions. These mobility rates vary considerably by family status. Couples with young children are most likely to move (14.7 per cent), both within (11.9 per cent) and between regions (2.8 per cent). Single individuals also have above-average mobility rates (14.3 per cent, 11.6 per cent and 2.7 per cent). Couples with school-age children have the lowest mobility propensities—only 5.7 per cent move house each year, with 1 per cent moving between regions. Therefore, it is not marital status per se that affects mobility rates; it is the presence and ages of dependent children. This reflects the importance of housing and household characteristics when raising a young family and the reluctance to disrupt the schooling and social networks of children. This is reinforced when looking at the factors inducing a preference to move. We do not show a table for these results, but we find that individuals in couples with preschool-aged children are most likely to report wanting to move (43.9 per cent) while those in couples with school-aged children are least likely to expect to move (35.8 per cent).

Table 10.2 shows mobility preferences by family structure but also in terms of the balance of agreement within couples. Couples with no children

Table 10.2   Subjective Measures of Neighbourhood Quality, Partnered Individuals: BHPS 1991–2004

Partnership status t-1	% want to move in t—1			N
	Neither wants	One wants	Both want	
No children	53.10	21.06	25.84	29,260
All children age < 5	45.62	21.08	33.30	7,871
All children age > = 5	52.30	23.86	23.84	20,187
Children of both ages	48.84	22.92	28.24	5,309

Table 10.3   Mobility rates *t*—1 to *t* by Subjective Neighbourhood Evaluations and Partnership Status at *t*—1: BHPS 1991–2004

| | Mobility rates *t*—1 to *t* | | | | | |
| | % like neighbourhood in *t*—1 | | | % want to move in *t*—1 | | |
Partnership status *t*—1	Neither like	One likes	Both like	Neither wants	One wants	Both want
Single	18.81	13.58	na	9.62	21.16	na
Partnership:						
No children	24.54	13.69	7.53	3.21	8.65	20.79
All children age < 5	32.64	21.91	12.48	4.93	14.17	28.39
All children age > = 5	15.81	8.18	4.79	2.72	6.23	11.80
Children of both ages	25.16	15.17	9.27	5.13	11.50	20.61
Total	20.76	13.42	7.42	5.35	13.94	19.36

or with school-aged children are most likely to agree on not wanting to move (53 per cent). In contrast, couples with preschool-aged children are most likely to agree on wanting to move (33 per cent). Disagreement among couples is most common for those with school-aged children (24 per cent). The presence of children and their ages are clearly important in affecting thoughts of neighbourhood quality and mobility preferences, and there is relatively little discrepancy in the views of both partners. Consensus seems the norm.

What about actual moves? Table 10.3 shows that mobility rates are highest among single individuals who did not like their neighbourhood, and for couples in which neither partner liked their neighbourhood. Almost one in three individuals in couples with preschool-aged children and in which neither partner liked the current neighbourhood subsequently moved, compared with 25 per cent of individuals in couples with no children and in couples with children of both ages, and 19 per cent of single individuals. Mobility rates are approximately halved in couples where there was disagreement, and almost halved again in couples where each partner agreed in liking the neighbourhood. Only 5 per cent of individuals in couple households with preschool-aged children and in which neither partner expressed a preference for moving actually moved in the following year. In contrast, almost 30 per cent of individuals in such couples that agreed in their preferences for wanting to move subsequently did so.[9]

These tables confirm that partnership status and the presence and ages of dependent children have large effects not only on preferences but on the likelihood of subsequently moving home. Do they also differentially affect any change in psychological well-being stemming from the move,

Table 10.4   GHQ Scores by Mobility Status, BHPS 1991–2004

| | GHQ: preferences and moving status | | | |
	t—1	*t*	*variation*	N
Single				
Want, not-move	12.18	11.91	−0.27	7,542
Not-want, not-move	11.00	10.96	−0.04	12,255
Want, move	11.99	11.46	−0.54	2,044
Not-want, move	10.99	10.66	−0.33	1,322
Partnership				
Want, not-move	11.66	11.79	0.13	18,952
Not-want, not-move	10.80	11.01	0.21	35,243
Want, move	11.38	11.19	−0.20	3,677
Not-want, move	11.18	11.36	0.18	1,558

or from unfulfilled expectations stemming from wanting but failing to move? Summarising GHQ scores gives an initial indication of the relationships between mobility preferences, mobility outcomes, family status and psychological well-being. Table 10.4 examines relationships between psychological health and fulfilled and unfulfilled mobility preferences and shows that unfulfilled expectations are important. On average, all single individuals experience an improvement in their mental well-being (a fall in GHQ scores) regardless of their mobility preferences and outcomes. The largest improvement is among those who expressed a preference for moving and who subsequently moved. Those who wanted to move but didn't had the lowest level of mental health. The same is true among individuals in partnerships—those who wanted to move but didn't had the lowest level of mental health, and on average their health deteriorated. Only individuals in partnerships whose preferences for moving were fulfilled experienced an improvement in their mental well-being. While these effects appear small given the range of the GHQ is 0–36, 80 per cent of the sample report a score of between 5 and 15, and of course these effects might be cumulative over time.

MOBILITY, FAMILY AND PSYCHOLOGICAL WELL-BEING

Economic theory indicates that an individual will attempt to sell his or her services in the market which offers the highest return—potential migrants contemplate the relationship between the immediate costs of moving and the stream of expected future benefits associated with the move. These depend at least partly on relative wages and employment growth in possible locations (Gordon 1990; Meen and Andrew 1998), as well as the condition and suitability of the current residence. Households will prefer to move if the expected gains to moving net of transaction costs exceed the expected utility from not moving.

Transaction costs associated with any move include the loss of location-specific human capital, information networks, and the psychological and direct costs of moving. However, family-level factors also have to be taken into account, including the potential loss of earnings of other household members, the costs of moving school-age children and the possible costs of changing job or employer. Such costs may create lock-in effects, substantial negative welfare effects and the suboptimal consumption of housing. They might also reduce job mobility and potentially increase unemployment (O'Sullivan et al. 1995; Oswald 1997; Van Ommeren et al. 2000; Van Ommeren and van Leuvensteijn 2005). These costs can be approximated by housing tenure, the number and ages of children, and the presence of a working spouse. These reflect a wide range of individual, household, job and housing characteristics and affect both the psychic and financial costs of moving home (Krieg and Bohara 1999; Van Ommeren et al. 2000).

From this simple discussion, the determinants of residential mobility emerge. In particular, it can be seen that the nature of the relationships within a household is of central importance. Thus, the decision to migrate is likely to be continuously revised as the household's situation changes, that is, as household members find and lose jobs, form or dissolve partnerships, and as children are born and age.

ESTIMATION STRATEGY AND MODEL SPECIFICATIONS

We now consider the joint effects of these factors and examine whether they are similar for men and women. Our aims are, first, to explain the basis of the migration decision, taking account in particular of differential preferences within the couple; and second, to look at the impact of the move on mental well-being, again examining differential effects.

Modelling Residential Mobility

Initially we examine the relationships between partnership status, the age of children and mobility preferences and actual residential mobility. To do this, we model the decision to move and study the impact of mobility preferences and household structure on this decision.[10] We adopt a random-effects probit procedure, modelling the decision to move as a function of a range of individual, household, job-related and housing characteristics.[11]

The dependent variable in this analysis takes the value 1 if the individual moves house between $t-1$ and t, and 0 if they remain at the same residence.[12] This approach allows us to benefit from the panel nature of the data by controlling for unobserved heterogeneity (under the assumption that the individual specific unobserved effect and observed characteristics are uncorrelated with each other).

We are interested in determining the extent to which the lower residential mobility rates of partnered individuals relative to single individuals can be explained by different mobility preferences, and above all whether or not these differentials depend on household structure and the set of relationships embodied within it. Therefore we include variables that capture household structure together with mobility preferences and subjective evaluations of local area quality of adults within the context of the family and the household. Our models also include a wide range of control variables that the previous literature has shown to be important determinants of residential mobility.[13]

Modelling Mental Well-Being

We are also interested in examining how residential mobility affects mental well-being and the extent to which this depends on mobility preferences and subjective evaluations of area quality prior to any move. Underlying psychological characteristics have been found to systematically influence reported well-being (De Neve and Cooper 1999), and therefore estimation methods that do not allow for such time-invariant unobservable individual traits are likely to result in biased estimates. Again we take advantage of the longitudinal nature of the data to control for such characteristics by approximating the GHQ score to be linear, and estimating the following specification:

$$GHQ_{it} = X_{it}\beta + Z_i + h_{it} \qquad (10.1)$$

$i = 1, \ldots n, t = 1, \ldots, T_i$ where GHQ_{it} is the reported GHQ score of individual i at time t, z_i is a vector of individual and household characteristics, z_i is a time invariant individual specific error term capturing the effects of unobservable characteristics, h_{it} is the random error term and β is a coefficient vector. We use within-group fixed effects estimation, equivalent to OLS estimation of the model in which variables are defined as deviations from their individual means. We estimate whether an individual's level of mental distress varies systematically with residential mobility and mobility preferences, controlling for changes in a wide range of personal, household, family, and housing-related characteristics. As we expect women to be more adversely affected by any residential mobility, we estimate these models separately by gender.

Table 10.5 Impacts of Family Structure, Mobility Preferences and Subjective Evaluations of Area Quality on Mobility, BHPS 1991–2004, Whole Sample (model 1) and Couples Only (model 2)

	Model [1]		Model [2]	
	Coeff	*t-stat*	*Coeff*	*t-stat*
No children	−0.000	(0.07)		
All children age < 5	0.007	(1.00)	0.005	(1.09)
All children age > = 5	−0.011*	(1.68)	−0.012***	(2.58)
Children of both ages	0.006	(0.79)	−0.002	(0.25)
Like neighbourhood				
Single, does	−0.009**	(2.37)		
Couple, one does	−0.016***	(4.23)		
Couple, both do	−0.037***	(9.09)		
Wants to move				
Single, does	0.081***	(21.50)		
Couple, one does	0.075***	(21.28)		
Couple, both do	0.170***	(41.60)		
Like neighbourhood				
Man does, woman doesn't			−0.013**	(2.43)
Man doesn't, woman does			−0.013**	(2.48)
Both do			−0.036***	(6.46)
Wants to move				
Man does, woman doesn't			0.055***	(10.31)
Man doesn't, woman does			0.072***	(12.68)
Both do			0.132***	(27.58)
rho	0.136		0.138	
Log likelihood	−23880		−7447	
Number of observations	87,409		31,116	
Number of groups	15,025		5,299	

Notes: Marginal effects calculated from random effects probit models. In model [1], dependent variable takes value 1 if individual moved house between *t*—1 and *t* and 0 otherwise. Model [2] focuses on couples only. The difference in the coefficients on the variables indicating man wanting to move, woman doesn't and woman wants to move, man doesn't are statistically significant. Other control variables in the models include: age, age squared, highest qualification, employment status of respondent and spouse (if partnered), number of children, household income, housing tenure, housing type, region, and year. *, **, *** indicate statistical significance at the 10%, 5% and 1% levels, respectively.

RESULTS

Mobility

Table 10.5 presents the estimated marginal effects from random effects probit models where the dependent variable takes the value 1 if the individual had moved house since the previous date of interview, and 0 if (s)he remained at the same residence. We estimate two models, both of which include the full set of controls. (We do not show the coefficients for the controls, which are consistent with previous research.)[14] Model [1] includes interaction terms between family status and the subjective evaluation and mobility preference variables to examine the extent to which matching preferences within couples affect behaviour. Model [2] focuses on couples only and examines whether the evaluations and preferences of the husband or the wife have the largest impact on subsequent mobility outcomes.[15]

In Model [1], which includes family structure and couple level evaluations and preferences, the family status variables have no statistical significance. This suggests that differences in mobility propensities by family structure can be explained by preferences and subjective evaluations of neighbourhoods of individuals within couples. A single individual who liked his or her current neighbourhood was one percentage point less likely to subsequently move than an otherwise similar single individual who did not like his or her current neighbourhood. Larger negative and statistically significant effects are also associated with being in a couple household in which one individual liked the current neighbourhood (reducing the probability by 1.6 percentage points), and particularly with being in a couple in which both partners liked the current neighbourhood (by almost 4 percentage points). These factors have the largest negative impacts on the propensity to move house.

Mobility outcomes are also strongly affected by preferences of both single individuals and individuals in couples. Single individuals who expressed a preference for moving and individuals in couples in which one partner expressed a preference for moving both have a higher propensity to subsequently move house than single individuals who did not express such a preference. These indicators have similar sized effects, increasing the propensity to move by about 8 percentage points. Individuals in couples in which both partners expressed a preference for moving are also significantly more likely than single individuals to subsequently move. The effect is very large, increasing the propensity to move house by 17 percentage points relative to a single individual who did not want to move. In fact, living in a couple in which both partners express a preference for moving has the largest positive impact on the probability of subsequently moving house.

In model [2] the unit of analysis is the couple.[16] The research question here becomes the extent to which family structure and the mobility preferences and subjective evaluations of each partner in the couple influence couples' mobility decisions. The estimates indicate that, consistent with previous findings (Krieg and Bohara 1979; Böheim and Taylor 2002), it is couples with school-age children that have the lowest propensity to move house, 1.2 percentage points lower than couples with no children. Couples with preschool-age children have similar propensities to move house as couples with no children. The effects of the subjective evaluation indicators are all negative relative to the omitted category of both partners not liking the current neighbourhood. The impacts of whether the man or the woman likes the current neighbourhood are of similar magnitude, reducing the probability of moving by 1.3 percentage points. This suggests that it makes little difference to the propensity to move whether the man or the woman dislikes the current locality. The impact of both partners liking the current neighbourhood is more negative (but the differences are not statistically significant), reducing the probability by 3.6 percentage points relative to a couple in which neither like the neighbourhood.

The final set of variables indicates the extent to which actual mobility is related to preferences of each partner in the couple. Couples in which at least one partner preferred to move are significantly more likely to subsequently move than those in which neither expressed a preference for moving—the coefficients are positive and highly significant. Whether it is the man or the woman that expressed a preference for moving makes little difference to the impact on actual behaviour—both increase the propensity to move (by 5.5 and 7.2 percentage points, although these effects are not significantly different). The impact of the variable indicating that both partners expressed a preference for moving is significantly larger, increasing the probability of moving by 13.2 percentage points. Therefore, couples in which both partners expressed a preference for moving are more likely to subsequently move than couples in which neither or just one partner expressed a preference for moving. In couples in which only one partner expressed a preference for moving, subsequent behaviour is similar whether it was the man or the woman that did so.

Our estimates suggest that the impact of family status on the propensity to move house largely disappears once mobility preferences and subjective evaluations of neighbourhood quality are taken into account. Single individuals and individuals in couples with and without children have similar propensities to move, although there is evidence that couples with school-aged children have lower mobility propensities than couples with no children. However, it is the subjective evaluations of neighbourhood quality and especially the mobility preferences of household members that have the largest impacts on mobility outcomes.

GHQ

Table 10.6 presents within-group fixed-effects estimates of the impact of mobility on GHQ scores.[17] Again, we estimate a series of different

Table 10.6   Impacts of Family Structure, Mobility Preferences and Subjective Evaluations of Area Quality on GHQ Scores, BHPS 1991–2004, Whole Sample (model 1) and Couples Only (model 2)

	Model [1]		Model [2]	
	Men	*Women*	*Men*	*Women*
Moved				
Likes neighbourhood	−0.662***	−0.828***	−0.474***	−0.908***
	(6.73)	(7.80)	(3.97)	(6.98)
Moving & preference status				
Moved, wanted to move	−0.172*	0.032	—	—
	(1.86)	(0.31)	—	—
Moved, didn't want to move	−0.017	0.047	—	—
	(0.14)	(0.33)	—	—
Didn't move, wanted to move	−0.065	0.058	—	—
	(1.06)	(0.82)	—	—
Moving & preference status in partnership				
Moved, wanted, partner didn't want	—	—	−0.391	−0.666**
	—	—	(1.42)	(2.32)
Moved, didn't want, partner wanted	—	—	−0.547*	0.092
	—	—	(1.94)	(0.30)
Move, both wanted	—	—	−0.239**	−0.089
	—	—	(1.99)	(0.65)
Moved, neither wanted	—	—	−0.073	−0.29
	—	—	(0.37)	(1.28)
Didn't move, wanted, partner didn't want	—	—	−0.029	0.342***
	—	—	(0.30)	(2.96)
Didn't move, didn't want, partner wanted	—	—	0.187*	−0.052
	—	—	(1.79)	(0.47)
Didn't move, both wanted	—	—	0.101	0.001
	—	—	(1.15)	(0.01)
R2	0.0123	0.0075	0.023	0.0144
R2 overall	0.0219	0.0287	0.0294	0.0175
Number of observations	40,120	42,473	28,913	30,517
Number of groups	7,121	7,314	5,032	5,260

Notes: Within-group fixed effects coefficients. Models [1] includes all individuals; model [2] focuses on couples only. Other control variables in the models include: age, age squared, highest qualification, employment status of respondent and spouse (if partnered), number of children, household income, housing tenure, housing type, region, and year. Absolute *t*-statistics are presented in parenthesis. *, **, *** indicate statistical significance at the 10%, 5% and 1% levels, respectively.

specifications each of them including a full set of control variables.[18] Model [1] examines whether the impact of mobility on mental health depends on mobility preferences at $t-1$—that is, do movers who expressed a preference for moving benefit in terms of their mental health relative to those who did not express such a preference? Model [2] focuses on men and women in couple households and examines the extent to which mobility status affects mental health depending on the mobility preferences of each partner.[19]

Model [1] includes mobility preferences at $t-1$ relative to mobility outcomes between $t-1$ and t.[20] Liking the neighbourhood has a large beneficial effect on mental well-being, particularly for women. However, it appears that considering mobility together with mobility preferences at $t-1$ has little impact on GHQ scores. The coefficients are generally small and not statistically significant, indicating that mobility has little impact on GHQ scores regardless of mobility preferences at $t-1$. There is some evidence that men who expressed a preference for moving at $t-1$ and who subsequently moved experienced an improvement in their mental well-being relative to those who did not want to move and remained at the same residence. The coefficient is negative, indicating a fall in GHQ score of 0.172 points, and is on the margins of statistical significance. Therefore, moving to fulfil preferences improves mental well-being for men.

Model [2] focuses on men and women in couple households and examines the extent to which mobility status affects mental health depending on the mobility preferences of each partner. The estimates indicate that mental well-being is affected by mobility preferences in the context of the household. For men, those who moved to meet the preferences of their partner rather than their own experienced an improvement in mental well-being of 0.547 GHQ points—which is equivalent in size to living in a liked neighbourhood. Also, men in couples that moved to meet both partners' preferences experienced a decline in their GHQ score of 0.239 points. Therefore, moving in response to preferences of either partner generally increases mental well-being for men in couples. There is some evidence that men in couples that did not move but whose partner expressed a preference for moving suffer an increase in mental distress of 0.187 points, which is on the margins of statistical significance. This indicates some association between a man's mental health and whether the preferences of his partner are met.

A different picture emerges among women. Women who moved to meet their preferences against the preferences of their partners experienced an improvement in mental health of 0.666 GHQ points. Women who were tied stayers, in that they expressed a preference for moving but whose partner did not express a preference for moving and who subsequently remained at the same address, suffered a fall in their mental well-being of 0.342 points. Therefore, in contrast to men, for women it is the extent to which their own mobility preferences are met that affects their mental well-being, as opposed to the preferences of their partner. It appears, therefore, that the traditional expectation that women follow men in their careers is not reflected in the balance of psychological well-being in the couple.

SUMMARY AND CONCLUSIONS

In this chapter we have examined the extent to which mobility rates vary across family types within the context of mobility preferences and subjective evaluations of area quality. Panel data from the BHPS allow identification of mobility preferences and subjective evaluations of area quality and of residential mobility within a household perspective. We then identify the impact of fulfilled and unfulfilled mobility preferences on psychological well-being, again within a household perspective.

Our results show it is not marital status alone that affects residential mobility, but that marital status, combined with the presence and ages of dependent children, subjective evaluations of local area quality, and mobility preferences of each partner, has large effects on the likelihood of subsequently moving home. It is the subjective evaluations of neighbourhood quality and especially the mobility preferences of household members that have the largest impacts on mobility outcomes. The interaction of residential mobility with mobility preferences and subjective evaluations of neighbourhood quality also have large impacts on psychological health. Therefore, relationships matter, in the sense that individuals in couples forgo their own preferences to meet those of their partner, and bear the psychological consequences of doing so, for the sake of their relationship.

Policy discussion in the UK continues to be focussed on the level and quality of available housing stock, with debates centred on the creation and location of new- build neighbourhoods. Working on the assumption that an increase in the quantity and quality of available housing reduces the costs of residential mobility, then a consequence of this policy is that households (and individuals within households) will be more able to meet their mobility preferences and have a higher chance of moving into neighbourhoods that match their needs. Our results suggest that this will increase the psychological well-being of adults and of couples, which could help strengthen relationships. Furthermore, it is likely that their children will also benefit both through the improved psychological health of their parents and through the quality of the neighbourhood in which they live.

NOTES

1. Studies include Böheim and Taylor (2002), Champion et al. (1998), Clark and Dieleman (1996) and Evans and McCormick (1994).
2. Previous research has shown that married persons migrate long distances less often than single people while dual-earner households migrate least (Böheim and Taylor 2002; Nivalainen 2004).

3. See, for example, Clark and Onaka (1983), Dieleman (2001), Mulder and Hooimeijer (1999).
4. Lansing and Mueller (1967), Long (1974), Böheim and Taylor (2007) report on reasons for moving home.
5. Examples include Boyle et al. (1999, 2001), Lee and Roseman (1999), Maxwell (1988), Morrison and Lichter (1988), Taylor (2007).
6. Relevant studies include Fanning (1967), Cappon (1971), Gillis (1977), Edwards et al. (1982), Lea et al. (1993), and Taylor et al. (2007).
7. Similar results to those presented here were obtained using an alternative Caseness scale.
8. Sample sizes are slightly smaller for the analysis of GHQ scores due to non-response among the GHQ component questions.
9. We have also examined mobility between standard regions. Although the proportions of movers are substantially reduced, the same patterns emerge.
10. It is becoming increasingly standard to jointly model housing tenure choice, the location decision and residential mobility in a nested multinomial logit framework (McFadden 1974; Quigley 1983). However, our primary interests lie in the factors that drive migration and influence departure choice, rather than those that determine the subsequent choice of housing tenure and destination. We therefore choose not to follow this route.
11. While it is clear that residential mobility decisions are not taken on an annual basis, the data lend themselves to the random-effects probit model on the grounds that they are collected annually.
12. We have also estimated a model in which the dependent variable takes the value 1 if the individual moved between regions since the previous date of interview and 0 otherwise. The results do not differ significantly from those presented here.
13. These include age, education, housing tenure, housing type, employment status of respondent and spouse (if partnered), number of children, household income, occupation (if employed), region and year.
14. We have also estimated these models separately by gender, but found no statistically significant differences in the impact of the key variables of interest. Full estimates, including for the control variables, are available from the authors on request.
15. We estimated two models before those presented here. The first included family structure variables. The second introduced the subjective neighbourhood evaluation indicators and the mobility preference variables. Introducing variables capturing subjective evaluations of the neighbourhood and mobility preferences (measured at t–1) reduced the sizes of family structure effects. Mobility preferences and subjective evaluations of the neighbourhood therefore play a major role in determining subsequent mobility behaviour.
16. Selection into this requires the couple to be intact at two consecutive dates of interview. Taylor et al. (2007) discuss potential biases that may result if this causes nonrandom selection.
17. We have estimated these separately for interregional migrants to examine whether longer distance moves have larger adverse effects on mental well-being. However, the coefficients on the key variables of interest were not statistically significantly different from those presented here.
18. These controls include age, age squared, highest qualification, employment status of respondent and spouse (if partnered), number of children, household income, housing tenure, housing type, region and year. The coefficients on these variables are consistent with previous research so are not presented here but are available from the authors on request.

19. We estimated two models before those presented here. The first included a variable indicating whether or not the individual moved house between $t-1$ and t with the subjective evaluation of the local neighbourhood (postmove) and a full set of control variables. The second model introduced interaction terms between mobility status and subjective evaluation. The estimates in the first model indicate that moving house has little impact on psychological well-being. However, living in a neighbourhood that the respondent likes significantly improves mental well-being. The estimates from the second model show that men and women who moved to neighbourhoods which they did not like from neighbourhoods they did like suffer a statistically significant increase in mental stress.
20. The impact on GHQ scores of moving to a liked neighbourhood is robust to the inclusion of the mobility preferences indicators.

REFERENCES

Argyle, M. (1989) *The psychology of happiness*, Routledge: London.

Bartel, A.P. (1979) The migration decision: what role does job mobility pay?' *American Economic Review*, 69(5): 775–86.

Bielby, W.T. and Bielby, D.D. (1992) I will follow him: family ties, gender-role beliefs, and reluctance to relocate for a better job, *American Journal of Sociology*, 97: 1241–67.

Blair, S.L. and Lichter, D.T (1991) Measuring the division of household labor: gender segregation of housework among American couples, *Journal of Family Issues*, 12: 91–113.

Böheim, R. and Taylor, M.P. (2002) Tied down or room to move? Investigating the relationships between housing tenure, employment status and residential mobility in Britain, *Scottish Journal of Political Economy*, 49 (4): 269–392.

———. (2007) From the dark end of the street to the bright side of the road? The wage returns to migration in Britain, *Labour Economics*, 14: 99–117.

Bolan, M. (1997) The mobility experience and neighbourhood attachment, *Demography*, 34 (2): 225–37.

Boyle, P., Cooke, T.J., Halfacree, K. and Smith, D. (1999) Gender inequality in employment status following family migration in GB and the US: the effect of relative occupational status, *International Journal of Sociology and Social Policy*, 19: 115–50.

———. (2001) A cross-national comparison of the impact of family migration on women's employment status, *Demography*, 38: 201–13.

Brett, J.M. (1980) The effect of job transfer on employees and their families, in C. L. Cooper and R. Payne (eds) *Current concerns in occupational stress*, New York: Wiley.

Buck, N. (2000) Using panel surveys to study migration and residential mobility, in D. Rose (ed.) *Researching social and economic change*, London: Routledge.

Cappon, D. (1971) Mental health in the high rise, *Canadian Journal of Public Health*, 62: 426–31.

Champion, A., Rees, P., Boyle, P. and Stillwell, J. (1998) The determinants of migration flows in England: a review of existing data and evidence, A report prepared for the Department of the Environment, Transport and the Regions, Department of Geography, University of Leeds.

Clark, W.A.V. and Dieleman, F.M. (1996) Households and housing: choice and outcomes in the housing market, Newark: Centre for Urban Policy Research, State University of New Jersey.

Clark, W.A.V. and Onaka, J.L. (1983) Life cycle and housing adjustment as explanations of residential mobility, *Urban Studies*, 28: 47–57.

De Neve, K.M. and Cooper, H. (1999) The happy personality: a meta analysis of 137 personality traits of subjective well-being, *Psychological Bulletin*, 125: 197–229.

Dieleman, F.M. (2001) Modelling residential mobility: a review of recent trends in research, *Journal of Housing and the Built Environment*, 16: 249–65.

Edwards, J.N., Booth, A. and Edwards P.K. (1982) Housing type, stress and family relations, *Social Forces*, 61: 241–57.

Evans, P. and McCormick, B. (1994) The new pattern of regional unemployment: causes and policy significance, *Economic Journal*, 104(424): 633–47.

Fanning, D.M. (1967) Families in flats, *British Medical Journal*, 18: 382–86.

Gillis, A.R. (1977) High rise housing and psychological strain, *Journal of Health and Social Behaviour*, 18: 418–31.

Gordon, I. (1990) Housing and labour market constraints on migration across the North-South divide, in J. Ermisch (ed.) *Housing and the national economy*, London: Avebury-Gower.

Gullotta, T.P. and Donohue, K.C. (1983) Families, relocation, and the corporation, in S.L. White (ed.), *Advances in occupational mental health,* San Francisco: Jossey-Bass.

Kan, K. (1999) Expected and unexpected residential mobility, *Journal of Urban Economics*, 45: 72–96.

Krieg, R.G. and Bohara, A.K. (1999) A simultaneous probit model of earnings, migration, job change, and wage heterogeneity, *The Annals of Regional Science*, 33: 453–67.

Lansing, J.B. and Mueller, E. (1967) *The geographic mobility of labor*, Ann Arbor, MI: Survey Research Center.

Lea, S.E.G., Webley, P. and Levine, R.M. (1993) The economic psychology of consumer debt, *Journal of Economic Psychology*, 14: 85–119.

Lee, B.A., Oropesa, R.S. and Kanan, J.W. (1994) Neighbourhood context and residential mobility, *Demography*, 31: 249–65.

Lee, S. and Roseman, C.C. (1999) Migration determinants and employment consequences of white and black families, 1985–1990, *Economic Geography*, 75: 109–33.

Long, L.H. (1974) Women's labor force participation and the residential mobility of families, *Social Forces*, 52: 342–48.

McCabe, C.J., Thomas, K.J., Brazier, J.E. and Coleman, P. (1996) Measuring the mental health status of a population: a comparison of the GHQ-12 and the SF-36, *British Journal of Psychiatry*, 169: 516–21.

McFadden, D. (1974) Conditional logit analysis of qualitative choice behaviour, in P. Zarembka (ed.) *Frontiers in econometrics*, New York: Academic Press.

Maxwell, N.L. (1988) Economic returns to migration: marital status and gender differences, *Social Science Quarterly*, 69: 108–21.

Meen, G. and Andrew, M. (1998) Modelling regional house prices: a review of the literature, Report prepared for Department of Environment, Transport and the Regions, Centre for Spatial and Real Estate Economics, University of Reading.

Morrison, D.R. and Lichter, D.T. (1988) Family migration and female employment: the problem of underemployment among migrant married women, *Journal of Marriage and the Family*, 50: 161–72.

Mulder, C.H. and Hooimeijer, P. (1999) Residential relocations in the life course, in L.J.G van Wissen and P.A. Dykstra (eds) *Population issues, an interdisciplinary focus*, New York: Kluwer Academic/Plenum Publishers.

Nivalainen, S. (2004) Determinants of family migration: short moves vs long moves, *Journal of Population Economics*, 17(1): 157–75.

O'Sullivan, A., Sedon, T.A., and Sheffin, S.M. (1995) Property taxes, mobility and homeownership, *Journal of Urban Economics*, 37: 107–29.

Oswald, A.J. (1997) *The missing piece of the unemployment puzzle: an inaugural lecture*, mimeo, University of Warwick.

Pevalin, D.J. (2000) Multiple applications of the GHQ-12 in a general population sample: an investigation of long-term retest effects, *Social Psychiatry and Psychiatric Epidemiology*, 35: 508–12.

Quigley, J. (1983) Estimates of a more general model of consumer choice in the housing market, in R. Greisan (ed.) *The urban economy of housing*, Lanham, MD: Lexington Books.

Rossi, P.H. (1955) *Why families move: a study in the social psychology of urban residential mobility*, Glencoe, IL: The Free Press.

Shihadeh, E.S. (1991) The prevalence of husband-centered migration: employment consequences for married mothers, *Journal of Marriage and the Family*, 53: 432–44.

Taylor, M.P. (2007). Tied migration and subsequent employment: evidence from couples in Britain, *Oxford Bulletin of Economics and Statistics*, 69 (6) 795–818.

Taylor, M.P., Pevalin, D.J. and Todd, J. (2007) The psychological costs of unsustainable housing commitments, *Psychological Medicine*, 37: 1027–36.

Turner, R.J. and Marino, F. (1994) Social support and social structure: a descriptive epidemiology, *Journal of Health and Social Behavior*, 35: 193–212.

Van Ommeren, J. and Van Leuvensteijn, M. (2005) New evidence of the effect of transaction costs on residential mobility, *Journal of Regional Science*, 45(4): 681–702.

Van Ommeren, J., Rietveld, P. and Nijkamp, P. (2000) Job mobility, residential mobility and commuting: a theoretical analysis using search theory, *Annals of Regional Science*, 34: 213–32.

Weissman, M.M. and Paykel, E.S. (1972) Moving and depression in women, *Society*, 9: 24–8.

Yankow, J.J. (2003) Migration, job change and wage growth: a new perspective on the pecuniary return to geographic mobility, *Journal of Regional Science*, 43(3): 483–516.

11 Early Labour Market Experience and the Timing of Family Formation

Emilia Del Bono

INTRODUCTION

As argued in the introduction to this volume, the increasing labour market participation of women is a major factor behind changes in the nature of the family and the relationships it comprises. Though much studied, the impact of employment, and in particular of early labour market experience, on marriage and fertility outcomes is of key importance in understanding the process of family formation.

Economic models of fertility behaviour predict that increases in schooling levels and wage rates of women lead to increases in their labour supply and reductions in the demand for children. The existence of an inverse relationship between fertility and participation was theoretically established by Becker (1960), Becker and Lewis (1973) and Willis (1973), and empirically documented by Butz and Ward (1979) for the US and by Mincer (1985) on a cross-country basis.

More recently, however, new research has suggested a weakening link between female employment and fertility due to the availability of formal childcare and the higher income effects arising from highly skilled female workers (Ermisch 1989, Rindfuss and Brewster 1996, Macunovich 1996, Hotz et al. 1997). It has even been shown that the cross-country correlation between fertility and female participation has changed sign since the emergence of high and persistent levels of unemployment in the mid-1980s (Bettio and Villa 1998; Ahn and Mira 2002).[1]

Following these developments, some authors have tried to explain the recent sharp declines in fertility in countries such as Italy or Spain by looking at the role of labour market constraints. These have been measured by unemployment rates (Ahn and Mira 2001; Adsera 2005), the scarce availability of part-time work (Del Boca 2002), and the widespread adoption of fixed-term contracts (de la Rica and Iza 2005). Others have focused more generally on the role of economic uncertainty, especially in relation to the sharp decline in birth rates experienced in many Eastern European countries as well as in the former Soviet republics (Ranjan 1999; Bhaumik and Nugent 2005).

Our analysis is closely related to this literature and in what follows we explore the empirical relationship between early labour market experience—in particular unemployment experience—and fertility. Since our data come from a sample of women born in 1958 and at that time fertility was largely synonymous with marital fertility, we look also at marriage decisions.

As well as studying the direct association between labour market experience and the outcomes of interest we also analyse how early labour market experience affects expectations of future earnings and employment opportunities and how these expectations affect the timing of family formation. Taking expected future employment opportunities as a measure of income uncertainty, we show how the latter strongly influences the process of family formation.

Our results show that unemployment has an unambiguous negative effect on the probability of marriage. As far as fertility is concerned, however, things are less clear-cut and the effect crucially depends on the timing of unemployment spells. As long as unemployment is short-lived and is followed by a period of subsequent employment, the effect on fertility can be positive. If, on the other hand, the woman experiences long periods of unemployment or recurring episodes of joblessness, the negative effect might dominate.

These results are also found in a more structural model, where the effect of labour market experience is mediated via its impact on future economic variables. Here we see that while expected future wages and employment probability are positively related to marriage decisions, these factors have opposite effects on fertility. In particular, we find that a higher expected future wage delays the birth of a child while a higher expected probability to be in employment increases the probability of observing a birth.

The chapter is organized as follows. The next section introduces the data set, the sample we derive from it, our measures of labour market experience and the empirical model. The following section discusses the main results, focusing on a specification in which we look at the direct effect of early labour market experience on fertility and marriage, and then considers the impact of expected future wage and employment opportunities. The last section concludes.

DATA AND MODEL SPECIFICATION

The National Child Development Study

Our sample is derived from the National Child Development Study (NCDS), a longitudinal study which takes as its subjects all those who were born in the week between 3 and 9 March 1958 in Great Britain. Since 1958, several follow-ups have been carried out in order to trace all the 17,000 original members of the NCDS and monitor their physical, educational and social development. The major face-to-face interviews took place when the cohort members were aged 7, 11, 16, 33 and 42, while telephone surveys were carried out at age 23 and most recently in 2004–5, when the cohort members were 46 years old. The data used in this chapter cover the period up to the fifth follow-up, which was conducted in 1991, when the subjects were 33 years old. This is because we are mainly interested in the relationship between early labour market experience and the process of family formation, in particular the event of marriage and the birth of the first child.

In 1991 approximately 11,000 individuals completed the retrospective questionnaire Your Life Since 1974, and 5,717 of these were women. This means that our data cover quite a long time period, precisely the timespan between age 16 and age 33. For this period, we have accurate information on births and marriages and monthly data on the respondent's experience in the labour market as a full- or part-time worker, the period spent in unemployment, as a full-time student or in other out-of-the-labour-force states. Data on individual wages and employment status in 1991 are taken from the main survey, while other background information on the individual and her family of origin is collected from previous waves as well as from the initial perinatal survey in 1958.

Sample Selection

The main disadvantage of using a retrospective questionnaire is the presence of memory-loss problems. The respondent is asked to recollect her memories over a long period of time and the information she provides tends to become less precise the further back in time she goes. As a consequence, we exclude from our sample individuals who have missing values for the earlier years (who did not fill in their employment, fertility or partnership histories completely) or those who provide inconsistent information, declaring, for example, they have been unemployed and working full-time in the same month. This reduces the sample to 5,084 observations

In order to capture the effect of labour market experience on fertility and marriage, we consider only individuals who had their first child or first marriage at least one year after the end of compulsory schooling and exclude the small number who started working before age 16. This reduces the sample size to 4,578 observations. Further observations are lost when checking information on wages and employment status in 1991 (at age 33), and when considering region of residence at age 16. The final sample consists of 2,320 individuals, only about 40 per cent of the original sample.[2]

The Main Variables of Interest and the Empirical Models

When we analyse fertility, the dependent variable is represented by the number of months elapsed between the beginning of the observation window and the birth of the first child. If the woman is still childless by age

33, which is the end of our period, the observation is considered *censored*. Similarly, when we look at marriage, the dependent variable is given by the number of months elapsed between the beginning of the observations period and the date of marriage. Individuals who do not get married before age 33 are considered as *censored observations*. The beginning of the observation window is set to be age 18, as the subjects are considered to be at risk of giving birth or of getting married only after completing full-time education (usually by age 17), and all our independent variables are lagged one year with respect to the event of a live birth or marriage.

When modelling events such as fertility or marriage, we are interested in the timing as well as the occurrence of the event itself. In this case it is common practice to use *duration* or *survival analysis* and describe the data by means of hazard functions. In a discrete time frame, the hazard function represents the probability that an individual will experience the event of interest (in this case the birth of a child or marriage) between time t and $t + 1$, given that the event has never occurred before time t. This is a conditional probability and it is the relevant statistical concept to use when we are interested in the timing of an event or the duration of the interval which precedes it.

About 76.4 per cent of women in our sample have had at least one child by 33, and for this cohort we observe a median age at motherhood slightly above 26 years.[3] Figure 11.1 shows the smoothed hazard function of a first

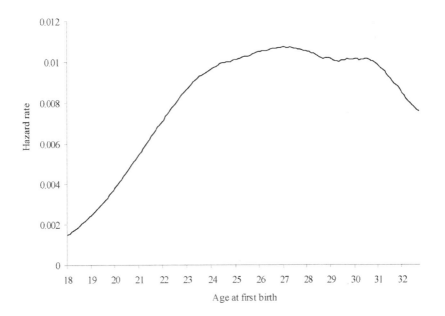

Figure 11.1 Smoothed hazard function—hazard of first child.

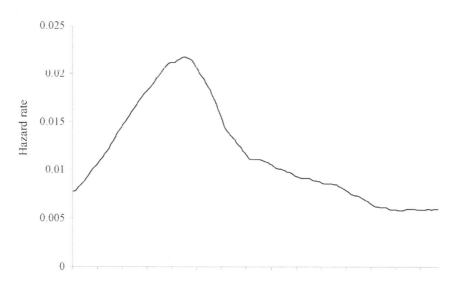

Figure 11.2   Smoothed hazard function—hazard of first marriage.

birth. The data clearly show that the conditional probability of having a first child increases (at a diminishing rate) between ages 18 and 27. After that age, the hazard drops slightly before declining sharply after age 30.

When considering marriage, the basic statistics are quite different. The percentage of women who have been married at least once before turning 33 is 87.5 per cent, while the median age at first marriage is about 22 years. This reflects the fact that for this cohort of women the event of marriage very frequently preceded the birth of the first child. Indeed, for the women in our NCDS sample the percentage of first births taking place within the first marriage is 86.9 per cent, while only 9.5 per cent of births occur to never-married women.[4] Accordingly, the shape of the hazard of first marriages is very different from the shape of the hazard for first births. Figure 11.2 shows that the conditional probability of getting married increases quite early on, in particular between ages 18 and 22, and then declines sharply to a much lower value for the rest of the observation period.

Our main explanatory variable is the individual labour market experience, which is coded as a monthly variable and divided into the following five different categories: full-time employment, part-time employment, unemployment (including government training), full-time education, and other out-of-the-labour-force states. There are different ways in which this information can be used. We first simply consider the individual labour market status in the current month; then we take the percentage of time the individual spent in the relevant labour market state from the beginning of the observation period to time t; finally, we split early labour market experience over time, considering the percentage of the period the individual spent in the relevant state the previous year, two years before, three years before, and so on. In all our specifications labour market experience variables are lagged one year with respect to the event of interest. In other words, we look at the effect of labour market experience up to one year before the event occurs in order to account for the fact that fertility and marriage decisions are taken some time before the event is actually observed.

In modelling the relationship between labour market experience and family formation we also consider some characteristics of the individual and of her family of origin which could explain some of the variation in the data. These background variables refer to the period up to age 16, so that they are predetermined with respect to the events of interest. In particular, we include the results of a mathematical test performed at age 11 and the type of secondary school attended in order to proxy for the level of education of the subject. Family background is captured by a variable reporting the father's social class and a variable indicating whether the family had experienced unemployment at the time the cohort member was aged 16. Differences across individuals in sexual maturity are captured by the age of menarche, while attitudes towards motherhood are proxied by the age of the mother (of the cohort member) at the birth of her first child.

An important variable for our purposes is information on local labour market conditions. This is obtained using regional unemployment rates computed on the basis of the claimant counts published by the Office of National Statistics (see www.nomisweb.co.uk). This variable varies over time on a monthly basis and is matched to each individual using the region of residence of the subject at age 16. Arguably, we could have used information on geographic residence at age 23 or at age 33, but since geographic mobility could be a response to early labour market outcomes we preferred to consider region of residence at an earlier point in time and take it as predetermined (i.e. exogenous).

Our aim is to analyse the effect of labour market status on marriage and fertility, but we want to pay particular attention to their relative timing. In order to do so, we conduct our analysis using survival or duration models and use the hazard function, a concept which is akin to the conditional probability of observing a certain event, in order to specify the relationship between the independent variables and the outcomes of interest.[5]

The first model we estimate is based on a proportional hazard specification. This means that the covariates enter the hazard multiplicatively, that is, the role is simply to shift up or down the baseline hazard, which represents the common pattern of durations in the data. In our specific case the model we estimate is given by the following expression:

$$\theta(t, X_t) = \theta_0(t)\exp(\beta'E_t + \gamma U_t + \delta Z) \qquad (11.1)$$

where $\theta(t, X_t)$ is the hazard of a birth or of marriage, t represents the number of months elapsed, and X_t is the vector of explanatory variables, which is divided into: a vector of time-varying variables representing experience in the labour market, E_t, a time-varying variable representing the regional unemployment rate, U_t, and a vector of time-invariant characteristics of the individual and her family, Z. The baseline hazard, here indicated by $\theta_0(t)$, is assumed to be the same for all individuals in the sample, and its functional form can be left free to vary. All the explanatory variables enter the model through an exponential function, although any other positive function could have been used instead.

Our second specification is what we refer to as our structural model. Here the aim is to take account of the effect of labour market experience on marriage and fertility indirectly through its impact on expected employment and wages. In order to do so, we divide the estimation process into two steps. In the first step we estimate the effect of labour market experience on the individual's wage rate and on the probability of being employed conditional on participating in the labour market at age 33. In the second step we use the predicted wages and the predicted employment probabilities at age 33 as covariates in the fertility and marriage hazard functions.

One possible concern is that wages and employment at age 33 are likely to be endogenous with respect to fertility and marriage events which occur in the period before. Assuming that labour market experience is exogenous with respect to *future* realizations of fertility and marriage, and using it in order to predict wages and employment at age 33, we can mitigate this problem and interpret the coefficients we obtain from the structural model as the effect of future expectations of earnings and employment opportunities on fertility and marriage. In particular, we are interested here in the effect of employment opportunities, as this may be seen as a measure of income uncertainty.[6]

Our structural model is specified as follows:

$$\theta(t, X_t) = \theta_0(t)\exp(p\hat{W}_{33,t} + \pi\hat{J}_{33,t} + \gamma U_t + \delta Z) \tag{11.2}$$

where $\hat{W}_{33,t}$ is the predicted wage at 33, obtained using information up to time t, and $\hat{J}_{33,t}$ is the predicted probability of having a job (conditional on being in the labour force) at 33, obtained using information up to time t. As the period of time over which we measure fertility and marriage goes from 18 to 33 (more precisely 32, as we stop shortly before the individual turns 33), and the vector of variables representing past labour force experience varies over this interval on a monthly basis, $\hat{W}_{33,t}$ and $\hat{J}_{33,t}$ vary over time.

Estimation of equations 11.1 and 11.2 is performed using a discrete time hazard framework. For both births and marriages the baseline hazard is specified as a polynomial of order four. Estimation of the expected future wages and job opportunities is achieved using standard models and including in the regressions all the covariates which appear on the right-hand side of equation 11.1. With the exception of early labour market experience, which is excluded to ensure identification of the model, all the other variables also appear in equation 11.2.

RESULTS

The Role of Labour Market Experience

In order to investigate the impact of early labour market experience on the process of family formation, we look at three different specifications. As shown in Table 11.1, we first consider simply the effect of current labour market status; then we take the whole history up to time *t* and calculate the percentage of time the individual spends in each labour market state; finally, we use a more flexible specification and look at the effect of labour market experience in different years preceding the event.[7] It is important to keep in mind that every covariate shown is lagged 12 months with respect to the actual event. So, when we talk about the current labour market state we are referring to the labour market status of the individual 12 months before the birth of the child or the event of marriage. Similarly, when we talk about cumulative experience, we consider only the experience cumulated up to 12 months before the event of interest.

Let us start by looking at the process leading to the birth of the first child. Column 1 of Table 11.1 shows that being in full-time employment (as opposed to being out of the labour force, which is the omitted category) does not significantly decrease the probability of having a child, and the same result holds with respect to unemployment. By contrast, being in part-time employment seems to be positively correlated with a first birth while being in full-time education has a significant delaying effect. Things change quite dramatically, however, when we consider the whole labour market experience of the individual up to time *t*. In this case, the results show that a higher percentage of time spent in full-time employment, part-time employment and unemployment are all positively related to the hazard of a birth, while time spent in full-time education continues to show a negative coefficient. It therefore seems that having accumulated any experience in the labour market, no matter what type, has a positive effect on fertility.

Would these results change if we adopted a more flexible representation of early labour market experience? After all, it is possible that having worked for a long time in a full-time position leads to career stability and higher income, but that when a birth is planned a woman may in fact prefer to switch to a part-time job, for example. In other words, is it possible to go beyond a simple model in which only current status matters (Model 1) and consider the whole past history in the labour market without giving the same weight to past and more recent events (Model 2)?

Model 3 addresses these questions adopting a more flexible representation of the individual past history in the labour market, which explains the different results obtained in Models 1 and 2. Here we consider the percentage of time the individual spent in the relevant state 1 year before time *t*, 2 years before time *t*, and so on up to 4 years.[8] As we can see, there are significant differences to highlight. While past experience in full-time employment shows a positive coefficient, a higher percentage of time recently spent in a full-time job is negatively correlated with the hazard of a birth. Similarly, we see that while recent experiences of unemployment have a strong negative impact on the hazard of a birth, past spells of joblessness have the opposite effect. Interestingly, once timing is taken into account, part-time experience is positively but not significantly correlated with fertility. Staying on in full-time education continues to show only a negative coefficient, as we might expect in this case.

The picture we observe in Model 3 is considerably richer as it highlights that the timing of early labour market experience is important in analysing the relationship between labour market events and fertility events. In order to give an idea of this, let us consider the effect of a spell of unemployment. In Model 1 this would not be captured at all unless the spell affects the current status (also, there would be no difference between a one-month spell and a six-month spell, for example), and in this case it would decrease the hazard of a birth. By contrast, in Model 2, a spell of unemployment would increase the hazard of a birth, but the effect would be the same whether the spell was recent or far away in the past. Model 3 tells us that if the spell of unemployment occurred in the last year, the hazard of a birth would be lower, but after three years the same spell would result in a higher conditional probability of having a first child.[9]

Table 11.1 also shows the effect of regional male unemployment rates, the only other time-varying covariate in the model. This is seen to have a significantly negative coefficient in Model 1 and Model 2 and a negative, but slightly less precisely estimated coefficient, in Model 3. Overall, it is possible to calculate that a one standard deviation increase in the unemployment rate would decrease the hazard of a birth by approximately 12.2 per cent.

All the other covariates exhibit coefficient in line with what we would expect from standard models of fertility, where proxies of human capital and earnings usually exhibit negative effects on fertility. In particular, a better performance in the mathematics test at age 11 reduces the hazard of a birth significantly, while the type of secondary school attended shows no significant impact. The lower is the social class of the father, the higher is the hazard, and so is the case when the woman experienced unemployment in her family, although these effects are not statistically significant. The age at menarche does not seem to correlate with fertility, while the age at which the mother of the cohort member had her first child is negatively related to the hazard of a birth.

Would we get different results if we accounted for the presence of unobserved heterogeneity? Model 4 addresses this questions and estimates our preferred specification, the one shown in Model 3, using a model which incorporates an additive random component which is assumed to follow a gamma distribution.[10] As we can see, the estimated coefficients change slightly—most notably we see a stronger effect of past part-time

Table 11.1   Early Labour Market Experience and the Hazard of the First Birth

	Model 1	Model 2	Model 3	Model 4
	Labour force state in period t	Total percentage of time spent up to period t	Year by year percentage of time spent up to period t	Year by year percentage of time spent up to period t & gamma distr. unobs. het
FT employment	−0.085	0.986**		
	(0.088)	(0.109)		
% time in FT emp. 1 year ago			−0.662**	−0.654**
			(0.170)	(0.172)
% time in FT emp. 2 years ago			0.522*	0.453*
			(0.2261)	(0.212)
% time in FT emp. 3 years ago			0.493*	0.467*
			(0.200)	(0.193)
% time in FT emp. 4 years ago			0.441**	0.509**
			(0.133)	(0.137)
PT employment	0.368**	1.441**		
	(0.127)	(0.194)		
% time in PT emp. 1 year ago			−0.006	0.001
			(0.251)	(0.272)
% time in PT emp. 2 years ago			0.250	0.243
			(0.347)	(0.364)
% time in PT emp. 3 years ago			0.639	0.685
			(0.330)	(0.366)
% time in PT emp. 4 years ago			0.424	0.702*
			(0.277)	(0.300)
Unemployment	−0.290	1.158**		
	(0.178)	(0.430)		
% time in unemp. 1 year ago			−0.725*	−0.711*
			(0.298)	(0.305)
% time in unemp. 2 years ago			0.438	0.413
			(0.345)	(0.334)
% time in unemp. 3 years ago			0.756*	0.711*
			(0.330)	(0.327)

(continued)

Table 11.1 (continued)

	Model 1	Model 2	Model 3	Model 4
	Labour force state in period t	Total percentage of time spent up to period t	Year by year percentage of time spent up to period t	Year by year percentage of time spent up to period t & gamma distr. unobs. het
% time in unemp. 4 years ago			0.083	0.254
			(0.298)	(0.331)
FT education	−2.101**	−1.426**		
	(0.343)	(0.342)		
% time in FT edu. 1 year ago			−1.284**	−1.084**
			(0.373)	(0.379)
% time in FT edu. 2 years ago			−0.713**	−0.616*
			(0.256)	(0.253)
% time in FT edu. 3 years ago			−0.075	−0.040
			(0.180)	(0.185)
% time in FT edu. 4 years ago			0.064	0.098
			(0.147)	(0.149)
Regional male unemployment	−0.040*	−0.039*	−0.035	−0.012
	(0.018)	(0.018)	(0.019)	(0.021)

Notes: Hazard model for first birth. Coefficients shown are estimated using a discrete time proportional hazard model where the baseline hazard is a quartic function of time. Heteroskedasticity robust standard errors shown. Other regressors include: results of maths test at age 11, type of secondary school attended, father social class at 16, experience of unemployment in the family by age 16, age at menarche, age of the mother at the birth of the first child and regional dummies. The number of monthly observations is 247,283 and the number of individuals is 2,320. Symbols: *significant at 5%; **significant at 1%.

employment experience and a reduction of the coefficient of local unemployment rates—but none of the qualitative findings is dramatically altered.[11]

Table 11.2 presents the same analysis but considers the timing of first marriage (in months) as the dependent variable. Here the difference across the various specifications of early labour market experience is less noticeable, and this implies that the timing of labour market events in this case matters less. For example, we see that having more experience in full-time employment leads to a higher conditional probability of marriage in all models and for all the different year-lags considered under Model 3. Similarly, we see generally positive and significant coefficients when looking at part-time employment, although recent part-time experience seems to matter most. As we would probably expect, unemployment exhibits a negative and very

Table 11.2 Early Labour Market Experience and the Hazard of the First Marriage

	Model 1	Model 2	Model 3	Model 4
				Year by year percentage of time spent up to period t & gamma distr. unobs. het
		Total percentage of time spent up to period t	*Year by year percentage of time spent up to period t*	
	Labour force state in period t			
FT employment	0.759**	0.984**		
	(0.087)	(0.085)		
% time in FT emp. 1 year ago			0.539**	0.554**
			(0.134)	(0.134)
% time in FT emp. 2 years ago			0.166	0.201
			(0.152)	(0.144)
% time in FT emp. 3 years ago			0.383*	0.435**
			(0.149)	(0.138)
% time in FT emp. 4 years ago			0.336**	0.551**
			(0.121)	(0.128)
PT employment	0.660**	0.931**		
	(0.150)	(0.224)		
% time in PT emp. 1 year ago			0.615*	0.568*
			(0.248)	(0.271)
% time in PT emp. 2 years ago			0.398	0.447
			(0.326)	(0.356)
% time in PT emp. 3 years ago			0.267	0.355
			(0.386)	(0.390)
% time in PT emp. 4 years ago			−0.329	−0.264
			(0.389)	(0.389)
Unemployment	0.163	−1.146*		
	(0.193)	(0.553)		
% time in unemp. 1 year ago			−0.291	−0.304
			(0.357)	(0.345)
% time in unemp. 2 years ago			−0.245	−0.296
			(0.358)	(0.369)
% time in unemp. 3 years ago			−0.969*	−1.081*
			(0.439)	(0.430)

(continued)

Table 11.2 (continued)

	Model 1	Model 2	Model 3	Model 4
				Year by year percentage of time
		Total	*Year by year*	*spent up to*
	Labour	*percentage of*	*percentage of*	*period t &*
	force state	*time spent up*	*time spent up*	*gamma distr.*
	in period t	*to period t*	*to period t*	*unobs. het*
% time in unemp. 4 years ago			0.636	0.577
			(0.348)	(0.358)
FT education	−0.352**	−0.485**		
	(0.133)	(0.118)		
% time in FT edu. 1 year ago			−0.428**	−0.431**
			(0.145)	(0.149)
% time in FT edu. 2 years ago			−0.014	−0.004
			(0.118)	(0.119)
% time in FT edu. 3 years ago			0.139	0.145
			(0.110)	(0.110)
% time in FT edu. 4 years ago			0.391**	0.452**
			(0.106)	(0.111)
Regional male unemployment	−0.058**	−0.052**	−0.055**	−0.056**
	(0.018)	(0.018)	(0.018)	(0.020)

Notes: Hazard model for first marriage. Coefficients shown are estimated using a discrete time proportional hazard model where the baseline hazard is a quartic function of time. Heteroskedasticity robust standard errors shown. Other regressors include: results of maths test at age 11, type of secondary school attended, father social class at 16, experience of unemployment in the family by age 16, age at menarche, age of the mother at the birth of the first child and regional dummies. The number of monthly observations is 154,326 and the number of individuals is 2,320. Symbols: *significant at 5%; **significant at 1%.

significant coefficient in Model 2 and this is generally true also of Model 3. If anything, in the latter specification a less recent experience of unemployment seems to matter most. Interestingly, and in contrast to what we saw in the previous case, there is evidence of timing effects when considering full-time education. Here, Model 3 indicates that the conditional probability of getting married is highest around four years after leaving school.

As for the remaining variables, we see that local area unemployment rates have a strong and significant negative effect on the hazard of marriage. Here the coefficient is higher (in absolute terms) than that we observed when considering fertility, indicating an even stronger discouragement effect of local labour market conditions. In this case a one standard deviation increase in unemployment translates into a 17.3 per cent lower conditional probability of getting married. None of the other covariates exhibits a statistically significant coefficient in this case. The only exception is represented by the father social class of the woman, where a lower social class is associated with a higher marriage hazard. As in our analysis of fertility, the contribution of unobserved heterogeneity is marginal.[12]

Future Wages and Employment Opportunities

The preceding models explain how early labour market experience directly effects fertility and marriage outcomes. However, it is plausible to think that the accumulation of human capital through full- and part-time employment or unemployment has its main direct effect on future wages and employability, that is, on future economic outcomes, and that only through these channels it affects fertility and marriage decisions.

The second specification of the hazard model for fertility and marriage therefore considers how early labour market experience affects future wages and job opportunities and if these variables then show a significant relationship with the family formation process. In other words, having analysed the direct relationship between labour market experience and fertility or marriage decisions, we now ask whether this relationship runs through the impact of labour market experience on future wages and employment.

The first step is to obtain predictions of future wages and employment opportunities using the set of variables representing early labour market experience. Since the NCDS collects information on wages only at the time of the main follow-up interview, we had no choice but to consider only the individual wage at age 33 as our measure of future wages. For consistency reasons we took the individual employment status at age 33 as the measure of future employment opportunities. So, the 'future' is represented by a fixed point in time, which slightly follows the last possible observed birth or marriage event. As labour market experience changes through time, assuming different values from the beginning of the observation period to the last available month, we can regress the wage (or employment) at age 33 on a different vector of regressors and obtain time-varying measures of expected future wages and employment opportunities at age 33. This procedure is meant to capture the idea that expectations of future economic opportunities change over time and are constantly updated as more information on an individual labour market history is revealed.

Regressing the wage at age 33 and the employment status at age 33 (conditional on participation to the labour force) on a time-varying vector of variables representing individual labour market experience means that we have a total of 189 cross-sectional equations for each individual (one for each observed month from January 1974 to January 1991). First we estimate the coefficients of interest by pooling together these equations. Then we calculate the predicted values of wages and employment probabilities

Table 11.3 Future Wages and Employment Opportunities

	Expected future wage	*Expected future employment (conditional on participation)*
% time in FT emp. 1 year ago	0.140**	−0.043
	(0.046)	(0.090)
% time in FT emp. 2 years ago	0.015**	0.023
	(0.003)	(0.019)
% time in FT emp. 3 years ago	0.022**	−0.045
	(0.006)	(0.040)
% time in FT emp. 4 years ago	0.029*	0.075
	(0.013)	(0.068)
% time in PT emp. 1 year ago	0.057	0.228
	(0.069)	(0.118)
% time in PT emp. 2 years ago	0.014*	0.043
	(0.007)	(0.046)
% time in PT emp. 3 years ago	0.017	0.001
	(0.014)	(0.063)
% time in PT emp. 4 years ago	0.024	−0.116
	(0.019)	(0.084)
% time in unemp. 1 year ago	−0.056*	−0.670**
	(0.027)	(0.133)
% time in unemp. 2 years ago	−0.035	−0.243**
	(0.019)	(0.054)
% time in unemp. 3 years ago	−0.047*	−0.328**
	(0.023)	(0.069)
% time in unemp. 4 years ago	−0.063*	−0.416**
	(0.031)	(0.130)
% time in FT edu. 1 year ago	0.200**	0.003
	(0.028)	(0.153)
% time in FT edu. 2 years ago	0.099**	0.001
	(0.019)	(0.046)
% time in FT edu. 3 years ago	0.016**	−0.024
	(0.004)	(0.025)
% time in FT edu. 4 years ago	0.023**	−0.039
	(0.010)	(0.066)

(continued)

Table 11.3 *(continued)*

	Expected future wage	Expected future employment (conditional on participation)
Regional male unemployment	0.003	−0.018
	(0.002)	(0.010)
Lambda	0.081	
	(0.144)	

Notes: The wage equation is estimated via maximum likelihood using a Heckman selection model, where the dependent variable is the female hourly wage in 1991. Other regressors include: results of maths test at age 11, type of secondary school attended, father social class at 16, experience of unemployment in the family by age 16, age at menarche, age of the mother at the birth of the first child. The selection equation (not shown) additionally includes information on the mother's labour force status at the time the cohort member was 5 years old. The lambda is the Heckman's lambda. The employment equation is estimated via maximum likelihood using a probit model where the dependent variable is represented by a dummy with value 1 if the individual is employed in 1991 where only individuals participating in the labour force in 1991 are considered. The numbers shown represent the estimated coefficients. All standard errors are clustered at the individual level. The number of monthly observations is 410,640 for the wage equation and 280,014 for the employment (conditional on participation) equation. Symbols: *significant at 5%; **significant at 1%.

using these coefficients and thus obtain time-varying measures of future wages and employment opportunities.

Since the results in Tables 11.1 and 11.2 reveal the importance of timing effects, we base our specification of the wage and employment equations on the vector of labour force experience variables shown in Model 3, which distinguishes between recent and earlier labour market history. We also include in the model the regional unemployment rate as an additional time-varying covariate, and all the other control variables seen in the reduced form hazard models.[13]

What we see in Table 11.3 is largely consistent with existing analysis of human capital. In particular, with respect to the wage equation the results show that time spent in full-time employment and full-time education contribute to higher wage rates, while time spent in part-time employment is only marginally significant. Unemployment has a negative and significant effect on wages, even after several years. Local unemployment rates, by contrast, seem not to matter much in this context. The coefficients on the mathematical test at age 11 show a positive effect of the latter on wages, and so does grammar school attendance. The expected wage rate is lower the lower the father's social class and in families with experience of unemployment, and it increases with the age of the mother (of the cohort member) at the birth of her first child. The coefficient for the Heckman's lambda indicates that the error terms of the wage and selection equations are positively correlated, although not significantly so.

By contrast, not much is significant in the probit model which captures the probability of being employed while participating to the labour market. Apart from the effect of individual unemployment experience, which is very significant, most of the other regressors show very weak or no correlation with the dependent variable. Even local unemployment rates appear to have a very weak association with our measure of future employment opportunities.

The Structural Model

The next step is to consider the impact of future wages and employment opportunities directly on the fertility and marriage hazards. Table 11.4 presents results for both fertility (panel A) and marriage (panel B). We first consider a model which only includes predicted future wages; then we look at a specification which considers only the predicted future probability of being employed; finally, we introduce both measures of future economic opportunities to gauge their relative importance. In all cases we also look at the effect of local labour market opportunities, as measured by the regional unemployment rates.

As we see in column 1 of Table 11.4, panel A, higher expected wages are negatively but not significantly related to the hazard of a birth. When we consider future employment opportunities instead, the effect has the opposite sign and the coefficient appears to be significant at the 5 per cent level of significance.[14] When both indicators are introduced, we obtain significant and somewhat larger coefficients on both variables. This is not surprising as the two measures of future economic opportunities are identified by the same set of variables and affect fertility in different directions. Once both in the model, the effects tend to reinforce each other. Interestingly, local unemployment rates have a negative but generally not statistically significant effect on fertility, especially once we include our measure for expected future employment opportunities.

Panel B of Table 11.4 presents the same set of results when the dependent variable is the time to first marriage. Here the effect of expected future wages is opposite to what we saw in the fertility hazard and the coefficient is strongly significant even in Model 1. In Model 2 we look at the effect of employment opportunities and we see that these have a positive and very strong association with marriage. When considering both indicators, the coefficients are slightly reduced as the two effects now go in the same direction, but both coefficients remain statistically significant at the conventional level.

Although we need to be careful in interpreting these results, as we are relying on the strong assumption that past labour force experience is exogenous, the comparison between the fertility and the marriage hazard reveals the different role that economic variables play in the process of

Table 11.4 The Impact of Economic Opportunities on the Hazard of a First Birth and of a First Marriage

Panel A: first birth	Model 1	Model 2	Model 3
Expected future wage	−0.654		−1.108**
	(0.355)		(0.383)
Expected future employment		2.219*	3.299**
		(1.118)	(1.217)
Regional male unemployment	−0.038*	−0.035	−0.031
	(0.018)	(0.018)	(0.018)
Panel B: first marriage			
Expected future wage	0.590*		0.420
	(0.288)		(0.294)
Expected future employment		4.877**	4.472*
		(1.765)	(1.781)
Regional male unemployment	−0.053**	−0.045*	−0.046*
	(0.018)	(0.018)	(0.018)

Notes: Hazard model for first birth in Panel A and for first marriage in Panel B. Coefficients shown are estimated using a discrete time proportional hazard model where the baseline hazard is a quartic function of time. Heteroskedasticity robust standard errors shown. Other regressors include: results of maths test at age 11, type of secondary school attended, father social class at 16, experience of unemployment in the family by age 16, age at menarche, age of the mother at the birth of the first child and regional dummies. For the hazard of a first birth the number of monthly observations is 247,283 and the number of individuals is 2,320. For the hazard of a first marriage the number of monthly observations is 154,326 and the number of individuals is 2,320. Symbols: *significant at 5%; **significant at 1%.

family formation. For instance, we see that a more positive labour market experience—whether represented by more full-time experience, less unemployment, or higher future wages and economic opportunities—has an unequivocal positive association with the conditional probability of marriage. This finding is consistent with much of the existing literature on marriage, as it emphasizes the importance of income in the couple's decision to get married and the positive association between socioeconomic status and marital status.

Fertility decisions are different from this point of view, however. Here, Table 11.4 shows that a more positive labour market experience has two different effects on the hazard of a birth. On the one hand, higher future wage opportunities exert a negative effect due to a higher opportunity cost of the woman's time. On the other hand, we see that higher employment opportunities encourage the decision to have a birth.

It is clear that although the opportunity-cost channel is important, income considerations matter in particular when capturing uncertainty about future employment. This could be because, unlike marriage, fertility is a form of irreversible investment, which once undertaken requires a significant amount of expenditure over a long period of time (Ranjan 1999).

DISCUSSION

In this chapter we analyse the role of labour market experience, and in particular the role of individual unemployment, in the process of family formation. We first look at the direct effect of labour market history on the decision to have a birth or to get married. Our results indicate that the timing of labour market events matters in explaining fertility decisions while it is less relevant when looking at the outcome of marriage. In particular, we see that while a recent experience of unemployment delays fertility, some years later the effect is reversed. This implies that as long as the period of joblessness is short and remains an isolated episode, postponement of fertility is small.

We also look at the impact of future expectations of wages and employment opportunities on the conditional probability of a birth and marriage. Here the aim is to build a more structural model, whereby past labour market history affects the process of family formation by changing long-term expectations of economic opportunities. We saw that while cost-opportunity considerations emerge when looking at the hazard of fertility, an increase in the uncertainty related to the future income stream (here represented by our measure of future employment opportunities) is positively related to the conditional probability of having a child.

Do these results help explain the sharp decrease in fertility experienced by countries such as Italy, Spain or the former Soviet bloc? This is still a difficult question to answer. Our data come from a sample of British women who experienced relatively short and isolated spells of employment during the observed period. For this reason, any quantitative predictions from this model would not be easily adapted to the experience of women in countries where unemployment is much higher and long lasting. Notwithstanding this limitation, we think that the results presented in this chapter contribute to the previous literature in that they clearly show the importance of individual labour market experience, and in particular the significant effect of spells of joblessness on the process of family formation. We also show that higher income uncertainty, here captured by future expected employment opportunities, is a significant economic variable in a model of fertility and marriage.

NOTES

1. See, however, Kögel (2004) for evidence that the negative time-series association between fertility and female labour force participation rates weakened but *did not* change its sign.

2. The issue of item nonresponse on key economic variables such as wages is often quite serious and in most cases the only approach available is simply to drop observations with missing values (Dearden 1998). Although this could be seen as a significant source of bias because individuals from lower socioeconomic backgrounds are underrepresented in the final sample, some research in this area has shown that incomplete information is in general not a major problem in the analysis of economic attainment of NCDS cohort members by age 33 (Harper and Haq 1997).

3. It is rather difficult to compare our data to official statistical sources, as we have information on a single cohort of women. A limited number of statistics by cohort is available in the ONS series Birth Statistics: Births and Patterns of Family Building England and Wales (FM1), and this indicates that about 20% of women born in 1960 were still childless by age 35 (see year 2000).

4. The remaining 3.7% births are to women who have been married more than once.

5. See Lancaster (1990).

6. This interpretation could be supported by a model in which future income is given by a variable y, which is equal to the wage w which is earned with probability p (the probability of being employed conditional on participating to the labour market), and to unemployment benefits b with probability (1-p). If we assume that benefits are nonstochastic, the expected value of this mixture distribution is $E[y] = pE[w] + (1-p)b$, and its variance is $Var(y) = pVar(w) + p(1-p)[E(w)-b]^2$. Since the variance is maximised for p approximately equal to 1/2, for values of p greater than 1/2 a decrease in the probability of employment (conditional on participation) increases the variance of the distribution of future income.

7. The latter specification basically allows us to take into account more precisely the timing of labour market events (Light and Ureta 1995).

8. The cutoff of 4 years was chosen by means of likelihood ratio tests starting with a specification going back 10 years.

9. Compared to a woman who is always employed in the past 4 years, the predicted hazard of a birth would be 6% lower if the woman is unemployed in the last year only, 30% higher if the woman is unemployed 3 years before time *t* but continuously employed afterwards, and 21% lower if the woman is always unemployed in the past 4 years.

10. For details, see Jenkin's lecture notes (http://www.iser.essex.ac.uk/teaching/degree/stephenj/ec968).

11. The likelihood ratio test of the gamma variance being equal to zero shows a chi-squared statistics of 21.262 (p—value = 0.000).

12. Despite the fact that a likelihood ratio test rejects the null hypothesis of a zero variance of the gamma distributed random component (chi-squared statistics of 16.0043, p—value = 0.0000) the estimated coefficients are only slightly affected and never change sign or level of significance.

13. We do not include dummies for region here.

14. The standard errors presented here do not take into account the fact that expected future wages and employment probabilities are generated regressors.

REFERENCES

Adsera, A. (2005) Vanishing children: from high unemployment to low fertility in developed countries, *American Economic Review* (papers and proceedings), 95: 189–93.

Ahn, N. and Mira, P. (2001) Job bust, baby bust?: evidence from Spanish data, *Journal of Population Economics*, 14: 505–21.

———. (2002) A note on the changing relationship between fertility and female employment rates in developed countries, *Journal of Population Economics*, 15: 667–82.

Becker, G. (1960) An economic analysis of fertility, in *Demographic and Economic Change in Developing Countries*, A conference of the Universities-National Bureau Committee for Economic Research (National Bureau of Economic Research, Special Conference Series, 11), Princeton, NJ: Princeton University Press.

Becker, G. and Lewis, H. (1973) On the interaction between quantity and quality of children, *Journal of Political Economy*, 81: S279–S288.

Bettio, F. and Villa, P. (1998) A Mediterranean perspective on the break-down of the relationship between female participation and fertility, *Cambridge Journal of Economics*, 22: 137–71.

Bhaumik, S. K. and Nugent, J. B. (2005) *Does economic uncertainty affect the decision to bear children? Evidence from East and West Germany*, Discussion Paper IZA, Paper 1746, Bonn: Institute for the Study of Labour (IZA).

Butz, W. and Ward, M. (1979) The emergence of countercyclical US fertility, *American Economic Review*, 69: 318–28.

Dearden, L. (1998) *Ability, families, education and earnings in Britain*, Working Paper Institute for Fiscal Studies, Paper 98/14, London: Institute for Fiscal Studies.

de la Rica, S. and Iza, A. (2005) Career planning in Spain: Do fixed-term contracts delay marriage and parenthood?, *Review of the Economics of the Household*, 3: 49–73.

Del Boca, D. (2002) The effect of child care and part-time opportunities on participation and fertility decisions in Italy, *Journal of Population Economics*, 15: 549–73.

Ermisch, J.F. (1989) Purchased child care, optimal family size and mother's employment: theory and econometric analysis, *Journal of Population Economics*, 2: 79–102.

Harper, B. and Haq, M. (1997) Occupational attainment of men in Britain, *Oxford Economic Papers*, 49: 638–50.

Hotz, V., Klerman, J. and Willis, R. (1997) The economics of fertility in developed countries, in M. Rosenzweig and O. Stark (eds) *Handbook of Population and Family Economics*, Amsterdam: Elsevier.

Kögel, T. (2004) Did the association between fertility and female employment within OECD countries really change its sign?, *Journal of Population Economics*, 17: 45–65.

Lancaster, T. (1990) *The econometric analysis of transition data*, Cambridge: Cambridge University Press.

Light, A. and Ureta, M. (1995) Early-career experience and gender wage differentials, *Journal of Labour Economics*, 13: 121–54.

Macunovich, D. J. (1996) Relative income and price of time: exploring their effects on US fertility and female labour participation, *Population and Development Review* (Suppl.), 22: 223–57.

Mincer, J. (1985) Intercountry comparisons of labour force trends and of related development: an overview, *Journal of Labour Economics*, 3: S1–S30.

Ranjan, P. (1999) Fertility behaviour under income uncertainty, *European Journal of Population*, 15: 25–43.

Rindfuss, R.J. and Brewster, K.L. (1996) Childrearing and fertility, *Population and Development Review* (Suppl.), 22: 258–89.

Willis, J. (1973) A new approach to the economic theory of fertility behaviour, *Journal of Political Economy*, 81: S14–S64.

12 Unemployment and Partnership Dissolution

Morten Blekesaune

The partners of relationships have expectations not only about affection and emotional support, but also about resources available in the relationship. What happens when these expectations come under strain? In this chapter we look at the effects of unemployment within partnerships. Does unemployment increase the risk of partnership dissolution?

This issue is investigated by following 3,586 partnerships in up to 15 waves of the British Household Panel Survey (BHPS). A partnership can be a marriage or cohabitation, or a cohabitation leading to a marriage. The probability of dissolving a partnership is investigated using discrete time hazard regression models. The analysis also investigates which types of partnerships are at risk of termination following unemployment of the man or the woman, and if unemployment effects are mediated by financial satisfaction and mental distress. Heterogeneity between unemployed and nonunemployed samples is also investigated using education level and random component models.

Previous research has shown that people hit by unemployment are at risk to suffer a number of other social problems as well, including partnership dissolution. Some studies have investigated a variety of social consequences of unemployment, particularly in periods of high unemployment such as the Great Depression of the 1930s (e.g. Jahoda, Lazarsfeld and Zeizel 1933; Liker and Elder 1983), the UK of the 1980s (e.g. Gallie, March and Vogler 1994) and transitional countries of the 1990s (e.g. Adler 1997; Smith 2000). Gallie, Gershuny and Vogler (1994) find that family conflicts are reported to be the most negative consequence of unemployment in the UK, even more so than economic problems and loss of self-respect. There is also a more specialised literature investigating the effects of unemployment on subsequent marital dissolution using longitudinal data for individuals or families (e.g. Jensen and Smith 1990; Hansen 2005). This chapter reviews this more specialised literature for arguments and findings before presenting an empirical analysis of 15 waves of the British Household Panel Survey (BHPS) spanning from 1991 to 2005.

RELATIONSHIPS BETWEEN UNEMPLOYMENT
AND PARTNERSHIP DISSOLUTION

Even if unemployed people are at enhanced risk of terminating their marital partnerships, it is not clear why these events coincide when comparing across people or when following them over time. One explanation could be that it is unemployment as such which leads to the dissolution of partnerships. The reason could be that low and uncertain income makes individuals less attractive as marital partners, or provides them with less influence in the partnership (Blood and Wolfe 1960), which in either case would put stress on a partnership. A somewhat associated reason is that unemployment leads to financial strain, which reduces the satisfaction derived from a partnership (Vinokur, Price and Caplan 1996). A third reason could be that unemployment leads to mental distress (Dooley, Fielding and Levi 1996), which in turn places stress on a partnership (Mastekaasa 1994) with dissolution as a possible outcome. Understanding the reasons why unemployment affects marital partnerships is important since some factors such as compensation levels are affected by social policies. If governments cannot always control unemployment, they can perhaps limit some of the social consequences of unemployment.

An alternative type of explanation, however, could be that it is marital dissolution which leads to unemployment. Research on marital dissolution and health indicates that marital dissolution is a stressful event; the incidence of both mental distress and sick leave peaks in the months surrounding marital dissolutions (Wade and Pevalin 2004; Blekesaune and Barrett 2005): some people are unable to carry out their jobs during the breakdown of a marital partnership. Research on unemployment and health indicates that poor physical and mental health can lead to unemployment (Dooley, Fielding and Levi 1996), and both types of health are likely to suffer as relationships break down. For these reasons, it is also plausible that marital dissolution could increase the risk of unemployment.

There could also be a third factor, or a set of factors, which leads to both unemployment and marital dissolution. People who are not able to hold on to their jobs could, for the very same reason, be unable to hold on to their marital partners as well. This could include stable characteristics of individuals such as a lack of income capability, social ability, or general efficacy, which could make them less attractive as both employees and marital partners.

The last explanation could also include more temporary problems such as a personal crisis or addiction to drugs or alcohol, which could lead to conflicts with employers as well as partners. But it is difficult to establish the causal order for other temporary problems than those associated with unemployment and partnership transitions. More stable characteristics of individuals, prevailing both before and after employment spells and a partnership dissolution, could at least technically help explain why some people experience both unemployment and partnership dissolution. It is more difficult to demonstrate that 'temporary' problems occurring simultaneously to these events can 'explain' job and partnership problems rather than merely reflecting such problems.

Thus, we have three types of causal relationships between unemployment and marital dissolution that we can investigate: unemployment leads to marital dissolution, marital dissolution leads to unemployment, and a third stable factor leads to both unemployment and marital dissolution. In real-life situations it can be difficult to distinguish between these processes, even for those involved. It is possible, however, to distinguish between these processes by studying the temporal order between the events of unemployment and marital dissolution. This approach can help to distinguish between the first two explanations: does unemployment lead to marital dissolution, or does marital dissolution lead to unemployment?

Another approach is to investigate if those experiencing unemployment and subsequent marital dissolution have stable characteristics which make them different from those not experiencing these events. Stable characteristics can be measured (e.g. education level) or unmeasured (i.e. represented by a random component), typically known as measured and unmeasured heterogeneity. This approach can help distinguish between the first and the last explanation: does unemployment lead to marital dissolution, or is there a third factor leading to both events?

We should also note, however, that unemployment could have the opposite effect to that predicted above. It might prevent people from ending their partnership. By living together, people can share expenses for housing and other consumer goods. It is thus more expensive for two adults to live apart than to live together. Low and uncertain income, which is associated with unemployment, could accordingly prevent some people from splitting up who would have moved apart if their financial situation had been stronger and/or if both parties had a secure income. Unemployment could thus destabilise some partnerships but stabilise others.

PREVIOUS FINDINGS

Research about the consequences of unemployment on family life date from at least the 1930s (e.g. Jahoda, Lazarsfeld and Zeizel 1933). But it is only during recent decades that it has been possible to investigate these issues more systematically using longitudinal data, which makes it possible to follow a large number of people or partnerships over time. Research in the USA and the UK has largely used panels of survey data, whereas Scandinavian research has largely used administrative data. These data sources have advantages and disadvantages regarding sample sizes, attrition problems and the extent of information available for each individual and family household. In general, survey data can provide more information about each individual or household (by including cohabitations, or data about mental distress and financial satisfaction) but at the expense of moderate samples and sometimes considerable attrition problems when people move apart, particularly for men.

In the UK, Lampard (1994) found that unemployment among both husbands and wives increased the odds of marital dissolution by 70 per cent in the following year. But marital dissolution could also predict later unemployment, indicating a two-way causality between unemployment and marital dissolution. The author argues that some marriages appear to dissolve as a result of unemployment, even though some individuals appear to have characteristics that can predict both unemployment and marital dissolution. March and Perry (2003) found that partnership dissolution was associated with male unemployment as well as economic hardship when following low- and moderate-income families over a two-year period.

Jensen and Smith (1990) found that unemployment among husbands, but not among wives, predicted the dissolution of married couples in Denmark. This effect could only be seen for the current year, however, and not in the years following male unemployment. Jalovaara (2003) found that unemployment among both husbands and wives predicted divorce among Finnish couples, but the effect of husbands' unemployment was stronger than that for wives. Similarly, Hansen (2005) found that unemployment of both husbands and wives predicted divorce among Norwegian couples, but the effect of husbands' unemployment was stronger than for that of wives. This study also indicates that economic problems can help explain these results, particularly following male unemployment, and that unemployment could catch unmeasured factors which increase the risk of divorce.

Some evidence is also provided by social-psychological research which has investigated a number of factors statistically associated with marital quality or marital satisfaction, some of which also include unemployment (e.g. Vinokur, Price and Caplan 1996). This literature suggests that financial hardship and mental distress can help explain why unemployed people have higher risk of terminating their partnerships (Vinokur, Price and Caplan 1996; McKee-Ryan et al. 2005).

HYPOTHESES

The principal hypothesis is that unemployment increases the risk of partnership dissolution. Secondly, we hypothesise that male unemployment has a stronger effect than female unemployment. This hypothesis stems partially from previous findings but can also be derived from a traditional division of labour between husbands and wives whereby men carry a principal responsibility for income whereas women are more likely to contribute unpaid work in the household when unemployed.

Beyond gender comparisons, previous research provides few indications of which types of partnerships are at a higher risk of dissolution following unemployment. We hypothesise that married people are at lower risk than cohabiters, and that parents are at lower risk than nonparents. Both hypotheses are based on an assumption that marriage and children provide 'glue' to a partnership, which reduces the impact of external shocks such as unemployment. We also investigate if unemployment effects vary by age of the partners, and the duration of a partnership.

A third set of hypotheses relates to which factors mediate the effect of unemployment on partnership dissolution. We hypothesise that financial dissatisfaction and any associated mental distress can help explain why unemployment is statically associated with a risk of ending a partnership. Finally, we also investigate if we have reasons to believe that characteristics of individuals or partnerships other than unemployment can help explain why people who have been unemployed are at greater risk of ending their partnerships. Such heterogeneity is investigated by the education level of the partners and by random components in hazard regression models.

DATA AND METHODS

The empirical analysis uses the first 15 waves of the British Household Panel Survey (BHPS), collected annually from 1991 to 2005. The analysis is done at the partnership level, as partnership dissolution applies to both parties. Since men are typically more difficult to trace after the dissolution of a partnership than women, the data matrix was constructed by following women over time. But information about the dissolution of a partnership could be provided by either partner in subsequent waves/interviews. Each woman can have up to four partnerships in the observation period from wave 2 (autumn 1992) to 14 (autumn 2005). The analysis includes 29,695 yearly observations for 3,586 partnerships representing 3,575 women and 3,586 men. No age limitations are applied.

The primary explanatory variable is unemployment during the previous year for the men or the women of a partnership.[1] All individual respondents were asked: 'I'd like to ask you a few questions now about what you might have been doing since September 1st [last year] in the way of paid work, unemployment [etc.].' Respondents were then given a hand calendar to help them fill in all spells of employment, unemployment, and so on. The vast majority of these interviews were carried out in September and October each year, but could be done in subsequent months as well. Unemployment was measured in a 12-month observation window from September in the previous year to September of the current year.

The dependent variable is partnership dissolution. This is a binary variable for the event of separation, divorce, or ending of a cohabitation union. This variable is based on a family history file which also uses information

Table 12.1 Descriptive Statistics of the BHPS Data

	Mean	S.D.	Low	High
Average age	47.0	14.5	18	92
Age difference	3.7	3.8	0	33
Years partnered	18.3	13.1	1	40
Log of years partnered	2.5	1.0	0	4
Married	88.0%		1	
Number of children	0.8	1.1	0	7
Man unemployed	6.3%		1	
Woman unemployed	2.8%		1	
Financial satisfaction[1] man)	3.9	1.0	1	5
Financial satisfaction[1] woman)	4.0	0.9	1	5
Mental distress[2] man	−0.1	0.9	−2.2	5.0
Mental distress[2] woman	0.1	1.1	−2.2	5.0
Observations	29,695			
Partnerships	3,407			

Notes: [1]coded 1–5 (5 indicating high satisfaction); [2]standardised variables.

from the BHPS retrospective marital history, prepared for 30,549 individuals participating in the survey in at least one panel wave (Pronzato 2007) and observed for a 12-month period, from September to September, in the year following each individual level interview. It is assumed that unemployment in one year would increase the risk of partnership dissolution in the following year. Further analysis also investigates same-year marital dissolution as well as marital dissolution two years after unemployment was recorded, but unfortunately, the timing of separation is not always available for those divorcing. When an individual had entered a new partnership with no data indicating when the previous partnership had ended, the dissolution of the previous partnership was set to one month before the new partnership started.

The statistical analysis is undertaken using discrete time hazard rate regression models based on yearly observations. Only partnerships lasting at least one year entered the analysis. All analyses control for the mean age of the two partners, the absolute age difference (in years) between them, the duration of the partnership, the legal status of the partnership (i.e. married or cohabiting), and the number of children aged below 16 years living in the household. In the regression analysis, mean age is measured through the use of splines as follows: for ages below 30, 30 to 40, 40 to 50, and age above 50. All age coefficients indicate a 10-year increase in age (using decimals for individual years).

Further variables control for financial satisfaction, mental distress, education level, and unobserved heterogeneity. Financial satisfaction was measured by a single item question: How well would you say you yourself are managing financially these days? Would you say you are 'living comfortably' (1), 'doing alright (2), 'just about getting by (3), 'finding it quite difficult (4), or 'finding it very difficult?' (5). This variable is treated as continuous in order to facilitate presentation and interpretation of the results, which are very similar if treated as a series of categories. Mental distress was measured using the General Health Questionnaire (GHQ), a measure of current mental health originally developed by Goldberg and Blackwell (1970). Each item asks whether the respondent has experienced a particular symptom or behaviour recently. This scale is standardised (with a mean of 0 and a standard deviation of 1). Education level is classified into five categories from degree to no qualification (or missing).

RESULTS

Unemployment and Partnership Dissolution

Unemployment is studied within periods of 12 months using three indicators: (1) the incidence of any unemployment in the period, (2) the number of unemployment spells in the period, and (3) the number of weeks unemployed in the period. We first investigate which of these three aspects of unemployment can predict marital dissolution best. More specifically, can the number of unemployment spells or the number of weeks in unemployment predict partnership dissolution better than the experience of a single unemployment spell of one week?

Table 12.2 indicates that the unemployment of a married or cohabiting man or woman increases the risk of partnership dissolution (left column). The unemployment coefficients presented in the tables can be recalculated to percentage differences to show that the probability of dissolution is 33 per cent larger when the man has been unemployed (exp(0.29) = 1.33) and 83 per cent larger when the woman has been unemployed (exp(0.60) = 1.83) compared to partnerships with no unemployment in a previous year. However, the difference between the effects of male and female unemployment is not statistically significant. Further, it is the presence of any unemployment in the previous year which predicts partnership dissolution. Adding the number of unemployment spells (beyond an initial spell in Model 2) or number of weeks (beyond an initial week in Model 3) does not predict partnership dissolution better than an initial spell of one week duration. Notice that the number of weeks unemployed indicates a 10-week increase in unemployment (using decimals for individual weeks). A relatively large coefficient could perhaps indicate that women having multiple unemployment spells is not associated with increased risk of partnership dissolution, but this is statistically very uncertain because of the low number of women with multiple unemployment spells. There is a tendency, at least in men, that long-lasting unemployment is less associated with partnership dissolution than shorter periods of unemployment.

Other explanatory variables in this analysis indicate that the risk of partnership dissolution declines with age at ages below 30 years and at ages above 40 years. As duration is being held constant, this picks up the effect of age at the start of the partnership. Partners with a large age difference between them are at higher risk of terminating their partnerships than similarly aged partners. There is little association between partnership duration and risk of dissolution when current age is controlled for. Married individuals are much less likely to move apart than cohabiters. Finally, children do not appear to stabilise partnerships since having more children is associated with increased risk of partnership dissolution. Most of these additional results are also known from previous analyses using BHPS data (e.g. Böheim and Ermisch 2001).

The analysis in Table 12.2 uses a time lag of one year from unemployment to a marital dissolution. Would these results change when using a

Table 12.2 Partnership Dissolution by Age and Unemployment, Hazard (cloglog) Coefficients

	Model 1	*Model 2*	*Model 3*
Mean age < 30	−0.82**	−0.80**	−0.86**
Mean age 30–40	−0.05	−0.06	−0.06
Mean age 40–50	−0.55*	−0.54*	−0.54*
Mean age 50+	−0.49*	−0.49*	−0.48*
Age difference	0.35**	0.35**	0.36**
Years partnered	−0.02	−0.02	−0.02
Married	−0.99**	−0.99**	−0.99**
Number of children	0.19**	0.19**	0.20**
Man unemployed	0.29*	0.24	0.65**
Woman unemployed	0.60**	0.64**	0.77**
Spells man (−1)		0.37	
Spells woman (−1)		−0.62	
Weeks (−1)/10 man			−0.14*
Weeks (−1)/10 woman			−0.09
Constant	−0.91	−0.94	−0.79

*p < 0.05 and **p < 0.01 in two-tailed tests.

longer time lag, or no time lag, between the two events? The short answer is not really. The statistical associations between unemployment and partnership dissolution are of similar magnitude when investigating effects of same year unemployment, previous year's unemployment, and unemployment two years before a partnership can end, at least for male unemployment. For female unemployment the tendency in the data is that same-year unemployment has a stronger effect than previous year's unemployment, but none of these differences are statistically significant. (These results are not shown in the tables.)

Who is at Risk?

Are all types of partnerships at enhanced risk of termination following unemployment of either partner? This is investigated by comparing marriages and cohabitations, partnerships with and without children, and the mean age of the partners as well as the duration of the partnership.

The results (presented in Table 12.3) indicate that female unemployment is associated with increased risk of partnership dissolution only when it occurs in partnerships which have lasted several years (Model 2). Notice that the interaction term between unemployment and partnership duration uses the natural logarithm of the number of years partnered since this fits the data well. The regression results indicate that female unemployment does not increase the risk of dissolving a partnership which has lasted only one year (−0.13), which is the starting value in this analysis since shorter partnerships are not investigated. But female unemployment does have a sizeable effect on partnerships that have lasted several years, for example, after five years female unemployment is associated with an 82 per cent increased risk of partnership dissolution ($\exp(-0.13 + 0.45*\ln(5)) = 1.82$), whereas after 15 years it is associated with a 200 per cent increased risk of dissolution ($\exp(-0.13 + 0.45*\ln(15)) = 3.00$).

Male unemployment has, on the other hand, similar effects on the risk of dissolution irrespective of the duration of a partnership. Across genders, unemployment has similar effects on the risk of dissolving partnerships irrespective of the age of the partners (Model 1), irrespective of being in a marriage rather than a cohabitation (Model 3), and irrespective of the number of children in the family (Model 4). A relatively large coefficient could perhaps indicate that female unemployment has more effect on marriages than cohabitations but this result is far from statistically significant.

Mediating Effects of Unemployment

Why are unemployed people more likely to terminate their partnerships than other people not experiencing unemployment? This is investigated by two factors which can potentially mediate the estimated effects of unemployment on partnership dissolution: (low) financial satisfaction and mental distress.

Table 12.3 Four Interaction Effects of Unemployment on Partnership Dissolution, Hazard (cloglog) Coefficients

	Model 1	Model 2	Model 3	Model 4
Mean age < 30	−0.82**	−0.86**	−0.82**	−0.82**
Mean age 30–40	−0.06	−0.05	−0.05	−0.06
Mean age 40–50	−0.56*	−0.55*	−0.56*	−0.55*
Mean age 50+	−0.49*	−0.45*	−0.48*	−0.49*
Age difference	0.35**	0.36**	0.35**	0.36**
Years partnered	−0.02	−0.02*	−0.02	−0.02
Married	−0.98**	−0.98**	−1.00**	−0.99**
Number of children	0.18**	0.18**	0.19**	0.19**
Man unemployed	0.56	0.32	0.34	0.43*
Woman unemployed	−0.08	−0.13	0.42	0.39
Age* man unemployed	−0.08			
Age* woman unemployed	0.20			
Log(years)* man unemployed		−0.02		
Log(years)* woman unemployed		0.45**		
Married* man unemployed			−0.12	
Married* woman unemployed			0.38	
Children* man unemployed				−0.10
Children* woman unemployed				0.20
Constant	−0.90	−0.75	−0.90	−0.91

*$p < 0.05$ and **$p < 0.01$ in two-tailed tests.

Both factors are measured separately in (partnered) men and women. Model 1 in Table 12.4 corresponds to Model 1 in Table 12.2, but this analysis includes only observations with valid data on financial satisfaction and mental distress in the men as well as the women.

Low financial satisfaction among women is strongly associated with increased risk of partnership dissolution (Model 2). But there is no correlation between men's financial satisfaction and the risk of partnership dissolution. Low financial satisfaction among partnered women can seemingly mediate 55 per cent of the effect of male unemployment on the risk of partnership dissolution (indicated by comparing the unemployment coefficients in Models 1 and 2). Low financial satisfaction among partnered women can only help explain a minor part of the effect of female unemployment on partnership dissolution (estimated as 12 per cent by comparing the female unemployment coefficient in Models 1 and 2).

Table 12.4 Two Mediating Effects of Unemployment on Partnership Dissolution, Hazard (cloglog) Coefficients

	Model 1	Model 2	Model 3	Model 4
Mean age < 30	−0.82**	−0.79**	−0.90**	−0.88**
Mean age 30–40	−0.06	−0.06	−0.10	−0.10
Mean age 40–50	−0.55*	−0.60*	−0.63*	−0.65**
Mean age 50+	−0.54*	−0.54*	−0.48*	−0.48**
Age difference	0.35**	0.32**	0.31**	0.30**
Years partnered	−0.02	−0.01	−0.02	−0.02
Married	−0.98**	−0.96**	−0.92**	−0.92**
Number of children	0.18**	0.14**	0.15**	0.13**
Man unemployed	0.29*	0.13	0.15	0.10
Woman unemployed	0.61**	0.53**	0.57**	0.54**
Financial satisfaction man		−0.04		0.05
Financial satisfaction woman		−0.21**		−0.14*
Mental distress man			0.26**	0.25**
Mental distress woman			0.22**	0.20**
Constant	−0.90	−0.02	−0.67	−0.38

*p < 0.05 and **p < 0.01 in two-tailed tests.

Mental distress in both men and women is associated with increased risk of partnership dissolution (Model 3).[2] Mental distress appears to mediate 47 per cent of the effect of male unemployment on partnership dissolution (when comparing Model 1 and Model 3). But mental distress cannot help explain why female unemployment is also associated with increased risk of partnership dissolution. Further, mental distress can only marginally help explain the effect of unemployment on the risk of partnership dissolution beyond what is already explained by low financial satisfaction (indicated by comparing Model 2 and Model 4). Thus, low financial satisfaction among partnered women appears to be the more important of these two factors in explaining why male unemployment is associated with increased risk of dissolution of partnerships. Neither financial satisfaction nor mental distress can help explain why female unemployment is associated with an increased risk of terminating partnerships.

Heterogeneity

Unemployment is associated with increased risk of partnership dissolution. But is it unemployment as such which is the reason that people who have been unemployed are more likely to have their partnerships terminated, or could there be a third factor which leads to both unemployment and partnership dissolution among these people? This is investigated by controlling for education level as well as normal and gamma distributed random components. Model 1 in Table 12.5 corresponds to Model 1 in Table 12.2 but is simplified by using a single linear slope for the mean age of the partners and it does not include the number of children living in the household. This simplification is done because the random component models used in this analysis are otherwise difficult to estimate. Model 2 also controls for education level of both partners (using four plus four dummy variables for the highest education of the two partners). The coefficients for education level are not shown in the table but they are far from being statistically significant, and by comparing Models 1 and 2 we can say that controlling for education level makes no difference for any of the other estimates in this analysis. Education cannot help explain why unemployment predicts partnership dissolution.

The other approach to controlling for time-invariant factors is the use of a random component which should capture nonobserved characteristics of the individuals being studied. The methodology literature labels this factor as 'frailty'; in our case, factors that lead to a persistently different rate of partnership dissolution. This is investigated assuming that the unmeasured variables (represented by random components) have a normal distribution (Model 3) or a gamma distribution (Model 4). The gamma distribution is more flexible and includes the normal distribution. Likelihood ratio tests (not shown in the table) indicate that the random components are statistically significant using either distribution. These results indicate that there are unmeasured factors which this analysis does not control for. But none of the results change much when controlling for unobserved heterogeneity either. The effects of male and female unemployment change only marginally. The difference between marriages and cohabitations is slightly larger

Table 12.5 Investigating Heterogeneity in the Analysis of Unemployment and Partnership Dissolution, Hazard (cloglog) Coefficients

	Model 1	Model 2	Model 3	Model 4
Mean age	−0.46**	−0.43**	−0.50**	−0.34**
Age difference	0.39**	0.36**	0.41**	0.34**
Years partnered	−0.01	−0.02	−0.01	−0.02
Married	−0.87**	−0.85**	−0.94**	−1.06**
Man unemployed	0.37**	0.35*	0.34*	0.37*
Woman unemployed	0.55**	0.55**	0.55**	0.58**
Constant	−1.66**	−1.76**	−1.86**	−2.31**

*p < 0.05 and **p < 0.01 in two-tailed tests.

when controlling for unobserved characteristics. Other results can vary somewhat between normal and gamma distributed random-effects models. In fact, of all characteristics investigated the unemployment effects appear to be those least affected by unobserved factors.

DISCUSSION

Our main finding is that unemployment increases the risk of partnership dissolution. It is the presence of any type of unemployment which increases the risk of partnership dissolution; the number of spells or the duration of unemployment spells does not seem to make much difference. However, at least in men, long-lasting unemployment is less associated with partnership dissolution than shorter periods of unemployment. Our estimates indicate that the effect on partnership dissolution is certainly not smaller when unemployment affects the women than when it affects the men in a marriage or cohabitation, even if the gender difference is never statistically significant. This finding is in line with the only similar study from the UK (Lampard 1994), but it is different from Scandinavian studies which indicate stronger effects of male than female unemployment on the dissolution of married partners (Jensen and Smith 1990; Jalovaara 2003; Hansen 2005).

The difference between British and Scandinavian research could reflect some differences between these countries. But it could also reflect a difference between survey data used in British research compared to administrative data used in Scandinavia. The BHPS used in this analysis provides an exceptionally rich source of information about each individual and household. For example, our analysis has compared marriages and cohabitations, and investigated if the effect of unemployment on partnership dissolution is explained by low financial satisfaction and mental distress. But this richness in information comes at the expense of a potential attrition problem which is virtually nonexistent in Scandinavian administrative data. Attrition poses a particular problem when investigating men leaving a partnership. It is possible that the effect of male unemployment on partnership dissolution is underestimated in this analysis. It is thus uncertain how the effects of male and female unemployment compare, and how these associations compare to those of Scandinavian countries.

Female unemployment increases the risk of ending partnerships which have lasted some years but not more recently established partnerships. No such differences by duration are found in the effect of male unemployment. The divorce literature has found that women's economic independence from their men increases the risk of partnership dissolution (Greenstein 1990), at least for less successful marriages (Schoen et al. 2002). It is thus likely that the effect of female unemployment on the dissolution of more mature partnerships reflects a process where some women seek economic independence from their men. A tendency in the data that the effect of female unemployment is stronger for same-year than subsequent-year partnership dissolution could also reflect similar processes.

The effect of male unemployment on partnership dissolution is to a considerable degree mediated by low financial satisfaction among their partners, but not their own financial satisfaction. The effect of female unemployment is, on the other hand, not mediated by low financial satisfaction. These results accord with Hansen's (2005) finding that the effect of male unemployment, but not the effect of female unemployment, is mediated by low income. From theory it is possible to argue that financial strain could stabilise and destabilise partnerships; stabilise because it is more expensive to live alone than sharing expenses with a partner, and destabilise because the gains from being partnered could be seen as less than satisfactory. To men it appears that these effects are of similar magnitude since the net effect of low financial satisfaction in men is not associated with partnership dissolution. To women it appears that low financial satisfaction in a partnership clearly outweighs the benefits of sharing expenses with a partner. The difference probably reflects that men and women have different roles in partnerships. Providing financial security is perhaps more important to men than to women.

NOTES

1. Homosexual partnerships are also included in the analysis, but because their numbers are small, we refer for convenience to the two partners as men and women.
2. The difference between the two coefficients for men and women is not statistically significant.

REFERENCES

Adler, M.A. (1997) Social change and declines in marriage and fertility in Eastern Germany, *Journal of Marriage and the Family*, 59(1): 37–49.

Blekesaune M. and Barrett, A. (2005) Marital dissolution and work disability: a longitudinal study of administrative data, *European Sociological Review*, 21(3): 259–71.

Blood, R.O. and Wolfe, D.M. (1960) *Husbands and wives*, New York: The Free Press.

Böheim, R. and Ermisch, J. (2001) Partnership dissolution in the UK—the role of economic circumstances, *Oxford Bulletin of Economics and Statistics*, 63(2): 197–208.

Dooley, D., Fielding, J. and Levi, L. (1996) Health and unemployment, *Annual Review of Public Health*, 17: 449–65.

Gallie, D., Gershuny, J. and Vogler, C. (1994) Unemployment, the household, and social networks, in D. Gallie, C. March and C. Vogler (eds) *Social change and the experience of unemployment*, Oxford: Oxford University Press, 231–63.

Gallie, D., March, C. and Vogler, C. (eds) (1994) *Social change and the experience of unemployment*, Oxford: Oxford University Press.

Goldberg, D.P. and Blackwell, B. (1970) Psychiatric illness in general practice: a detailed study using a new method of case identification, *British Medical Journal*, 2(5707): 439–43.

Greenstein, T.N. (1990) Marital disruption and the employment of married-women, *Journal of Marriage and the Family*, 52(3): 657–76.

Hansen, H.T. (2005) Unemployment and marital dissolution: a panel data study of Norway, *European Sociological Review*, 21(2): 135–48.

Jahoda, M., Lazarsfeld, P. and Zeizel, H. (1933) *Marienthal: the sociology of an unemployed community*, (In English Translation from 1972:) London: Tavistock.

Jalovaara, M. (2003) The joint effects of marriage partners' socioeconomic positions on the risk of divorce, *Demography*, 40(1): 67–81.

Jensen, P. and Smith, N. (1990) Unemployment and marital dissolution, *Journal of Population Economics*, 3(3): 215–29.

Lampard, R. (1994) An examination of the relationship between marital dissolution and unemployment, in D. Gallie, C. March and C. Vogler (eds) *Social change and the experience of unemployment*, Oxford: Oxford University Press.

Liker, J.K. and Elder, G.H. (1983) Economic hardship and marital relations in the 1930s, *American Sociological Review*, 48(3): 343–59.

March, A. and Perry, J. (2003) *Family change 1991 to 2001*, Department for Work and Pensions. Research Report No. 180.

Mastekaasa, A. (1994) The subjective well-being of the previously married: the importance of unmarried cohabitation and time since widowhood or divorce, *Social Forces*, 73(2): 665–92.

McKee-Ryan, F.M., Song, Z.L., Wanberg, C.R. and Kinicki, A.J. (2005) Psychological and physical well-being during unemployment: a meta-analytic study, *Journal of Applied Psychology*, 90(1): 53–76.

Pronzato, C. (2007) Family histories from BHPS. British Household Panel Survey Consolidated Marital, Cohabitation and Fertility Histories, 1991–2005, Online. HTTP: <http://www.data-archive.ac.uk>. Accessed on July 2007.

Schoen, R., Astone, N.M., Rothert, K., Standish, N.J. and Kim, Y.J. (2002) Women's employment, marital happiness, and divorce, *Social Forces*, 81(2): 643–62.

Smith, A. (2000) Employment restructuring and household survival in 'postcommunist transition': rethinking economic practices in Eastern Europe, *Environment and Planning A*, 32(1): 1759–80.

Vinokur, A.D., Price, R.H. and Caplan, R.D. (1996) Hard times and hurtful partners: how financial strain affects depression and relationship satisfaction of unemployed persons and their spouses, *Journal of Personality and Social Psychology*, 71(1): 166–79.

Wade, T.J. and Pevalin, D.J. (2004) Marital transitions and mental health, *Journal of Health and Social Behavior*, 45(2): 155–70.

13 Marital Splits and Income Changes over the Longer Term

Stephen P. Jenkins

INTRODUCTION

In the past two decades, as panel surveys have become widespread, substantial evidence has accumulated concerning the economic consequences of marital disruption measured in terms of the change in some measure of net household income adjusted for differences in household size and composition. Almost without exception, these studies have found large falls in income in the year after a marital split for separating women. National studies covering Britain, Canada, and the USA include Bianchi and McArthur (1989), Bianchi et al. (1999), David and Flory (1989), Duncan and Hoffman (1985), Finnie (1993), Hoffman (1977), Jarvis and Jenkins (1998, 1999), McKeever and Wolfinger (2001), and Smock (1993, 1994). Cross-national comparative studies have also become more common, building on the pioneering study of Germany and the USA by Burkhauser et al. (1990, 1991). See Andreß et al. (2006) comparing Belgium, Britain, Germany, Italy and Sweden using national panel surveys, and Uunk (2004) and Aassve et al. (2007) comparing member states of the European Union using the European Community Household Panel.

This paper contributes to this literature in two ways, drawing on data from waves 1–14 (survey years 1991–2004) of the British Household Panel Survey. First, it is the only study of the trends over time in Britain of the short-term changes in income associated with a marital split. As in most previous studies, I calculate the average year t and year $t + 1$ income change for persons experiencing a marital split between t to $t + 1$, pooling multiple waves of panel data to ensure sample sizes are not too small. With a long run of panel data, however, I do not have to pool all waves of data, and can compare earlier periods with later periods. I focus on 1991–1997 compared with 1998–2003 (the years mentioned refer to year t). Previous studies of trends in short-term income changes, all for the USA as far as I am aware, have either utilised different surveys to draw conclusions about trends (e.g. McKeever and Wolfinger 2001) or, for the same survey, examined trends relatively long ago (e.g. Smock 1993). With the BHPS, I am able to use consistently defined data from the same survey, and they refer to the relatively recent past.

The second contribution of the chapter arises from its use of the long run of BHPS panel data in a different way. I examine six-year trajectories, analysing how incomes evolve from the year prior to the marital split (t) over the five years following the split ($t + 1$ to $t + 5$). This longer-run perspective on the economic consequences of marital splits has also been taken by Andreß et al. (2006) using data from five European panel surveys and, in much greater detail, by Duncan and Hoffman (1985) using the US Panel Study of Income Dynamics. My contribution is its focus on Britain, and examination in detail of women who have dependent children prior to the marital split.

In the next section, I explain key definitions such as a 'marital split' and 'income', and how data about these were derived from the BHPS, and report sample numbers. In the third section, I update the analysis of Jarvis and Jenkins (1999), which was based on four waves of BHPS data. I show that marital splits continue to be associated with substantial declines in income for separating wives and children relative to separating husbands. However, the analysis of trends reveals that the size of the drop in income declined in the late 1990s, and I argue that the most likely explanation for this was secular increases in labour force participation rates and—closely associated—changes to the social security benefit system at that time, notably the introduction of Working Families Tax Credit. The analysis of six-year income trajectories is presented in the fourth section. The estimates suggest that, in the five years following a marital split, incomes for separating wives recover but not to their previous levels, on average. Women in paid work or who have a new partner fare best. The final section provides concluding remarks.

DATA AND DEFINITIONS[1]

I analyse longitudinal data from the first 14 waves of the BHPS (survey years 1991–2004).[2] (For a detailed discussion of the BHPS, see Lynn 2006.) All the adults and children in the wave 1 sample were designated as original sample members (OSMs). Ongoing population representativeness has been maintained by using a following rule typical of household panel surveys: at the second and subsequent waves, all OSMs are 'followed' (even if they move house, or if the household splits up), and there are interviews, at approximately one-year intervals, with all adult members of all households containing either an OSM or an individual born to an OSM whether or not they were members of the original sample. New panel members who subsequently stop living with an OSM are, however, not followed and interviewed again. Thus, for example, if a non-OSM married an OSM at wave 2, and the partnership subsequently dissolved, the OSM is followed, but the non-OSM is not. There are some exceptions: new panel members who have children with OSMs become 'permanent sample members' (PSMs) and continue to be followed. These PSMs are included in the analysis.

Following Jarvis and Jenkins (1999) and most other studies, I define a marital split as a transition from a legal marriage or cohabiting union observed at the wave t interview to living apart from the wave t spouse or partner at the wave $t + 1$ interview, where t runs from 1 (wave 1) to 13 (wave 13). Calculations are based on three main subsamples of persons experiencing a marital split: (1) separating men, (2) separating women, and (3) the dependent children present at wave t of parents who separated between t and $t + 1$.[3] Adults who repartner between wave t and wave $t + 1$ are included in the analysis. As with a number of other studies, I consider only the first marital split that is observed in the panel (this accounts for almost 90 per cent of all observed splits.)

An individual's economic circumstances in each year is measured in terms of the equivalized household net income of the household to which the individual belongs. Net income is the sum across household members of income from employment and self-employment, investments and savings, private and occupational pensions, other market income and private transfers (including maintenance income), plus cash social security and social assistance receipts from the state, less income tax payments, employee National Insurance contributions, and local taxes.[4] Net income is the most widely used income measure in the UK, and the basis of official income distribution statistics (see, e.g., Department for Work and Pensions 2007).[5]

The reference period over which most income components are measured is the month prior to the interview or the most recent relevant period,[6] with all figures converted to a comparable pounds per week basis pro rata. The use of this current income measure increases the chance that observed income changes reflect transitory variations.[7] However, there are also significant advantages to using a relatively short reference period. First, we can be more confident that the household income measure is based on information for the people who are present in the household during the income reference period. Second, we maximise sample size, because fewer interviews are required to measure pre- and postsplit income change.

In order to derive comparable measures of real income over time, all incomes have been indexed to April 2007 price levels using an appropriate monthly price deflator (the index of retail prices excluding local taxes).

Net household income was adjusted to take account of differences in composition and size between households using the McClements (before housing costs) equivalence scale, which has scale rates which depend on the number of adults and the number and age of dependent children: see Department for Work and Pensions (2007) for details. I normalise the scale rates so that the rate has the value of one for single-adult households.

Although the McClements scale has been the most commonly used in Britain, there is no single 'correct' equivalence scale from a conceptual or an empirical point of view (Coulter et al. 1992). Estimates of the size and direction of the income change resulting from a marital split may be sensitive to the equivalence scale chosen. When a couple separate, they typically form separate households of a smaller size and so, if there are large economies of scale, the consequences of a marital split for living standards are much more deleterious than were there only minor economies of scale. Moreover, inbuilt assumptions about economies of scale affect income change estimates more for separating husbands than wives (or children) because the change in household size with a marital split is greater for husbands: children of separating couples typically reside with their mothers after the split. For a detailed analysis of the sensitivity of results to changes in the equivalence scale, see Jarvis and Jenkins (1999).

Sample Numbers and Characteristics

The numbers of separating husbands, wives and children who experienced a marital split in BHPS waves 1–14 are summarized in Table 13.1. Column 1 shows the number of individuals for the case where at least one partner of a splitting couple was traced at the wave after the split. (If both partners attrit, one cannot tell if they also split up.) Column 2 shows the numbers of individuals providing some form of response at interview, and Column 3 shows the numbers for whom valid net income measures could be derived. Clearly, sample dropout is substantial, especially for separating husbands and those with dependent children at wave t in particular.[8] For only 67 per cent of separating husbands is any kind of interview achieved (77 per cent for those without children at t; 60 per cent for those with children at t). By contrast, there are interviews with 89 per cent of separating wives, and this fraction does not vary between mothers and childless women. These figures may be compared with the overall wave-on-wave response rates to the BHPS of around 90 per cent for wave 2, and several percentage points higher for each wave thereafter. Incomplete response to income questions reduces sample numbers further, as a comparison with column 3 shows. However, the proportionate reduction is broadly the same for separating husbands and wives.

Despite sample dropout, there remain relatively large numbers of cases for analysis, an advantage of having a long run of panel data. With 14 waves, there are about four times as many cases as there were for Jarvis and Jenkins (1999), who used BHPS waves 1–4: 610 children compared with 151, 392 separating husbands compared with 105, and 513 separating wives compared with 148. With the larger sample sizes, some analysis of subsamples is also possible: I compare the experiences of separating husbands and wives with and without children prior to the marital split, and also between different periods especially between waves 1–7 (survey years 1991–1997) and waves 8–13 (1998–2003). It remains the case, however, that although subsample numbers are relatively large for this kind of study, they are relatively small by the standards of much survey analysis, and the estimates need to be treated with appropriate caution. I limit the number subsamples that I analyse and, to minimise the influence of outlier values, I work mostly with medians rather than means.

Table 13.1   Numbers of Persons Experiencing a Marital Split

Persons experiencing a marital split	Original Sample Members at wave t eligible to be interviewed at wave t + 1	As (1), and with an interview of any kind at wave t + 1 (full, proxy, telephone)	As (1), and with valid net income data at waves t and t + 1		
	Waves 1–13	Waves 1–13	Waves 1–13	Waves 1–7	Waves 8–13
	(1)	(2)	(3)	(4)	(5)
Husbands	803	539	392	234	158
Wives	845	748	513	311	202
Husbands with no children at *t*	327	252	182	112	70
Wives with no children at *t*	346	305	199	124	75
Husbands with child(ren) at *t*	476	287	210	122	88
Wives with child(ren) at *t*	499	443	314	187	127
Children	849	748	610	357	253

Notes: For the definitions of an Original Sample Member, a marital split, and net income, see text. 'Children' refers to the dependent children of couples experiencing a marital split (see text). Table excludes cases where neither partner of the splitting partnership provided an interview at *t* + 1. Numbers refer to first marital split observed in the panel. If all marital splits in the panel are used, the Column 1 numbers are 911 for separating husbands, 995 for separating wives, and 963 for affected children.

In addition to the small numbers, Table 13.1 raises questions about the possibility of bias in estimated statistics from nonrandom attrition. The relatively high attrition rates for separating husbands compared to separating wives is typical in studies of this kind (see, e.g., Burkhauser et al. 1990). The standard method for controlling for attrition biases and cross-sectional non-response potential attrition bias is to use an appropriate sample weight when calculating statistics. Jarvis and Jenkins (1999), for example, used the BHPS longitudinal enumerated individual weights for wave *t* + 1 to derive their estimates, though they also noted that their conclusions were unchanged when unweighted data were used.

I report unweighted estimates of short-term income changes following a marital split. This is because the BHPS longitudinal weights were not designed for this type of analysis and this unsuitability is exacerbated the longer the panel. The longitudinal weights for wave *s* are nonzero only for OSMs who are respondents at every annual interview between wave 1 and wave *s* inclusive, or their children (Lynn 2006, section 8.1.2). They are zero for PSMs, for non-OSMs who join the panel after wave 1, and for any OSM with intermittent panel response. As the panel matures, increasing numbers of persons at each wave do not have a valid longitudinal weight or, put another way, applying the longitudinal weights systematically excludes cases from later waves.[9] Although unweighted estimates are reported, I also calculated weighted estimates and these yielded similar conclusions.

For analysis of longer-term income trajectories, the possibility of attrition bias was larger because of the stringent selection criteria for membership of the analysis sample, namely, responding and having valid net income values at six consecutive waves. I estimated the probability of inclusion in the analysis sample using probit regression and, for each member of the analysis sample, calculated an individual-specific weight equal to the inverse of the probability predicted from the regression.

SHORT-TERM INCOME CHANGES FOR PERSONS EXPERIENCING A MARITAL SPLIT

Patterns of Income Change, by Subgroup and over Time

For each individual experiencing a marital split, I calculated the percentage change in net income between the interview before the split (year *t*) and the interview after the split (year *t* + 1). Figure 13.1 summarizes the median of the distribution of these changes for each of a number of subgroups and time periods. The horizontal axis shows time periods defined in terms of the waves for the calculations. For example, 'All' refers to all waves (*t* = 1–13), 'w1-w7' to waves 1–7 (*t* = 1–7), and so on. Thus, what is plotted is a form of temporal moving average. Each line shows the median percentage change for a particular group. Also shown, for reference, is the corresponding median percentage income change for all persons in the panel, including those not affected by a marital split ('All persons'), which is consistently between 1½ and 2 per cent per year.

The patterns of income changes between men, women and children correspond closely to those found in earlier studies, and Jarvis and Jenkins (1999) in particular. Separating wives and children fare much worse than separating husbands. According to the 'all waves' estimates, the median income change for separating wives is–22 per cent, for separating husbands +13 per cent, and for children–19 per cent. For separating wives, there is little difference in the median change according to whether there were dependent children present at the presplit interview:–21 per cent for those without children, and–23 per cent for those with children. By contrast, there is a large difference for separating husbands: for those without dependent children at *t*, the median change is 0 per cent; for those with dependent children, it is +32 per cent.[10] As explained by Jarvis and Jenkins (1999), this

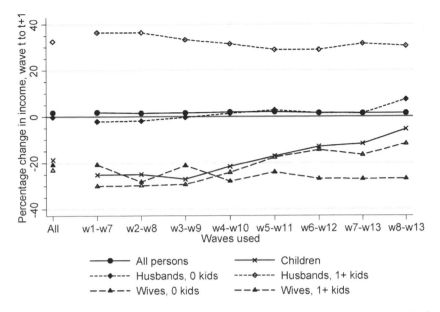

Figure 13.1   Median percentage change in net income, wave *t* to wave *t* + 1, for persons experiencing a marital split, by period.
Notes: Net income is defined in text. 'Waves used' refers to waves pooled for calculations. The median is the 50th percentile (middle value) of a distribution.

differential is in part due to changes in household composition rather than changes in money income. Changes in incomes that are unadjusted for differences in household size and composition are similar for the two groups, but, because children mostly live with their mother rather than their father after a marital split, the equivalence scale factor for fathers falls markedly, thereby increasing equivalised income.

How have income changes associated with a marital split varied within the 14-year period? Figure 13.1 shows that there was little trend in the median change for separating wives without dependent children at *t*, or for separating husbands regardless of whether they had children at *t*. By contrast, there have been marked trends for separating wives with children, and for children. For both groups, the median percentage change in income associated with a marital split has become less negative, and this starts once calculations involve wave 9 and later waves ('w3–w9' onwards). For example, for separating wives with children, the median change is –30 per cent for 1991–1997 but –12 per cent for 1998–2003. For children, the corresponding estimates are –25 per cent and –6 per cent. So, there appears to have been a substantial reduction on average in the adverse consequences of a marital split for these two groups. Are these patterns replicated across the full distribution of changes rather than only the median?

Table 13.2 shows, in addition to the median income change, the lower quartile and the upper quartile of the distribution of income changes for each subgroup, where the calculations have been undertaken separately for waves 1–7 and for waves 8–13. The table shows that for separating wives with children, and for children, there has been a rightward shift in the distribution of income changes: for both groups, each of the lower quartile, median, and upper quartile has become less negative or more positive. This cannot be said for the other groups. Kernel density estimates of the entire distribution of income changes (not shown) confirm these differential trends over time for the different groups.

In addition to providing information about trends over time, Table 13.2 reemphasises Jarvis and Jenkins's remarks that 'there is much heterogeneity in income change associated with a marital split, regardless of gender, in addition to the clearcut average changes' (1999: 244). Small sample numbers constrain the use of cross tabulations to investigate who the gainers and losers are. A median regression of the percentage change in net income for separating wives with dependent children at t suggests few systematic associations with their characteristics measured at t. For instance, neither age, legal marital status, academic qualifications, number of children, whether UK-born, or housing tenure appeared to have a statistically significant association for this group. Two factors did have an association. The percentage change in net income after a marital split was smaller (i.e. less negative on average) for women whose former partner did not work (22 per

Table 13.2   Percentage Change in Net Income, Wave t to Wave $t + 1$, for Persons Experiencing a Marital Split, by Period

	Waves 1–7			Waves 8–13		
	Lower quartile	*Median*	*Upper quartile*	*Lower quartile*	*Median*	*Upper quartile*
All persons[*]	−13	2	20	−12	2	18
Persons experiencing a marital split						
Children	−50	−25	11	−37	−6	25
Husbands	−25	9	55	−20	17	59
Wives	−53	−27	12	−43	−17	14
Husbands, no children at t	−30	−2	35	−24	7	46
Wives, no children at t	−51	−21	24	−48	−27	11
Husbands, child(ren) at t	−15	36	82	−15	31	76
Wives, child(ren) at t	−56	−30	8	−39	−12	18

Note: Net income is defined in text. [*]All BHPS respondents regardless of whether experienced a marital split or not. The lower quartile is the 25th percentile, the median is the 50th percentile, and the upper quartile is the 75th percentile of a distribution.

cent of the estimation sample), and for women with marital splits in later years rather than earlier years.

Towards an Explanation of the Trends

Why have the economic costs of a marital split declined for women with dependent children? (Since most children stay with their mother after a marital split, answers to this question will also explain the improved fortunes of children experiencing parental marital splits.)

The most likely explanations of the trends are increases in attachment to paid work, and increases in the rewards to paid work relative to not working, both of which are associated with the various changes in the late 1990s to the system of in-work support. These changes specifically aimed to increase the employment rates of families of children and to 'make work pay'.

Family Credit (FC), the programme providing means-tested support to low-income working families, was replaced by Working Families Tax Credit (WFTC) in October 1999 and fully phased in by April 2000. WFTC was more generous than FC (Brewer et al. 2006): it paid higher benefits ('credits') especially for families with young children; more could be earned before benefits tapered off; there were credits for childcare; and maintenance income from nonresident parents was disregarding when assessing income. (WFTC was itself replaced by the Working Tax Credit and Child Tax Credit programmes from April 2003. As this is at the end of my sample period, it is less relevant to an explanation of the trends I report.) By design, WFTC raised incentives to work for lone parents who were not in paid work, or working fewer than 16 hours per week, the minimum number required for WFTC receipt. See, inter alia, Brewer and Shephard (2004) for further details.

There were a number of other changes during this period that raised support for families with children, notably increases in Child Benefit (paid regardless of parental work status), and increases in the child allowances in Income Support, the principal means-tested social benefit for families and individuals not in paid work.[11] These provided disincentives to paid work that could potentially have offset the effects of WFTC. What was the net effect on employment rates?

According to Labour Force Survey data, the proportion of lone parents in paid work increased steadily over the 1990s from around 40 per cent in 1993 to around 51 per cent in 2002 (Gregg et al. 2007; see also Brewer and Shephard 2004, Figure 11), with a notable increase in the rate of increase after 1998, especially for those with young children. The employment rate of married mothers also rose over the same period, but the rate of increase levelled off in the late 1990s (Gregg et al. 2007). The marked reduction in the gap in employment rates between married mothers and lone parents, and its timing, suggests that the introduction of WFTC did indeed stimulate increases in lone mothers' employment rates.

More sophisticated analytical methods, controlling for the changes in the composition of the lone parent population, the pre-1998 employment trends, and for the effects of the other reforms, confirm that WFTC's introduction had a causal effect. Three different studies suggest that 4–5 percentage points of the increase in lone mothers' employment rates could be attributed to WFTC: see Brewer et al. (2006), Francesconi and van der Klaauw (2007), and Gregg et al. (2007). For example, Gregg et al. write that the policy change 'lay behind more than two thirds of the rise in employment [of lone mothers] from 1998 to 2003' (2007: 10).

So, over the sample period there was an increase in employment rates for lone parents and a particular spurt closely associated with WFTC introduction. There was also a marked increase in WFTC take-up relative to FC take-up, and an increase in the average award made (Gregg and Harkness 2003, Figure 7). The combination of these changes provides a good prima facie explanation for the trends in the economic consequences of a marital split for women with children and is consistent with the timing of the onset of the trend (Figure 13.1).

Changing Income Sources

I now consider the extent to which this story is corroborated by the experiences of women experiencing marital splits, and examine changes in rates of employment, receipt of social assistance and in-work benefits, and other sources. I use the term 'in-work benefits' to refer to FC, WFTC or Working Tax Credit. 'Social assistance' refers to means-tested social security benefits: Income Support, Unemployment Benefit or Job Seekers Allowance (contribution or income based),[12] and 'housing benefits' (Housing Benefit or Council Tax Benefit). In Table 13.3, I report results for all separating wives and for wives with children prior to the split, and compare changes between waves 1–7 and waves 8–13. (More detailed breakdowns were ruled out on sample size grounds.) Contrasts between the two periods should be indicative of the effects of the policy changes introduced by the Labour government.

Employment rates clearly increased between the periods. Two-thirds (66 per cent) of all separating wives were in paid work at the interview prior to the marital split over waves 1–7, but three-quarters (74 per cent) over waves 8–13, an increase in the rate of about an eighth. For separating women with children present, the corresponding proportions are 57 per cent and 67 per cent, which is an increase in the rate of 16 per cent. Looking at the employment transition rates instead reveals that the proportion of women with dependent children who stop working after a marital split almost halved between the two periods, from 16 per cent to 9 per cent, and the proportion remaining in work increased sharply from 41 per cent to 58 per cent. (These changes are much larger in proportionate terms than the changes in transition rates for all separating women.) The second panel shows employment transition rates for employment defined as working at least 16 hours

Table 13.3 Participation in Paid Work, Receipt of Social Assistance and In-Work Benefits, Before and After a Marital Split

Column percentages	All separating wives		Separating wives with children at t	
	Waves 1–7	Waves 8–14	Waves 1–7	Waves 8–14
Paid work (weekly work hours > 0)				
not working at t, not working at $t + 1$	26	20	33	24
not working at t, working at $t + 1$	8	6	10	8
working at t, not working at $t + 1$	13	8	16	9
working at t, working at $t + 1$	53	66	41	58
Paid work (weekly work hours ≥ 16)				
not working at t, not working at $t + 1$	47	32	64	58
not working at t, working at $t + 1$	10	15	6	9
working at t, not working at $t + 1$	13	11	10	3
working at t, working at $t + 1$	31	43	21	30
In-work benefits				
not receiving at t, not receiving at $t + 1$	90	75	83	60
not receiving at t, receiving at $t + 1$	6	17	10	27
receiving at t, not receiving at $t + 1$	3	3	4	5
receiving at t, receiving at $t + 1$	2	5	3	8
Social assistance benefits				
not receiving at t, not receiving at $t + 1$	63	76	51	68
not receiving at t, receiving at $t + 1$	20	9	26	15
receiving at t, not receiving at $t + 1$	5	5	5	5
receiving at t, receiving at $t + 1$	13	10	18	12
Social assistance benefits, including housing benefits				
not receiving at t, not receiving at $t + 1$	53	65	40	53
not receiving at t, receiving at $t + 1$	25	17	34	25
receiving at t, not receiving at $t + 1$	4	6	3	7
receiving at t, receiving at $t + 1$	18	12	23	15
Receives maintenance at $t + 1$				
Yes	25	30	26	31
Repartnered at $t + 1$				
Yes	21	21	18	21

Note: *For the definitions of in-work benefits, social assistance benefits and housing benefits, see main text. Receipt refers to receipt by the respondent or respondent's partner.

per week, the eligibility threshold for WFTC receipt. The same trends are apparent: the rise in cross-sectional employment rates and in employment retention rates, with the changes being larger for mothers compared to all separating wives. Gregg et al. (2007) have also remarked on the increased likelihood of job retention for employed mothers around the time of a marital split, and show that this trend is not due to changes in the characteristics of employed mothers over time. Paull's (2007) analysis of partnership and employment histories using monthly calendar data from the BHPS and the Family and Children's Study also concluded that 'the relationships between partnership transitions and the work behaviour of mothers have become less dramatic, particularly in the post-1996 period' (2007: 2–3).

How receipt of in-work benefits and social assistance changed is shown in the next three panels of Table 13.3. (Since the family is the unit of assessment, receipt refers to receipt by either partner.) For women with dependent children, there is a substantial rise in receipt of in-work benefits between the year before and the year after the marital split, in both periods. What changed between the two periods is that presplit receipt rates were higher (13 per cent rather than 7 per cent) and the take-up after a marital split was higher still: 35 per cent rather than 13 per cent, that is, more than twice rather than less than twice the presplit rate. Correspondingly, the chances of not being in receipt in both the year before and the year after the split fell between the two periods, from 83 per cent to 63 per cent.

The patterns of receipt of social assistance are the inverse of those for in-work benefits. That is, there is marked rise in receipt between the year before and the year after the marital split in both periods, but the association between receipt and separation declined between the two periods. For example, for waves 1–7, the proportion of wives with children receiving social assistance including housing benefits was more than twice as high in the year after the split as before the split (57 per cent rather than 26 per cent), but for waves 8–13 the corresponding proportions were 40 per cent and 22 per cent. So, the relative chances of receipt associated with a separation declined from 2.2 to 1 to 1.8 to 1. Correspondingly, the proportion who did not receive social assistance including housing benefits before and after the split rose from 40 per cent to 53 per cent.

Labour market earnings, social assistance and in-work benefits form the major part of most families' income packages. For lone parents, maintenance payments from a former partner and income from a new partner are other potential sources of income. The bottom two panels of Table 13.3 provide an indication of the importance of these sources. The proportion of separating mothers who receive maintenance from a former partner increased from 26 per cent to 31 per cent between the two periods, and the proportion who found a new partner within a year of separation increased only slightly, from just below one-fifth to just above one-fifth. Since the repartnering rate hardly changed, it is unlikely that repartnering can play a substantial role in explaining the decline in the income loss associated with a marital split for women with children. The change in the proportion receiving maintenance is also not large. Its effects are likely to have been indirect, via its interactions with the policy changes aiming to make work pay. In particular, maintenance was counted as income in assessments of eligibility for Income Support, but was not counted in assessments for WFTC eligibility.

CHANGES IN INCOME OVER THE FIVE YEARS FOLLOWING A MARITAL SPLIT

What do income trajectories look like when the focus is changed from the immediate short-term (one year after the split) to a longer period (from one through five years after the split)? I look in particular at the evolving circumstances of women with dependent children prior to the split. Small sample sizes are an important constraint on the analysis.[13] For instance, it is not possible to examine how the shape of the six-year trajectories changed over time.[14] Almost all of the trajectories analyzed next began in waves 1–7, and so most refer to the period before the Labour government's policy changes. It should be borne in mind that some of the reported relationships between income and time since the marital split may reflect the effects of these policy changes.

The requirement for response and valid household net income at six consecutive annual interviews is a stringent criterion; with differential attrition, the analysis sample may be unrepresentative. Because the BHPS longitudinal weights were not designed to be applied in this context, I developed a special purpose set in the following way. I defined an 'at-risk' sample to be all adults living as man and wife at wave t, where t could be any of waves 1 to 8 (some of whom separated from their marital partner by wave $t + 1$) and with valid household net income data at t, and then modelled the probability of having valid household net income data at waves $t + 1$, $t + 2$, $t + 3$, $t + 4$ and $t + 5$, using probit regression. A weight for the analysis of trajectories was then constructed for each individual equal to the inverse of the probability predicted from the regression. The probability of having valid household net income data for the full sequence was estimated to be higher for women, for those legally married rather than cohabiting, for older persons, for those UK-born, with higher academic qualifications, with a lower income, with fewer children or fewer adults in the household, or living in owner-occupied accommodation. There were also differences by region of residence and survey year.[15] All the calculations reported following are based on these weights. I also repeated the analysis without using the weights and, reassuringly, the patterns derived were similar.

Income trajectories are summarised in Figures 13.2(a) and 13.2(b). I calculated for each individual his or her income in each of the five years after the marital split and expressed that income as a ratio of his or her income at

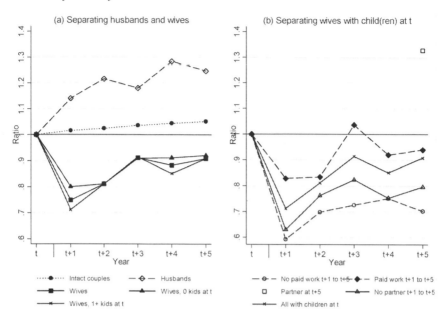

Figure 13.2 Net income of selected groups after a marital split as a fraction of net income in year prior to marital split (wave *t*)

wave *t*. The figures report, by subgroup, the subgroup median income ratio year by year. For comparison, I also show the corresponding income ratios for intact couples in Figure 13.2(a). Overall, average incomes increased by 1 to 2 percentage points per year in real terms.

Figure 13.2(a) highlights stark differences in the experiences of separating husbands and wives. Differentials between the sexes remain in the longer term. Five years after a marital split, separating husbands have an income that is 25 per cent higher on average than their income prior to the marital split, whereas for separating wives, income at *t* + 5 is 9 per cent lower on average. If poverty is defined as having an income less than 60 per cent of the whole-sample median in the relevant year, then the poverty rate among separating husbands at *t* + 5 is 10 per cent, just below the poverty rate for intact couples of 13 per cent. For separating husbands, incomes appear to rise almost continuously on average in the years following the marital split, whereas for separating women, the sharp fall in income experienced immediately after the marital split is followed by a gradual improvement in the subsequent four years, but not to presplit levels. The poverty rate among separating wives at *t* + 5, is 27 per cent, almost three times that of separating husbands. Interestingly, the income trajectories for women who have children at *t* appear quite similar to those without children.

Figure 13.2(b) examines the circumstances of separating wives with children in more detail, showing differences related to participation in paid work and partnership. The figure shows that women who are not in paid work in any of the five years after a marital split experience the largest income fall initially, and, although their incomes subsequently improve slightly, they remain worse off than the other groups. In fact, all of them have incomes below the poverty line for each of the five postsplit years. At the opposite extreme, women in paid work at every interview following the split experience relatively small income falls initially and almost recover their original income by $t + 5$. None of them have incomes below the poverty line in any year. (The subsample size of 56 means that these estimates should be treated with caution.) Lack of partner is not as deleterious as lack of paid work: the income trajectory for those without a partner at all five waves following the marital split lies between that for all mothers and all who do not have a job at any of the postsplit interviews. Almost no women are observed with a partner at every wave after the split. However, some indications of the possibilities of regaining income through repartnering are illustrated by the income ratio for women who have a partner at $t + 5$, for whom income at $t + 5$ is one-third higher than their presplit income.

Underlying these income trajectories are changes in the sources of income. These variations are summarized in Figure 13.3 for women with dependent children at wave t. After the initial rise in receipt of social assistance, including housing benefits associated with the marital split, from 31 per cent at t to 62 per cent at $t + 1$, there is then a decline in to 40 per cent at $t + 5$. The proportion in paid work increases from 48 per cent to 58 per cent between $t + 1$ and $t + 5$, and the proportion working at least 16 hours per week increases from 41 per cent to 49 per cent. The proportion receiving in-work benefits increases from 11 per cent before the marital split to 19 per cent in the year after the split, but then stays much the same: the proportion is 20 per cent at $t + 5$. This may simply reflect the fact that most of the sample trajectories cover the early to mid-1990s (see above). The chances of receiving maintenance from a former partner also increase most noticeably between the year before and the year after the split—the proportion in receipt increases from 4 per cent to 27 per cent—but hardly changes thereafter (it is 30 per cent at $t + 5$). Repartnership rates rise steadily after the marital split, from 10 per cent to 38 per cent.

These trajectories in income sources are consistent with the short-term picture painted earlier, in that a rising income trajectory is associated with increasing participation in paid work combined with growing receipt of in-work benefits and declining receipt of social assistance. What is different between the longer-term and short-term pictures is that, over the longer term, repartnership appears to play a larger potential role in securing income. I return to this issue shortly.

These six-year trajectories for Britain may be compared with the six-year trajectories estimated for US men and women by Duncan and Hoffman (1985), using waves 1–14 of the Panel Study of Income Dynamics (income years 1967–1981). There are similarities and differences between their results and mine. Both studies find that incomes after a marital split rise

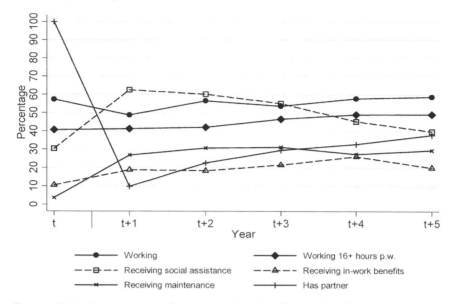

Legend:
— ● — Working   — ◆ — Working 16+ hours p.w.
— ⊟ — Receiving social assistance   — △ — Receiving in-work benefits
— ✕ — Receiving maintenance   — ┼ — Has partner

Figure 13.3 Percentage working, receiving benefits, and with a partner: wives with dependent children at wave *t* who experienced a marital split between waves *t* and *t* + 1.
Note: Percentages shown for year *t* + *s*, for *s* = 1–5, are median ratios among the relevant groups. Data weighted by inverse probability of remaining in panel and having valid net income waves *t* through *t* + 5 (see text). Social assistance includes housing benefits. See main text for definitions of social assistance, housing benefits, and in-work benefits.

for separating husbands but, for separating women, fall initially though subsequently recover, even if not to presplit levels (see their Figures 14.3 and 14.4). The principal difference between us is that they emphasise repartnership rather than work as a source of income replacement.[16] An explanation for this emphasis could be that the labour force participation rates for separating women in the US were high in the years after a marital split—and higher than those for comparable British women—and hence there was less opportunity to increase income by raising labour force participation rates further.

Given their emphasis, Duncan and Hoffman were motivated to develop an empirical model of the gains for remarriage for women. They estimate jointly an equation for the probability of repartnership within the five years after the marital split and, for women who do repartner, an equation for the new partner's labour income, using the Heckman (1979) sample selection modelling approach.

For Britain, my results about the longer-term changes after a marital split suggest that a different approach would be more appropriate—one that examines the correlates of not only repartnership but also of labour force participation and the interrelationships between the processes. And it would be of interest to examine not only whether there is a repartnership or (re-)employment, but also how long it takes for these events to occur for women with different characteristics. All of these aspects can be estimated using a bivariate duration model: see, for example, the discussion of multivariate mixed proportional hazard models by van den Berg (2001). One would not need to limit the observation window to a fixed width— spells may be shorter or longer than five years—and this would also lead to larger sample sizes. Another potential advantage is that sample dropout can be modelled jointly with the other processes of substantive interest. Development of this approach is the subject of my current research and will be reported elsewhere in due course. The work complements that of Paull (2007), who examined the timings of partnership and employment transitions relative to each using monthly history data but with separate univariate duration models for each process.

CONCLUDING REMARKS

Fourteen waves of BHPS panel data reveal interesting new findings about the economic consequences of a marital split in Britain. First, the short-term income loss associated with a marital split has declined over time for women with dependent children and for the children of separating parents, and by a substantial amount. The most plausible explanations for these trends are the secular rise in women's labour force participation rates and, related, the changes to the social security system, especially to in-work benefits, introduced by the Labour government in the late 1990s which stimulated lone mothers' employment rates and made work pay. Second, women's income trajectories over the longer term follow a distinct upward trend on average after the initial fall associated with the marital split. Women with children who have a job in the year after their marital split and retain it in each of the following five years come close to recovering their presplit incomes after five years.

These findings can be interpreted as Good News. There is also some Bad News. There remain large gaps on average between the short-term income losses of separating husbands and of separating women. This is despite the improvement in the circumstances of women with children. Observe too that the average short-term income loss for childless separating women has remained fairly constant over the last 15 years. Gender remains a good predictor of whether an adult's income rises or falls after experiencing a marital split.

NOTES

1. This section draws on Jarvis and Jenkins (1999).
2. I use only the original sample which began in 1991. Data from the later extension samples for Scotland, Wales, and Northern Ireland are not used.

3. A dependent child is aged less than 16 years, or more than 16 years but under 19 years and unmarried, in full-time nonadvanced education and living with parents. When looking at income changes for dependent children experiencing a marital split, I also required that the child be dependent at both waves t and $t + 1$.

4. For a more detailed discussion of the construction of the BHPS net income variables, see Levy et al. (2006).

5. See Jarvis and Jenkins (1999) for analysis of pretax pretransfer ('original') income and pretax posttransfer ('gross') income.

6. The principal exceptions are employment earnings which are 'usual earnings', and income from investments and savings which are annual measures.

7. But see Böheim and Jenkins (2006), who show that the distributions of BHPS current and annual income measure are very similar.

8. The differential attrition rates are not a BHPS peculiarity; they are typical in panel studies of this kind. See, e.g., Burkhauser et al. (1990), using data from the US Panel Study of Income Dynamics and the German Socio-Economic Panel.

9. There is another issue about using BHPS longitudinal weights. They are not designed for the case where analysts pool pairs of waves, as here. Although this case is common, it does not appear to have been addressed in the statistical literature.

10. In principle, income gains for separating fathers may be overestimated, because child support payments are not deducted from my definition of income. However, in practice, the bias is likely to be small: see the sensitivity analysis undertaken by Jarvis and Jenkins (1999).

11. Other changes included the introduction of a National Minimum Wage (which had negligible employment effects), and the New Deal for Lone Parents, which aimed to improve job search and work readiness. See Brewer and Shephard (2004).

12. Job Seekers Allowance replaced Unemployment Benefit from October 1996. Unemployment Benefit and contribution-based JSA are not means-tested, but many recipients also received means-tested benefits. It is not possible to distinguish between the two types of JSA receipt in the BHPS and so, for consistency, Unemployment Benefit was also included in the definition of social assistance benefits used here.

13. The number of separating husbands with valid household net income data at waves t through $t + 5$ is 181. For separating wives, the corresponding number is 260, and for separating wives with dependent children at t, it is 161. Of these, 90 have no partner at each wave t to $t + 5$; 38 are not in paid work at each wave t to $t + 5$; 56 are in paid work at each wave t to $t + 5$; 97 are in paid work at $t + 5$, and 61 have a partner at $t + 5$. These sample numbers are similar to those in Duncan and Hoffman's (1985) analysis of 14 waves of PSID data.

14. E.g. there are only 29 separating wives with children with six-year trajectories beginning in 1998 (wave 8 interview).

15. I also experimented with separate regressions for men and for women, but analysis undertaken with weights derived from these regressions led to conclusions that differed little from those reported.

16. In their study, like mine, 'divorce' refers to separations of legally married as well as cohabiting partners.

REFERENCES

Aassve, A., Betti, G., Mazzuco, S. and Mencarini, L. (2007) Marital disruption and economic well-being: a comparative analysis, *Journal of the Royal Statistical Society, Series A*, 170: 781–99.

Andreß, H.-J., Borgloh, B., Bröckel, M., Gisselmann, M. and Hummelsheim, D. (2006) The economic consequences of partnership dissolution—a comparative analysis of panel studies from Belgium, Germany, Great Britain, and Sweden, *European Sociological Review*, 22: 533–60.

Bianchi, S. and McArthur, E. (1989) The relationship between family compositional change and the economic status of children: SIPP and PSID, in *Individuals and families in transition: understanding change through longitudinal data*, Washington DC: U.S. Bureau of the Census, 43–67.

Bianchi, S., Subaiya, L. and Kahn, J.R. (1999) The gender gap in the economic well-being of non-resident fathers and custodial mothers, *Demography*, 36: 195–203.

Böheim, R. and Jenkins, S.P. (2006) A comparison of current annual measures of income in the British Household Panel Survey, *Journal of Official Statistics*, 22: 733–58.

Brewer, M., Duncan, A., Shephard, A. and Suarez, M.J. (2006) Did working families' tax credit work? The impact of in-work support on labour supply in Britain, *Labour Economics*, 13: 699–720.

Brewer, M. and Shephard, A. (2004) *Has Labour made work pay?* York, UK: York Publishing Services for the Joseph Rowntree Foundation.

Burkhauser, R.V., Duncan, G.J., Hauser, R. and Berntsen, R. (1990) Economic burdens of marital disruptions: a comparison of the United States and the Federal Republic of Germany, *Review of Income and Wealth*, 36: 319–33.

———. (1991) 'Wife or frau, women do worse: a comparison of men and women in the United States and Germany after marital dissolution, *Demography*, 28: 353–60.

Coulter, F.A.E., Cowell, F.A. and Jenkins, S.P. (1992) Differences in needs and assessment of income distributions, *Bulletin of Economic Research*, 44: 77–124.

David, M.H. and Flory, T.S. (1989) Changes in marital status and short-term income dynamics, in *Individuals and families in transition: understanding change through longitudinal data*, Washington, DC: U.S. Bureau of the Census, 15–22.

Department for Work and Pensions (2007) *Households below average income 1994/95–2005/06*, London: Department for Work and Pensions.

Duncan, G.J. and Hoffman, S.D. (1985) Economic consequences of marital instability, in M. David and T.M. Smeeding (eds) *Horizontal inequity, uncertainty and well-being*, Chicago: University of Chicago Press, 427–70.

Finnie, R. (1993) Women, men, and the economic consequences of divorce: evidence from Canadian longitudinal data, *Canadian Review of Sociology and Anthropology*, 30: 205–41.

Francesconi, M. and van der Klaauw, W. (2007) The socioeconomic consequences of in-work benefit reform for British lone mothers, *Journal of Human Resources*, 42: 1–31.

Gregg, P. and Harkness, S. (2003) Welfare reform and lone parents employment in the UK, Working Paper 03/72, Bristol, UK: Centre for Market and Public Organisation, University of Bristol.

Gregg, P., Harkness, S. and Smith, S. (2007) Welfare reform and lone parents in the UK, Working Paper 07/182, Bristol, UK: Centre for Market and Public Organisation, University of Bristol.

Heckman, J.J. (1979) Sample selection bias as a specification error, Econometrica, 47: 153–61.

Hoffman, S. (1977) Marital instability and women's economic status, *Demography*, 14: 67–76.

Jarvis, S. and Jenkins, S.P. (1998) Marital dissolution and income change: evidence for Britain, in R. Ford and J.I. Millar (eds) *Private lives and public responses: lone parenthood and future policy in the U.K.*, London: Policy Studies Institute.

———. (1999) Marital splits and income changes: evidence from the British Household Panel Survey, *Population Studies*, 53: 237–54.

Levy, H., Zantomio, F., Sutherland, H. and Jenkins, S.P. (2006) Derived net current and annual income variables to accompany BHPS waves 1–14, Data deposited at the UK Data Archive (SN3909), December 2006.

Lynn, P. (ed.) (2006) *Quality profile: British Household Panel Survey. Version 2.0: Waves 1 to 13: 1991–2003*, Colchester, UK: Institute for Social and Economic Research, University of Essex. Online. HTTP: <http://www.iser.essex.ac.uk/ulsc/bhps/quality-profiles/BHPS-QP-01–03–06-v2.pdf> Accessed on 16 December 2007.

McKeever, M. and Wolfinger, N.H. (2001) Reexamining the economic costs of marital disruption for women, *Social Science Quarterly*, 82: 202–17.

Paull, G. (2007) *Partnership transitions and mothers' employment*, Department for Work and Pensions Research Report No 452, Leeds, UK: Corporate Document Services.

Smock, P.J. (1993) The economic costs of marital disruption for young women over the past two decades, *Demography*, 30: 353–71.

———. (1994) Gender and the short-run economic consequences of marital disruption, *Social Forces*, 73: 243–62.

Uunk, W. (2004) The economic consequences of divorce for women in the European Union: the impact of welfare state arrangements, *European Journal of Population*, 20: 251–85.

van den Berg, G.J. (2001) Duration models: specification, identification, identification and multiple durations, Chapter 55 in J.J. Heckman and E. Leamer (eds) *Handbook of econometrics, Volume 5*, Amsterdam: Elsevier, 3381–3459.≥

Contributors

Michèle Belot is currently at Nuffield College, Oxford. From 2004-8 she was in the Department of Economics at the University of Essex. She received her PhD in 2003 from Tilburg University (CentER). Her research is mainly in the area of labour and behavioural economics, with specific interests in the formation of social ties (friendships, partnerships and teams) and the determinants of geographical mobility in developed countries. Her previous work took a more macroeconomic approach to the functioning of the labour market and the determinants of labour mobility in European countries. She has recent publications in *Oxford Economic Papers, Economica* and *Empirical Economics*.

Morten Blekesaune is a researcher at Norwegian Social Research (NOVA), and was formerly a chief research officer at the Institute for Social and Economic Research, University of Essex. He has completed research on marital transitions related to health, employment, and benefit receipt, ageing and retirement, and public attitudes to welfare policies.

Malcolm Brynin is a sociologist and principal research officer at the Institute for Social and Economic Research, University of Essex, with research interests in education and skills; the family and young people; and the transmission of social values. He has published in sociology, political science and economics journals.

Emilia Del Bono is a senior researcher at the Institute for Social and Economic Research, University of Essex. Prior to joining ISER she was a visiting scholar at the University of California, Berkeley, and a junior research fellow in economics at Queen's College, Oxford. She is a labour economist whose research interests include fertility, partnership formation, early childhood outcomes, education and gender. Her main research area is the impact of economic opportunities on fertility outcomes. Current projects include the effect of unemployment on single motherhood and the impact of job displacement on the probability of having a child.

John Ermisch is a professor of economics at the Institute for Social and Economic Research, University of Essex, and a fellow of the British Academy. Formerly, he was Bonar-Macfie Professor in the Department of Political Economy at the University of Glasgow (1991–94) and a senior research officer at the National Institute of Economic and Social Research. From 1991 to 2001, he was one of the coeditors of the *Journal of Population Economics*, and was president of the European Society for Population Economics in 1989. His research is broadly concerned with how the family and markets interact. He is the author of *An Economic Analysis of the Family* (Princeton University Press, 2003), *Lone Parenthood: An Economic Analysis* (Cambridge University Press, 1991) and *The Political Economy of Demographic Change* (Heinemann, 1983), as well as numerous articles in economic and demographic journals.

Priscila Ferreira is currently a PhD student at the University of Essex, having completed her first degree and master in economics at the University of Minho. Her research interests are in the field of labour economics and applied microeconometrics. Currently she is working on the determinants and consequences of job mobility using linked employer-employee data.

Jonathan Gershuny is chair of the Sociology, Demography and Social Statistics Section of the British Academy. He is a professor in Oxford University's Sociology Department, and a professorial fellow of St Hugh's College. He was previously a senior fellow of the Science Policy Research Unit, Sussex University; professor of sociology at University of Bath; and a fellow of Nuffield College, Oxford. He was the director of the Institute for Social and Economic Research, University of Essex, from 1993 to 2005. His research interests are the analysis of narrative data sets (life and work histories, time-use diaries); interconnections between household organisation, labour force participation, and household formation and dissolution; and relationships between individual-level behaviour and socioeconomic structure.

Maria Iacovou is a chief research officer at the Institute for Social and Economic Research, University of Essex. Her research interests include youth and the transition to adulthood, and most recently poverty and deprivation among young people. She is also interested in family formation and living arrangements, and has worked extensively on cross-national comparative research, particularly across Europe.

Stephen P. Jenkins is professor of economics and director of the Institute for Social and Economic Research, University of Essex, chair of the Council of the International Association for Research on Income and Wealth, research professor of DIW Berlin, and research fellow of IZA,

Bonn. His current research focuses on income dynamics, labour market transitions, and survival analysis.

Man Yee Kan is a British Academy Postdoctoral Fellow and Research Councils UK Academic Fellow in the Department of Sociology, and a Junior Research Fellow of St. Hugh's College, University of Oxford. Her current research interests include the domestic division of labour, the gender wage gap, and empirical and methodological issues in time use research.

Simonetta Longhi is a senior researcher at the Institute for Social and Economic Research, University of Essex. Her current research projects include pay gaps across ethnicity, religion, and disability; job search behaviour and occupational change; and housing choices. She is also interested in returns to education in the UK and in Europe; and in the determinants and impact of national and international migration.

Lavinia Parisi is an economics PhD student at the Institute for Social and Economic Research in the University of Essex.

Álvaro Martínez Pérez, based at the Juan March Institute in Madrid and also at the Institute for Social and Economic Research in the University of Essex, where he is undertaking his PhD. The research for this covers family values, the couple relationship, and homogamy. He is also interested in the analysis of political behaviour.

Thomas Siedler is a researcher of the DIW, Berlin, and a senior research officer at the Institute for Social and Economic Research at the University of Essex. His research interests include intergenerational links, political values and geographic mobility.

Mark Taylor is a principal research officer at the Institute for Social and Economic Research, University of Essex. His research interests include labour economics, the causes and consequences of labour market and residential mobility, and relationships between these different forms of mobility and mental health. He has recently published in *Economica*, *Journal of the Royal Statistical Society* and *Psychological Medicine*.

Index

NB: 'n' after a page number refers to a note.

Printed in the USA/Agawam, MA
October 4, 2012

569533.118